THE SOURCES OF HISTORY:
STUDIES IN THE USES OF HISTORICAL EVIDENCE

GENERAL EDITOR: G. R. ELTON

The Sources of History:
Studies in the Uses of Historical Evidence

The Western European Powers, 1500–1700

by
CHARLES CARTER

CORNELL PAPERBACKS
CORNELL UNIVERSITY PRESS
Ithaca, New York

First published 1971

First printing, Cornell Paperbacks, 1971

International Standard Book Number 0-8014-9114-2
Library of Congress Catalog Card Number 75-146276
Printed in Great Britain

in memory of
my
beloved father
Ernest H. Carter

Contents

General Editor's Introduction

By what right do historians claim that their reconstructions of the past are true, or at least on the road to truth? How much of the past can they hope to recover: are there areas that will remain for ever dark, questions that will never receive an answer? These are problems which should and do engage not only the scholar and student but every serious reader of history. In the debates on the nature of history, however, attention commonly concentrates on philosophic doubts about the nature of historical knowledge and explanation, or on the progress that might be made by adopting supposedly new methods of analysis. The disputants hardly ever turn to consider the materials with which historians work and which must always lie at the foundation of their structures. Yet, whatever theories or methods the scholar may embrace, unless he knows his sources and rests upon them he will not deserve the name of historian. The bulk of historical evidence is much larger and more complex than most laymen and some professionals seem to know, and a proper acquaintance with it tends to prove both exhilarating and sobering—exhilarating because it opens the road to unending enquiry, and sobering because it reduces the inspiring theory and the new method to their proper subordinate place in the scheme of things. It is the purpose of this series to bring this fact to notice by showing what we have and how it may be used.

G. R. ELTON

A Reader's Prospectus

The scope and intent of this book may best be understood within the framework of the series of which it is a part: dealing with a particular type of 'Sources of History' in a given period, with the treatment reflected in the series' subtitle: *Studies in the Uses of Historical Evidence.*

The sources in question are diplomatic sources, a straightforward term that might seem to require no definition but in fact has two. It is a convenient but ambiguous label with two overlapping but very different meanings: sources of *diplomatic origin* (which might be about anything) and the sources of *diplomatic history* (which may be of non-diplomatic origin). Though the former documents are basic to the latter purpose, they are neither limited to it nor, by themselves, sufficient for it. On the one hand, the documents produced by diplomatic activity include important sources for a good many kinds of history besides diplomatic. On the other hand, the sources essential for writing diplomatic history, though those of diplomatic origin are naturally central, include various other kinds, some not manuscript in form nor even documentary in nature. 'Diplomatic sources' under both of these definitions are dealt with herein. Both types, one may add, must be dealt with in the context of the diplomatic machinery that was developing in the period and the evolving 'state system' it served, which are discussed in Chapter 1.

Both 'developing' and 'evolving' are appropriate terms both for the organisation and composition of European political units in the period (as in others) and for the system by which they conducted their affairs with each other. In 1500 the latter bore little resemblance to what it has been in more recent times; in 1700 it did. Actually, of course, neither date has any such particular meaning in that development as 1454 or 1494 or 1713–14 would have, but that is as it should be. Evolution, almost by definition, knows no precise beginning nor final perfection: a crucial factor which even merely symbolic terminal dates might obscure and which wholly arbitrary ones serve far better. In sum, one is concerned not with beginnings and ends but with a span of time during which essential developments took place, the span that lies between the Middle Ages, as that term applies to diplomacy, and the eighteenth century, itself not a very precise chronological term as used by historians.

It is not this book's intention to provide a comprehensive guide to diplomatic archives nor a detailed inventory of diplomatic sources (in either sense). The former has already been done,[1] and the latter is patently impossible in a single volume, since it involves dozens of archives, hundreds of collections and millions of documents (some individual catalogues of which are discussed in Chapter 3). Instead, my purpose is to describe various types of diplomatic sources, collections and repositories, and discuss their nature and use.

To give this treatment greater depth of coverage, its lateral reach has been mainly confined to four states: Spain and France, as the two truly great powers of the period; England, as an emerging power and the only one of importance that continued so throughout this period (and perhaps the one of greatest interest to readers of this English language book); and the Spanish Netherlands, not only as an excellent example of an aborted 'state' but as the principal territorial focus of international

---

[1] See Daniel H. Thomas and Lynn M. Case, *Guide to the Diplomatic archives of western Europe* (Philadelphia, 1959). There are individual published guides for most of the major archives and many lesser ones, some countries have published specialised guides to specific foreign archives or collections (mainly for research in the publishing country's own history), and there are, of course, catalogues to many collections; some of the more useful of these various aids are cited in Chapter 3.

disputes in this period and in consequence a principal locus of historical sources about them. One may justify this on the grounds that the book's main focus is upon great powers, and that others, such as Sweden and Denmark, hold that status for relatively brief periods at best. Germany is a double anomaly, its individual states being below the sovereign status associated with regular diplomatic activity and the Emperor above it; the latter anomaly is further complicated by the close post-1556 ties with the senior branch of the house of Habsburg, the distinction having been for a time obliterated by the king of Spain's holding the imperial throne himself in 1519–56. (Moreover, a volume on Central Europe and its historical sources is planned for this series.) The papacy is a further supra-national anomaly in inter-national affairs. With the exception of Savoy and Venice at the northern corners, the 'states' of Italy were very soon either Spanish domains or satellites or too weak to count for much in European diplomacy except as victims and pawns. As scholars and students of the history of any of these will well understand, it has required some self-discipline to resist the siren songs of the north, the east and the Italian scene and maintain a focus-in-depth upon the four named (the eagle-eyed reader will in fact notice an occasional lapse). This, however, is with regard to specifics described; the characteristics which they illustrate and generalisations made with regard to types of source materials, problems of use, etc., have of course more general application.

For this sort of analytical discussion one must naturally resort to examples. As, even within the above delimitations, the available ones are usually enormous in number, the criteria used for their selection should perhaps be specified. Although there are some inevitable and intentional exceptions in specific cases, a thin (chronological and geographical) veneer has, where possible, been abjured in favour of concentration, expending, with regard to a given matter, one's necessarily limited quota of examples on a concise period, a particular country, one or two archives, etc. The purpose is to illustrate types, and obviously concentration allows more adequate illustration.

An adequate degree of such concentration precludes an egalitarian national balance within every individual topic, but that has little to recommend it anyway. I have sought instead, by selectively rotating the emphasis—French published documents, Belgian serials, English and Spanish archives, etc.—an over-all balance which I hope will also give an adequate picture of national strengths, shortcomings and other special considerations worthy of note.

This procedure also facilitates a limited departure from the standard cliché citations, a matter which, to this historian's view at least, seems seriously pressing. A thin spread of the most conspicuous examples of some types would result in merely one more listing of well-known items, which would not only be pointlessly redundant since they are already easy to find but in many cases undesirable: some are so overused, that they would be far better forgotten. To speak bluntly, it is of vital importance that the long-established canon of sources, for diplomatic history and for other categories—always inadequate and now worn threadbare to boot, yet still strangely sanctified—be radically expanded if historical knowledge (of at least many aspects of this period) is ever to emerge from its superannuated embryo. If this volume aspires to be a guide to anything it is to possible outward passages over the walls, beyond the sanctified sources, problems, issues, questions (and answers) and *Dramatis Personae*—which have never been more than partial at best, nor revealed more than part of the truth.

Regarding examples (illustrations), there is chronologically something of a bulge in the middle of the period, again for several reasons: in any period a 'middle' example is apt to be more applicable to the whole than one taken from either chronological extreme; some specific developing factors—the techniques of document production, some types of early publication, etc.—cannot be exemplified satisfactorily until they are fairly well along; and more detailed examples, necessary in certain connections, can obviously be taken more reliably from the period of one's own more detailed research, which here happens to be in the early seventeenth century—with due attention to appropriateness, naturally, when broader application is intended. This is especially pertinent when describing comparatively *nuancé* problems. To illustrate such things as the uses of trivia in handling documents, one's choice is obviously limited to citing instances from one's own experience or relating those of others at second hand. I have naturally chosen the former (especially since this consideration is reinforced by those already noted), hoping that the reader will forgive the intrusion of personal examples, and (since references to 'the present writer' and such become tiresome) even an occasional use of the perpendicular pronoun in doing so. Where the actual text of documents is used for illustration, English ones have usually been chosen to avoid the almost inevitable damage to nuance in translation. Within the above considerations, specific examples of types of documents, collections, etc., and of problems involved in the use of diplomatic sources have been, to the degree that seems necessary, selected for their interrelatedness in order to give a more coherent broader picture and not merely relevant but isolated detail.

C. H. C.

CHAPTER 1

The Subject and the Sources

Modern diplomacy differs from its medieval predecessor on three important levels: theoretical, institutional, and—for lack of a better word—technological. The political theory that justified, and thus to a degree shaped, diplomatic activity had earlier defined its legitimate end as the peace of Christendom, but defined it now as whatever was in the interest of the individual state. To the structure of the old occasional diplomacy was now added the permanent resident ambassador, and with him continuous diplomatic relations. And where before diplomacy had been an adjunct of medieval monarchy it now belonged to the rapidly-developing administrative state.

The former, the shift in attitude of political theorists (of whom Machiavelli is only the best known—the most influential but also, in his adjectival form, a 'mere' symbol for a widespread new wave of political theorists who successfully gained the field), analogous to developments in the 'real' world—whether cause or effect or both—is too well known to require going into here.[1] But one cannot seriously discuss the diplomatic documents of the 'early modern' period—certainly not as historical evidence— without giving some attention to the latter two aspects of the context in which they were produced and served their historical function and of which they themselves are evidence.

[1] The classic analysis of this shift in rationale is Garrett Mattingly, *Renaissance Diplomacy* (London and Boston, 1955). The numerous writers who, drawing upon traditional Christian morality, mounted a substantial but unsuccessful opposition to the 'Machiavellian' rationale, have of course been granted no place in the historical canon: intellectual history, like political and military, is not kind to losers.

THE DIPLOMATIC SYSTEM

During the fifteenth century, what were to be the three major European powers in the succeeding period (Spain, France, and, on a lesser scale, England) were, when not preoccupied with fighting each other, scenes of internal power struggles, and of territorial consolidation. The eventual outcome in each case was a stronger and more effective monarchical government, increasingly well organised for both domestic rule and foreign adventure, with an expanded and improved territorial base, and—no small matter—with internal disruption at least temporarily under control (though all three were to experience domestic risings in both of the following centuries). Analogous processes were going on elsewhere in transalpine Europe, the most important, in the role it was subsequently to play, being the Netherlandish 'state' being pieced together by successive dukes of Burgundy.

Meanwhile, while the cats were busy at this, the mice were playing in Italy—playing (the old historical clichés are quite right about this) at being independent sovereign states, playing at small-scale power politics in a miniature international 'world', and in the process developing (inventing or adapting from the past) a new set of instrumentalities and procedures—those of permanent diplomatic representation—for dealing with relationships between and among independent states in that sort of world, in effect (though of course not by intent) working out the rules in advance for the great powers who would soon take over the game.[1]

---

[1] The question of whether the Western powers *owe* the institution of permanent diplomacy to Italian invention is as specious as the analogous one regarding the 'Renaissance State'. There seems no reason and no need to suppose that fifteenth-century Venetians or Florentines were more responsive to the institutional needs of the state than, say, Ferdinand of Aragon: that if they had not adopted permanent diplomacy no one else would have. But the point is irrelevant here: what is relevant, extremely so as regards the state of development of the European diplomatic system (and the sources it would produce) at some given later date, is that by the time the transalpine powers took up its use others had already had considerable experience with it and so had had time to work the initial bugs out of it.

The historical conditions which allowed this, however, were not limited to the abnormal hiatus that thus occurred in the usual (past and future) domination of Italian affairs by outsiders.[1] For reasons still perhaps not fully understood, while a process of territorial consolidation on a large-state basis was going on in most parts of the West, with small units being absorbed (as in France) or combined (as in Spain and the Netherlands) into larger ones, in Italy most of the small existing 'states' were able to maintain their separate identity[2] and to sustain their claims as independent sovereign powers.

One result, as noted, was to create an 'international' society within the confines of Italy, coincidental with (and no doubt partly the result of) a period of freedom from outside interference from greater powers. An indispensable aspect of this was that this world was made up of states sufficiently small to be operable as such at a comparatively early level of administration development, and to be prepared for such operation fairly quickly. Centralisation of government power was here a comparatively simple matter: the Medici, for example, had a considerably smaller landed aristocracy to deal with than, say, the Valois. Territorial consolidation was a similarly limited problem: the outlying region of a city state was relatively small—anything beyond that was a matter of 'foreign affairs'. And perhaps most importantly, administration of so small a state (and its foreign affairs) sufficiently effectively for it to function *viably* in diplomacy and war was sufficiently simple for such a condition of operability to be reached at a much earlier stage of administrative development than would be the case in meeting the larger and more complex administrative demands of a France or a Spain. This difference affected both sides of the equation: those greater

[1] There was, of course, still some occasional dabbling. Myron P. Gilmore, *The World of Humanism, 1453–1517* (New York; Harper Torchbook edition, 1962, pp. 293–5), provides a convenient brief bibliography.

[2] To the degree that the effectiveness of the imperial superstructure may be credited with the failure of states to achieve full sovereignty in the similar situation of non-consolidation in Germany, its converse ineffectiveness perhaps should be credited in Italy.

powers stayed out of Italy (a distant adventure far different from their usual disputes over contiguous territory) until they were ready, which included being sufficiently well organised, and meanwhile the Italian states were sufficiently ready to function as 'modern bureaucratic states', including the ability to maintain the sophisticated machinery of permanent diplomacy, and proceeded to do so.

This 'international' Italy saw several decades of inter-state warfare which apparently led to the conclusion that the state's natural instinct for competition with other states was not always best served on the battlefield, and that security, aggrandisement and the state's lesser goals might, at least a worthwhile part of the time, be gained through continuous peaceful liaison between governments. The institution of ambassador was of course an old one, well known to the ancient world, as old as kingdoms, as old as history. In the Middle Ages they were frequently employed,[1] but only for specific occasions. One medieval ruler might send another a herald, who was essentially a messenger, to deliver congratulations or condolences, a declaration of friendship or (more likely) war, or some message, and to receive (but not respond to) an answer. Or he might send a *legatus*, an envoy authorised to *discuss* certain specific matters in his name, such as negotiating an alliance or the settlement of a dispute; although

[1] The frequency is reflected in, for example: L. Mirot and E. Deprez, *Les ambassades anglaises pendant la guerre de cent ans* (Paris, 1900), which covers 687 English embassies; see also, e.g., J. Calmette, *La diplomatie Carolingienne* [843–77] (Paris, 1901). For the substantial recent European background in diplomacy see e.g., P. Champion and P. de Thoisy, *Bourgogne, France, Angleterre au traité de Troyes* [1420] (Paris, 1943); J. Toussaint, *Les relations diplomatiques de Philippe le Bon avec le Concile de Bâle, 1431–1449* (Louvain, 1942); J. M. Madurell Marimón, *Mensajeros Barceloneses en la corte de Nápoles de Alfonso V de Aragón 1435–1458* (Barcelona, 1963); P. M. Perret, *Histoire des relations de la France avec Venise du XIIIᵉ siècle à l'avènement de Charles VIII* (2 vols. Paris, 1896); Baron F. de Gingins la Sarra, *Dépêches des ambassadeurs Milanais sur les campagnes de Charles-le-Hardi, duc de Bourgogne, de 1474 à 1477* (2 vols. Paris, 1858); R. Rey, *Louis XI et les Etats Pontificaux de France au XVᵉ siècle d'après des documents inédits* (Grenoble, 1899); J. Calmette and G. Périnelle, *Louis XI et l'Angleterre 1461–1483* (Paris, 1930); E. Toutey, *Charles le Téméraire et la Ligue de Constance* [1474] (Paris, 1902).

such a legate might have to stay for a considerable length of time, the duration of his embassy was still normally limited to that of the negotiations or the special set of circumstances that had occasioned his being sent. Ambassadors might also be sent to a neutral site to negotiate peace. The innovation which the Italians were first to experiment with, among themselves (first Venice, then the Papacy, then others) was not merely to send an ambassador *to* another court but to *keep* one there on a permanent basis, which soon also became one of mutual exchange. What institutionally differentiates 'medieval' diplomacy from 'modern' is the employment of the resident ambassador.

There were already some useful antecedents for this. Most states, as circumstances required and their resources allowed, kept spies at other courts on a continuing basis: in effect, permanent agents maintained there to pursue their employers' interests, though not such as could be formally acknowledged—though they were in practice covertly 'exchanged'. Commercial and banking firms maintained agents abroad—openly, of course— who served as eyes and ears for the home government, sending along not only whatever state secrets they could learn but general information as well, the value of which as a basis for making policy decisions governments were increasingly appreciative of, and were occasionally authorised to act as mouthpiece as well. In states such as Florence or Venice there was little enough distinction between the leading merchants and the government anyway, while the Papacy had the special advantage of the apparatus that already necessarily existed for liaison with the Church hierarchies in the various states. It was thus no very great jump from the old to the 'new', from a customary practice that included both the fairly common maintenance of 'regular' but non-ambassadorial agents abroad and the fairly frequent sending of official but temporary ones, to the maintenance of fully-accredited ambassadors at foreign courts on a permanent basis.

The crucial time for this phase was the forty years after the Peace of Lodi in 1554, during which the permanent, regular diplomatic network thus created became the principal channel of interstate relations, increasingly used for the settlement of territorial disputes, the negotiation of ever-shifting alliances, etc. By the time Charles VIII invaded Italy in 1494—the start of the Great Italian Wars and the end of Italy's unwonted freedom from outside domination—it was a well-established and well-proven institution, with the rules, rituals and techniques of its use already quite fully developed.[1] The transalpine powers fairly quickly adopted its use, though the quickness and pattern of their doing so was naturally much affected by the long period of warfare among them then commencing.

Before the sixteenth century was many years old, however, most of the important powers had residents in several capitals of particular importance to them, and received residents from them in return since it was a bilateral exchange, a matter of establishing permanent (increasingly understood to be 'regular', normal) diplomatic relations *between* states. Each of these capitals thus was simultaneously the centre of its own network of permanent embassies abroad and the locus of a corollary community of foreign ambassadors to it. Since this permanent network was the mechanism used for handling most of the affairs between the more important states (when not at war with one another) it can properly be called the principal element in the diplomatic system from the time of its Europe-wide adoption. But—an important point—that is not to say universal adoption in Europe: employment of the permanent embassy did not extend quite so far or so fast as one might suppose.

For example, when Ferdinand of Aragon, one of the readiest exploiters of this new instrument of state, sent Rodrigo González de la Puebla to London in 1495 he was both the first resident

[1] That the basic *institution* of modern diplomacy—the permanent residency —was first developed in Italy there is no question, but one is on shakier ground in saying the same for some of the basic diplomatic *concepts* traditionally associated with the same period: see, e.g., E. W. Nelson, 'Origins of modern balance of power politics', *Medievalia and Humanistica*, I (1943), pp. 124–42. By the late fifteenth century some of the Italian states, especially Venice, already had resident ambassadors beyond the Alps.

ambassador in England and the first Spanish resident anywhere except Rome.[1] But by contrast, although Ferdinand sent at least ten major embassies to France (usually two or three persons) in the period 1498–1514 and Charles V at least three thereafter, there seems to have been no Spanish *resident* there until Juan de Hannart in 1531. They had of course been at war during much of that time, but even during the peaceful period between the sixteenth-century wars of religion and the Thirty Years' War, Spain, the predominant power in Europe (and at the same time a weakening one, increasingly dependent upon diplomacy) usually had only eight or ten residents abroad: at Paris and London, Brussels and the Empire, and in Italy Rome, Venice, Savoy and two or three varying lesser states. In a comparable period of French preponderance (but significantly without the same wide spread of territorial domains abroad) Louis XIV maintained twenty-one permanent embassies, but this was exceptional. England, far more typically, kept only five in the period 1660–88—while sending diplomatic missions to a total of thirty separate rulers.[2]

The reasons are not hard to find. Not many states could afford to maintain many (or any) permanent embassies abroad, or needed to; a state such as Genoa, for example, with middling resources and not much involved in Europe-wide affairs, was apt to compromise, maintaining residents with some of its neighbours (where it counted most) but only one or two at any distance from home. Conversely, most principal powers did not consider very many states important enough, or important enough to their

[1] On this much abused figure (a large part of whose papers are at Simancas, *Est.* 52–4, 806) see Garrett Mattingly, 'The reputation of Dr. de Puebla', *English Historical Review*, 55 (1940), pp. 27–46; see also 'The first resident embassies: medieval Italian origins of modern diplomacy', *Speculum*, 12 (1937), pp. 423–29.

[2] Phyllis S. Lachs, *The diplomatic corps under Charles II and James II* (New Brunswick, N.J. [1965]), pp. 4–5. I have used Professor Lachs's representative French figure (the actual number at any given moment would fluctuate slightly), for which she cites Louis Batiffol, 'Charge d'ambassadeurs du 17e siècle', *Revue d'Histoire Diplomatique*, XXV (1911), pp. 339–55—a very fundamental contribution to diplomatic history.

own interests, to warrant maintaining a permanent embassy there. Numerous others were, but continued so for only a brief time, then subsided into comparative unimportance again, to be replaced on the scene by some other transitory 'power': there were a good many such during the period 1500–1700, but, in the affairs of a given state, seldom more than a couple at any one time. A state of war, religious incompatibility, and other inhibitions reduced the number of available, eligible, and acceptable states still further.

In sum, the web of permanent embassies that stretched across Europe in this period was basic to the diplomatic system because it handled much of the basic business among the 'basic' states. It also gave the system its altered character, in two important ways. The existence and customary use of this network of permanent diplomacy, even though only partial in coverage, established and maintained a custom and context of permanent diplomacy for the system as a whole: the normal peaceful relationship between states of any consequence was that of permanent diplomatic liaison through the exchange of permanent diplomatic representatives; anything else was irregular, and the handling of relations through any other channel, whether from motives of friendship or the reverse, was considered and treated accordingly. And secondly, it was the permanent embassies (because they had a larger apparatus, and operated it on a continuing basis) that performed what in the broad view (and definitely that of the researcher) may be considered any ambassador's most significant function in the period: the production of diplomatic reports. But this same overwhelming influence on the entire system makes it necessary to remind oneself that the network of permanent representation and the diplomatic system were not the same thing. There was, in fact, a good deal else to diplomatic activity in the period: it was not only not confined to resident ambassadors—it was not even confined to states.

The participants in the broader system of diplomatic activity were both multifarious and subject to fairly frequent change. In pre-1494 Italy it included almost everyone: the Kingdom of Naples, Rome, Florence, Venice and Milan (the peninsular 'Big

26

Five'), a few middle-size powers (on the Italian scale) such as Genoa, and a shifting congeries of smaller states, some only tiny fragments, many of which were gobbled up by the others (or remained to be fought over later). After the incursion of the great powers most of these were eliminated from the diplomatic scene. By 1503 Naples was a Spanish viceroyalty, by 1535 Milan a reclaimed imperial fief, by 1540 a Spanish governorship. Though they continued to be active in diplomacy, Florence, Genoa, and the like became increasingly minor actors and even satellites; the Papacy, like the others unable to match armies with the great powers, was soon reduced to being merely a moral force in the world—an unaccustomed role, but not necessarily a bad thing. By the Peace of Cateau Cambrésis in 1559, of the old Italian powers only Venice, her naval strength a diplomatic asset, remained of real consideration, though by then Savoy, who had earlier functioned mainly in the French orbit, must be added to the Italian one, and, along with Venice, to the European one, where both can be rated as middle-sized powers which in pragmatic terms might be defined as neither fearsome nor negligible.[1]

Outside Italy the fifteenth and sixteenth centuries witnessed a dramatic reduction in the number of independent entities even available for participation in international affairs. In France, territorial consolidation removed Provence, Brittany, Béarne, etc., while in Spain two important powers, Aragon and Castile, became one far greater one. The Netherlandish state (which, with its dense population and highly developed economy, was potentially the third or fourth greatest power in Europe) was not yet quite rounded out in 1516 when the Duke of Burgundy became also King of Spain (already consolidated), and three years later Holy Roman Emperor as well. By the time the Spanish and Imperial crowns were again separated in 1556 the new emperor had already added Bohemia and Hungary to *his* holdings, and

[1] It is a truistic paradox that a state's importance in diplomacy, the peaceful alternative to war, is normally measured in military terms, the source of its diplomatic effectiveness consisting in unequal parts of the rightness of its policy, the quality of its ambassadors, and the size of its armies.

the Netherlands remained a Spanish domain. A new participant was added when the northern provinces split off, but about the same time Portugal was incorporated into the Spanish crown; long before Portugal had become a separate state again (and host to one of the five later-Stuart resident embassies), Scotland had ceased to be; and so on.

On the other hand, this attrition of the number of states available for 'diplomatic' activity was partially offset by religious conflict, civil war and such, and the consequent addition of several groups that had no sovereign-state identity but still managed to send and receive ambassadors (though almost never a resident one) and to participate actively in the diplomatic affairs of their time: the Huguenots and the League in France, the League and the Evangelical Union in Germany, and insurgent factions everywhere.[1] During the hundred years or so from the mid-sixteenth to the mid-seventeenth centuries, for example, there were probably no more than two or three sovereigns with whom the king of France had more negotiations and made more treaties than with the successive Princes of Condé—though under Louis XIII the palm may go to the king's own mother.

THE MODERN BUREAUCRATIC STATE

To discuss the sources of diplomatic history or the sources produced by diplomatic activity or, as here, both of those mainly overlapping but not identical bodies of sources, requires making one essential distinction: that diplomatic relations and international relations are not the same thing. 'Diplomacy' in

[1] The Dutch rebels fall naturally into this irregular category at the beginning of their revolt, but clearly cease to long before 1648 and probably well before 1609. Though perhaps technically incorrect, it seems reasonable to date that shift (necessarily arbitrarily) with England's beginning to keep a 'commissioner' in the States General (Henry Killigrew, then Thomas Wilkes) in the mid-1580s; the States conversely kept a resident agent in London from an early date— Noel Caron, seigneur de Schoonwale.

The Hanse towns of Hamburg, Bremen and Lübeck had long been a semi-regular case; in this period they for example received (together) one of the only five late-Stuart resident embassies.

the sense of the doings of diplomats is only the symptom, the surface detail, the crucial contact point, the ultimate stage of consummation and implementation of diplomacy in the broader, proper, and meaningful sense. It should not be confused, as it often is, with 'diplomacy' in the sense of international relations or, from the point of view of an individual state, foreign relations. An ambassador is only an infantryman, or at best a field general, waging battles but not waging war. In the military analogy his role is tactical; he is not, except incidentally, a deviser of strategy or a decider of ultimate goals. Those roles belong to the state—or, more properly, to another and more central part of it. Ambassadorial activity is only one phase, basic though it is, of a broader process that can be called a state's diplomacy, the conduct of its foreign affairs, the *whole* of which process is a function of the state, and which, just as foreign affairs are only a part of a state's total affairs, is only a part of the state's total function.

We are all inclined to fall back on convenient clichés that describe the modern diplomatic system, or the individual government's system of diplomatic representation abroad, as 'the handmaiden of the modern state'. It is of course no such thing. The cliché notion in fact manages to be totally inaccurate on two levels. Representation abroad is part of a total diplomatic process, of which the representation is one essential part and decision-making the other. One need not argue that one is superior to the other to assert without qualification that the formation and the execution of foreign policy (or anything else) are distinct but complementary parts of a single process: as it is a highly integrated process, the machinery by which it works must be viewed as a single integrated whole as well. But affairs of state as a whole—interests, aims, needs, resources, and influences upon these things—are also an integrated complex; the conduct of them is necessarily an integrated process, and the machinery for it an integrated one. Diplomacy is not the handmaiden of the state; it is one of the things the state does.

The *way* a state does this is the way it does almost everything else: by shuttling paper back and forth along a two-way channel and taking a distinct type of action with regard to it at either end. At one end persons possessing that role make a policy decision and send notice of it in the form of written orders to the other end—to an ambassador abroad, for example, or a provincial tax official. He in turn executes the policy decision (obeys the order), or tries to, and reports back in writing on the results (this king says he will agree to your demand A but not B or C; I have begun collecting the new tax but Smith refuses to pay). The decision makers read this and respond (tell him that if he will agree to B we will not insist on C; arrest Smith and tell him he will be imprisoned until he pays). The implementor reads, acts, and replies (the king will agree to B only if we agree to D; we applied the thumbscrews to Smith but he still refuses to pay). (Agreed—draw up the treaty; give him a fair trial and then hang him) (done; done).

Essential to this process of decision and execution was a corollary one, conducted through the same channels, whereby each end continually transmitted information to the other to assist the other in the performance of its respective role. The decision-making end sent, in addition to orders, whatever backgrounding, explanation or other information might be necessary or useful in their implementation (including the execution of continuing routine duties). Conversely, the official at the implementing end had as a principal continuing responsibility that of transmitting whatever information might be necessary or useful in the making of policy decisions. An ambassador might report that the host government was negotiating a potentially hostile alliance; the tax collector that the current tax rates were hurting the local economy and so might result in declining revenues. This (and supporting information) would provide the basis for a decision to attempt to abort the alliance by threats or courtship, and to lower the tax rates—and, of course, for orders to implement the decisions.

In such pure cases as this, one has the absolute ultimate in integration of the system: the implementor provides the informational basis for the very orders he executes, while the policymakers base their decisions on information supplied by the ultimate implementors. The channels are in constant counter-flow. Each end takes in paper as raw material for the production of more paper; for each, the supplier of its raw material and the consumer of its own paper product are identical—the opposite end of the channel.

In practice, of course, the system is (and was in the early modern period) more highly articulated than this. One may retain the metaphor of various two-way-channels, but they in fact run between a single (though perhaps departmentalised) governmental centre and a multitude of 'outlying' officials—in the provinces, on lower levels of central government, ambassadors abroad, etc.; between one decision-making, order-giving complex and many widely scattered agents of implementation (and of information gathering, as a basis for further decision-making). There is an obvious difference in scope of purview and need. The centre (or some department of it) deals with all things, the individual agent 'implements' in a fairly restricted sphere. Outlying officials require orders and information only about a comparatively limited area of business, and that is ordinarily all they get from the centre. The centre requires information about all things to aid it in guiding all aspects of the state's affairs, and, for confirmation and completeness, from as many different sources as possible; thus the information the centre expects from any outlying official—including ambassadors—is limited only by his competence (a tax official would be expected to know little about road engineering) or the opportunities available (an ambassador to Denmark will learn less about Turkey than Sweden).

From the researcher's point of view, the effect upon the documentation produced is threefold. The two sides of this correspondence—from decision-making centre to implementor, and vice versa—are different in nature, as between master and servant, commander and commanded. They are very different in diversity of subject matter, the former hewing very closely to the recipient's restricted area of business, the latter being potentially as broad as the centre's unlimited interests and needs. And there is inevitably far more of the latter than of the former. (The documentation of the decision-making process itself—that which lies between receiving an ambassador's dispatches and replying to them—is discussed in Chapter 2.)

The ambassadorial side of this system has already been touched upon, and further aspects of it are discussed later on. But one cannot hope to understand either the diplomacy or the diplomatic documents of the time without substantial familiarity with the policymaking side of it, as well, or, in the alternative metaphor, with the decision-making centre as well as the implementary periphery, and with the whole—in sum, with the 'administrative state' itself.

This is not the place to discuss the emerging 'modern state' from either a political or philosophical point of view. The concern here is necessarily with the state as a consumer and producer of documents, a complex organisation whose basic function, from the pragmatic point of view of the researcher, is that of a gigantic paper-making machine.

Given the slipperiness of the term 'state', dealing with it as a functioning machine may in any case be the only way that is not instantly open to qualitative debate. Perhaps the most useful euphemism for the phenomenon in this period is 'power aggregate'; with regard to the present pragmatic concern, this might be redefined, or further characterised, as organised resources of power—with emphasis not only on the possession of such resources but the role played by organisation in converting those resources into power, or, stated differently, transforming potential power into actual power, in terms of effective action. That is, not merely the state's administration but the state *as* administration. In this period the key is a high degree of rationalisation, departmentalisation, professionalisation—that is to say bureaucracy, which in its consequences should perhaps be ranked right after the wheel and the zero among important human inventions.

One special relevance of the inseparability of power and administration is their close two-way relationship with regard to magnitude: increased resources—e.g., acquiring Italian domains or English monastic lands—require and so call into being improved administrative machinery, while improved administrative machinery harnesses existing resources more effectively and thus increases real (usable) power. The double general rule that applies is therefore not very surprising: that the greater the state the more highly developed the administration, and the more highly developed the administration the greater the power a given state is able to bring into play. This double axiom of response and result of course applies not only to a state's affairs in general but to its specific diplomatic needs and performance.

As a result of this inseparability of what and how, one obviously cannot work very intelligently with these documents without some familiarity with the principal administrative office involved, that of Secretary of State; with what was at certain times and places the principal administrative and/or policymaking body; with the role of the monarch or other chief of state; and with the role of chief minister. How much of this familiarity can be obtained from existing historical studies varies greatly with country, period, and aspect involved.

For England, A. V. Dicey's early study of *The Privy Council* (London, 1860; reprinted London and New York, 1887) and J. F. Baldwin's *Kings Council in England during the Middle Ages* (Oxford, 1913), which is most exhaustive for the fourteenth and fifteenth centuries but goes to the reign of Henry VIII, were followed by E. R. Turner's *The Privy Council of England in the Seventeenth and Eighteenth Centuries, 1603–1784* (2 vols, Baltimore, 1927–8) and *The Cabinet Council of England . . . 1622–1784* (2 vols, Baltimore, 1930–2).[1]

Oddly, some three decades lapsed before interest in administrative history caught up with the pioneering work of F. M. G.

[1] E. R. Turner having died 31 December 1929, the latter was published posthumously, ed. Gaudence Megaro, with a useful summary of further literature to date on the subject in E. R. Adair's introduction to Vol. II, pp. ix–xviii; see also Adair's *The sources for the history of the council in the 16th and 17th centuries* (London, 1924). On both the council and the secretariat of state see G. R. Elton, *England, 1200–1640*, pp. 66–81.

Evans (afterwards Mrs Higham) on *The Principal Secretary of State. A survey of the office from 1558 to 1680* (Manchester, 1923 [Manchester Historical Series, No. 43]), which might serve as a model of the genre, devoting a chapter each to the king's secretary (which, in England as elsewhere, may be considered the office of secretary of state *in ovo*), the reign of Henry VIII, 'The Great Elizabethans', 'The Age of Experiment' (the reign of James I), 'Charles I and his secretaries', 'John Thurloe, Secretary of State to the Protector', and the period 1660–80, then some forty-two pages on the office in general, and individual chapters on half a dozen special aspects of it; the very useful appendices include nine pages of bibliography—a rather sobering reminder of how much there is to be learned, considering that it naturally excludes everything written since 1923.

The most influential work on English administrative history is clearly G. R. Elton's *The Tudor Revolution in Government: administrative change in the reign of Henry VIII* (Cambridge, 1953), itself revolutionary (and controversial: see especially the extended debate in *Past and Present*, 1963–5), which argues the establishment of modern bureaucratic government in England during Thomas Cromwell's tenure as secretary of state in the 1530s (or, in the present narrower context, the establishment of that office as the functional hub of administration).[1]

A general work such as Mrs Higham's is inevitably limited in the detailed treatment possible for any given time within the long period covered, and Professor Elton would be the first to insist that the administrative revolution of the 1530s was not a switch from one rigidity to another. Fortunately, the need for detailed familiarity with personnel and procedures (which changed not only with progressive refinement of method but with temporary shifts in political circumstance) at specific times has in recent years begun to be filled in by specialised works on individual administrators, such as F. E. Emmison, *Tudor Secretary* (London, 1961), on Sir William Petre; Mary Dewar, *Sir Thomas*

[1] See also the almost simultaneous contribution of W. C. Richardson, *Tudor Chamber Administration, 1485–1547* (Baton Rouge, 1952).

The Subject and the Sources

Smith: a Tudor intellectual (London, 1964); S. E. Lehmberg, Sir Walter Mildway and Tudor Government (Austin, Texas, 1964); and a growing richness of works on Stuart secretaries and other ministers by members of the Joel Hurstfield seminar at the Institute for Historical Research.[1]

For France the secretariats have been covered for two substantial periods by N. M. Sutherland, The French Secretaries of State in the age of Catherine de Medici (London, 1962) and Orest A. Ranum, Richelieu and the councillors of Louis XIII: a study of the secretaries of state and superintendents of finance in the ministry of Richelieu, 1635-1642 (Oxford, 1963). There have been occasional works on individuals, such as J. Nouillac, Villeroy, secrétaire d'Etat et ministre de Charles IX, Henri III et Henri IV (Paris, 1909), but perhaps inevitably such work has focused upon the periods of the great chief ministers, ranging from Charles Vialart's History of the government of France under . . . Richelieu, in English translation as early as 1657, to J. Caillet, De l'administration en France sous le ministère de Richelieu (Paris, 1857), and Louis Dollot, Les cardinaux-ministres sous la monarchie française (Paris, 1952).

The French bent for institutional analysis has produced a substantial and valuable literature for the period, including Georges Pagès, 'L'évolution des institutions administratives', Revue d'Histoire Moderne, (1932); Gaston Zeller, Les institutions de la France au 16ᵉ siècle (Paris, 1948); R. Doucet, Les institutions de la France au XVIᵉ siècle (2 vols, Paris, 1948); Roland Mousnier, 'Le Conseil du roi de la mort de Henri IV au gouvernement de Louis XIV', Etudes d'Histoire Moderne et Contemporaine (1947) and his classic La vénalité des offices sous Henri IV et Louis XIII (Rouen, 1946); and Pagès' brief but perceptive sketch of La monarchie d'ancien régime en France, de Henri IV à Louis XIV (Paris, 1946).

[1] For north of the border see especially, Maurice Lee Jr., John Maitland of Thirlestane and the foundation of the Stewart despotism in Scotland (Princeton, 1959); Maitland was secretary 1584-95. On England see also G. E. Aylmer, 'Attempts at administrative reform, 1625-1640', English Historical Review, LXXII (1957), pp. 229-59, and The king's servants: the civil service under Charles I, 1625-1642 (London, 1961).

For Spain, the preponderant power in the period, there is no really satisfactory modern general treatment of central administrative institutions, and what exists for individual administrators is extremely spotty in both coverage and quality. Elsewhere one has a scattering of useful works, such as H. F. Schwarts, *The Imperial Privy Council in the 17th century* (Cambridge, Mass., 1943), but one still has to get down to greater detail for one's own briefer period to reach the sort of familiarity necessary for actual knowledgeable work in the documents; not many specific brief periods for given states have actually been given detailed study, so that one's period is far more apt to coincide with a gap in the literature; and when there is a certain amount of literature for the administration one is concerned with, the odds are greatly against its being of the quality and usefulness of Sutherland's or Ranum's. When it comes down to the *specifics* of how government business was actually being handled—who was being consulted, and how; who made the decisions or contributed to them, and how—the odds are instead that the existing literature will be insufficient because too general, or simply wrong, based upon faulty inferences or misinformation.

Fortunately, the answer to the problem of knowing what procedures were at a given time and place is built into the problem itself. Just as 'the pearl is the autobiography of the oyster', so government documents are of the bureaucratic machine that produced them, especially since that autobiography —where the documents survive, of course—records all phases of production, from intake through processing to output. For this reason one cannot emphasise too strongly the importance of this special role of the conciliar documents discussed in Chapter 2.[1]

---

[1] A NOTE ON TERMINOLOGY. Either ordinary or extraordinary envoys might hold the higher rank of 'ambassador' or the lesser rank of 'agent', for reasons which I have attempted to spell out (along with other aspects of the subject) in 'The Ambassadors of Early Modern Europe: Patterns of Diplomatic Representation in the Early Seventeenth Century', *From the Renaissance to the Counter-Reformation: Essays in Honor of Garrett Mattingly* (ed. C. H. Carter, New York, 1965, London, 1966). During the course of the seventeenth century there was increasingly inserted between these two an intermediate rank of 'minister',

and an additional (and confusing) one of 'resident'. Although differences in rank (as in kind) naturally affect the nature and contents of diplomatic documents, the term 'ambassador' is used throughout in this volume in the generic sense, indicating a diplomatic representative of any rank, and 'resident' in the generic sense of a resident envoy of any rank.

As monarchy was the most usual form of government in the period, the term 'monarch' or 'king' is often used for simplicity in contexts which equally apply to non-monarchs in a chief-of-state position; similarly, for 'king' read (where relevant) monarchs of any rank. Conversely, to avoid ambiguity and conflict within the wide variety of functional arrangements and power distribution that existed, the conveniently broad term 'government' is used in order to embrace generically whatever combination of monarch, ministers, councils, etc., may have been running diplomatic affairs in a given state at a given time.

CHAPTER 2

Archival Materials

The essential inseparability of the origin, nature, purpose and use of diplomatic documents is closely reflected in the many-sidedness of the archival terminology conventionally attached to them. This is a *mélange* that variously refers to them in terms of purpose and function (Instructions to ambassadors), of form, both general (letter) and specific (*Avis, consulta*), and of manufacture. Much of the discussion that follows is necessarily couched in the latter set of terms. These are of three principal types: the 'original', which is the formal, official version of a given document; the one or more drafts that may have preceded it; and copies and other later versions that may have followed it.

Draft

A document whose wording and precise contents were sufficiently critical might go through several drafts before the final version was finally arrived at. Even where this was not the case—a fairly straightforward letter to an ambassador, for example, on a fairly simple matter—it would normally be dictated in rough to a secretary or scribbled out by the writer for copying, in either case producing, in effect if not in technical fact, a 'draft', from which a clean copy was made for sending (the 'fair copy' or 'original'). In a secretariat where such drafts were produced with reliable frequency they were quite sensibly preserved as the sender's file copy.

Where this system existed, regularly producing drafts in the process of producing 'originals' and thus automatically producing available ready-made file copies, accompanied by the converse tendency to preserve drafts in the files (even when there were several, and even when they were early drafts and thus not accurate as 'file copies'), the historian gains two priceless benefits. First of all (obviously): a voluminous body of copies of letters sent, not dependent upon scribes having actually made all the file copies they were supposed to, and (for government correspondence, where such a system was most likely to exist anyway) tucked away in government archives, where the prospect of survival was very good, while the fair copy sent off was probably being passed from hand to hand at the receiving end with an excellent chance of getting lost, and while analogous file copies in private hands were beginning a less sheltered existence often far less conducive to their survival. To appreciate the value to the historian of the systematic preservation of such draft copies of out letters one has only to pursue an applicable research project at the Archivo General at Simancas, where they exist in vast numbers, and then at the Public Record Office in London, where one is limited almost exclusively to in letters—comparable to hearing one side of a telephone call.

Secondly, through the revisions that are revealed in a draft— additions, deletions, alterations of wording—one is often able to trace the course of policy formation (or at least a part of the course), detect changes of attitude, nuance of feeling, about particular issues, persons, states, etc., and learn a good deal else that the historian ought to know but would have no evidence of if only the fair copy were available to him. The possibilities for this are of course even greater if several drafts, at several stages of development, are available. (Some various specific drafts are discussed in the following section.)

'Original' or 'fair copy'

Of the several versions that a given document may appear in, the 'signed fair copy' or 'original'—in the case of a letter, the version actually sent by the author and normally the one read by the addressee or by someone acting for him—is often considered the principal version. Perhaps properly so in the main, but just because the supposition is so wisely accepted, one must note that this pride of place is not always wholly justified. As noted above, more of importance can often be learned from drafts than from the fair copy—aesthetically more pleasing, no doubt, but for that very reason often too aseptic for the historian's purposes, and of course containing nothing (beyond confirmation that it was sent, and when) not to be found in a reliable final draft. And in the special realm of ambassadors' reports on which policy decisions were based, the latter were in fact often based on versions of the report (discussed later in this chapter) other than the original and often substantially different from it. (Neither of the conventional names for this official version is directly appropriate to the case, both being relative to some other version. It is a 'fair copy' of course of an earlier draft, a transcription of the usually-messy final draft neat and clean enough for official use. Conversely, when previous drafts were made it is 'original' only with respect to the copies of it made afterwards.)

Copies

For various reasons, transcriptions might be made of the original, by the recipient or sometimes by the sender; properly used, the term 'copy', unqualified, refers only to these. (The specific term 'fair copy' refers only to the original. A duplicate for one's own use was sometimes made of a draft, which presumably one might refer to as a 'draft copy'; in practice the term is almost never used except improperly, for a simple draft version that is not a copy *of* anything at all.) In the following discussion of various types of archival materials, the term 'copy' is used only in the sense of transcription.

Contemporary secretaries filed documents in folders or packets, limited in size either by the subject matter or the need for easy handling in subsequent consultation (both readier location of individual documents and the ability to pull a whole packet without taking too many more documents than were actually desired). In reorganising documents (from policy or necessity) modern archivists have also put them in small individual bunches. In this, there are rough parameters of practical size. On the one hand, too small a group is almost as apt to get mislaid as an individual document is, and a multiplicity of them would simply multiply the task of cataloguing. On the other hand, too big a group cannot be given proper protective cover nor be handled very efficiently: with increasing size a group of documents usually becomes not only increasingly unmanageable physically but decreasingly useful to researchers who typically deal with a particular problem or period; few would be apt to want a series of diplomatic reports for, say, an entire century. Thus most documents of this sort are stored in bunches usually ranging roughly from two to six or eight inches thick; when they are bound (a crime that is widely but fortunately not universally practised) the physical limitations of the process usually limit thickness to three inches or so.

Archival terminology with regard to such 'bunches' of documents—the basic unit of archival organisation and cataloguing— is theoretically precise, but the usage is not. The French *liasse* or Spanish *legajo* (the two non-English languages most pertinent to the present discussion) literally means 'a loose bundle of papers', while the term 'volume' is understood in strict usage to mean *bound* volume, but the terms are commonly used generically to refer to either kind (presumably because the English 'bundle' is not very elegant, the English generic usage is usually 'volume'); in discussing documents here I have followed that convenient precedent of loose usage. The more specific term 'register', which should be some form of entry book, is also sometimes used generically, but I have used it here only in its specific sense.

When a continuous chronological series is involved, division into such groups is usually by even years (one or several) or half-years. One result of this logical procedure is its obvious and desirable orderliness; another is to make a *liasse* or 'volume' fairly meaningless as a measure of quantity: the correspondence for a given year may have an individual volume only because the ones before and after are too fat to allow even a few more documents to be squeezed in, or may be split into two volumes only because it is half an inch too thick to be bound as one. The point is not a trivial one for the researcher. A contemplated topic for research may require, say, 3,000 or 4,000 pages of documentation to be handled properly, but not be important enough to justify ploughing through twice that amount; if one knew that the available documentation was either inadequate or impracticably extensive one would undertake some other task instead of this inappropriate one. Yet to know from published catalogues that ten relevant *liasses* exist for the subject is little help, since that may mean anything from 2,000 to 10,000 pages. In addition, one usually does not even know whether both sides of the paper have been written on (they have in most copybooks; it is also an indication that they probably have when a volume is known to be *paginated* —every page numbered; but when it is foliated—only the leaves numbered—one has no such indication unless there are references to versos of folios—fo. 246v., etc.), halving or doubling the alternative possible wordage; the presence or absence of blanks introduces a further uncertainty. Taken together, the variables add up to a possible quantitative variation of perhaps ten to one: a potential margin of error of 1,000 per cent provides a fairly shaky basis for planning—and one more argument in favour of letting the documentation dictate the ultimate shape of research, and against *a priori* definition of subject.

INSTRUCTIONS AND RELATED DOCUMENTS

Every ambassador began his mission armed with a Letter of Credence and a set of formal written Instructions.[1] The former, a ritual letter of introduction to the receiving monarch (which

[1] With some variations. A plenipotentiary sent to negotiate a treaty additionally carried 'full powers', which (1) sometimes obviated the need for a separate Letter of Credence and (2) might in cases where the business to be negotiated was fairly straightforward require no further detailed Instructions. At the other end of the scale of importance, a formally credentialled envoy might be sent on a diplomatic errand so simple that his Letter of Credence might also provide sufficient written instruction. Late in this period there was also an infrequently used 'recredential' document (*lettre de recréance*), used when a resident was transferred directly from one court to another without the usual return home; the novelty of this form even as late as 1676 is emphasised in Phyllis S. Lachs, *The Diplomatic Corps under Charles II and James II*, p. 23.

literally asked him to 'believe' the named person as the sender's ambassador—hence the document's name) was merely the official document of accreditation that diplomatic custom required for the quasi-sacramental conferring of ambassadorial status and capacity on an otherwise private person, and need not detain us here. The formal Instructions, whose virtues as sources are exceeded only by their shortcomings, require some attention.

There is no other single diplomatic document more useful than an ambassador's formal Instructions—and none more over-used and over-rated, or more subject to misuse and misunderstanding. It is a particularly useful document because it contains so much in such brief compass. In structure it is simply an itemised list of directions and explanations regarding anything from a few to twenty or more specific matters. Though it is somewhat artificial to separate policy from even the most prosaic aspects of its execution, one may distinguish, broadly speaking, between two types of concern: (1) routine activities ranging from high ritual to the most mundane practical matters, and (2) various items and areas of specific diplomatic business—issues between countries, etc.—which are to be negotiated, communicated, monitored, or otherwise attended to in some appropriate fashion.

The former can provide the historian with a valuable picture of current protocol, practical aspects of an ambassador's activities, etc., and frequently an indispensable insight into the nuances of relations with the particular country in question; even when the picture is not complete it provides context for issues, negotiations, etc., without which they cannot properly be understood.

The second type is both more useful and more risky as evidence. Collectively they provide a succinct overview of issues, problems, concerns, etc., involved in relations with the host country and with some others, and to some degree in the home government's foreign relations in general, and in the process provide a summary statement of decided-upon policy regarding these things. It is here that the document's most conspicuous value lies—and its most dangerous pitfalls.

Both types often fill in a good deal of background on individual matters when it is pertinent, and often tell the ambassador not only what to do but how to go about it (and how not to), features which, with all the above, make an ambassador's instructions a veritable storehouse of information. Or misinformation, as the case may be.

The initial problem is that the coverage of various duties and issues, though wide, may be incomplete, and that what *is* there may be pure hokum. This is necessarily so, given the nature and conventions of diplomatic representation. Few ambassadors (and almost never a resident) had full powers. Without such plenipotentiary status an accredited ambassador could indeed deal in a general way with many things, and had certain basic powers inherent in his office, but he could properly engage in serious negotiation on matters of substance only if he had been specifically empowered to do so, and those powers at the beginning of his mission were normally incorporated into his formal Instructions. The receiving monarch could insist on seeing these powers before agreeing to such negotiations, as without them nothing the ambassador negotiated would have any official standing, for which reason they were commonly and quite appropriately called *public* Instructions. Thus, though much they contain is perfectly accurate, one did not ordinarily include there any topics that might cause offence or alarm or reveal state secrets, nor any aspects of otherwise includable topics that might. Those things were normally—and as a matter of course— consigned to a separate set of Secret Instructions, often substantially longer than the public ones. Thus the historian simply does not know what he has in his hand as 'evidence' until he has seen both sets.

Even then, however, the evidence is not necessarily (nor even very often) complete. The ambassador may have been given some special or last-minute instructions in a completely separate document; he was probably given further documentation of a sort more properly described as briefing than as instructions; and he was almost certainly given still further briefing and/or instructions orally. The Secret Instructions will deal with items

47

beyond those in the public ones, and will tell the historian that some of the public ones are false, but, equipped with just these two documents, one cannot be sure of having in hand the full range of topics actually dealt with, nor the correct version of all the false or misleading public ones. It is not unusual, for example, to find in an ambassador's public Instructions full powers to negotiate a specific treaty and orders to do so, with nothing in the Secret Instructions superseding this or even qualifying it, yet to discover elsewhere, in his or someone else's correspondence, that he was orally (but bindingly) forbidden to conclude any treaty at all.

Even if one is reasonably certain of having all of the documentation, however, or sufficient to be sure of what government policy was and what were the real instructions given, at least regarding a specific issue, the applicability of this as evidence of policy or instructions 'currently' in force is or can be far more limited than would support the overly-sanguine generalisations that historians have sometimes attempted to make it serve. On the one hand conditions can (and probably will) change at some later date, and the corresponding instructions can (and probably will) be superseded by others; as this can be both quite sudden and quite soon, the assured *continued* validity of any given instruction on any given matter is, without continuing evidence, extremely and increasingly slight. On the other hand, there is no assurance that present policy as indicated in a new ambassador's Instructions was also previous policy (i.e., a continuing one); the odds in fact are quite good that the reverse is true, as quite often (but again not always: it requires further evidence either way) it is a change of policy that occasions the change of residents, the previous resident having been associated with the previous policy and perhaps with its failure.

At Simancas, *Estado* 2863 is a small *legajo* catalogued as 'Instructions to Ambassadors, 1605–1617'. It includes a folder whose contemporary label reads, 'Despatch [i.e., in the sense of 'the group of papers'] that was given to Don Pedro de Zúñiga for [i.e., in connection with his appointment to and assumption of] the ordinary embassy in England, signed at Valladolid 20 April 1605.' It contains Zúñiga's public Instructions, his Secret Instructions, and a number of other items related to his appointment. As this comes sufficiently late in the period 1500–1700 for such forms to have become well developed, as Instructions for that embassy at that time would predictably involve numerous matters of importance,[1] and as Zúñiga provides another type of example elsewhere, this is a more than usually useful and convenient example of this type of documentation—of some of the virtues, limitations and pitfalls discussed above. In addition, a *coup d'œil* cast over both the instructions and the other contents of the folder provides a convenient one-place illustration of certain characteristics of diplomatic documents in general, of other comments made elsewhere about the nature and use of diplomatic documents, and of some problems of historical evidence as encountered in diplomatic sources.

It will be noted in the discussion that follows that drafting of this routine batch of documents was begun in time for an expected use in April: some are dated 20 April (the date on the overall folder label) or 27, and some bear an open date, never filled in; some were redated 15 June, which is clearly the ultimately pertinent date, while some remain with the April date unchanged, leaving the correct date for those particular items uncertain for the researcher. What is most important, however, is not the

---

[1] For present purposes it was a conveniently critical time, Spain having made peace with England only the year before and with France in 1598, with relations still very uncertain with both, and with some sort of settlement with the Dutch (eventually, the Twelve Years' Truce of 1609), much wanted by Spain, still to be achieved.

The following details are pertinent to this and a later discussion. The Treaty of London (1604) had been negotiated for Spain by a delegation headed by the Constable of Castile and the Count of Villamediana. After the Treaty was concluded, the Constable returned to Spain, leaving Villamediana as interim ambassador until a regular resident, Zúñiga, could be sent. Zúñiga (1605–7), who (by then Marqués de Floresdavilla) also went to England as an extraordinary ambassador in 1612, was replaced by Alonso de Valasco (1607–13) and he by Diego Sarmiento de Acuña (later) Conde de Gondomar (1613–18, 1620–2).

correct date of particular individual drafts but the clear indication that the new ambassador's departure was delayed for eight weeks after having been firmly set to the point of dating at least some of his credentials: the careful researcher will want to find out why.

As a document for reading the set of Instructions is somewhat above average. Clearly a final draft, it has almost no corrections and these very minor—here and there, e.g., a pronoun inserted that may very well have been merely left out in making this copy of the draft. Only one paragraph is a later insert, and this too could have been a copyist's omission. The handwriting is a bit scrawley and slapdash, but large and open and therefore quite easy to read. The *o*'s look like *a*'s, the final '-*nos*' (as in *algunos* or *años*) is unnecessarily convoluted, and the *r*'s are sometimes no more than hinted, but in the main the hand is fairly conventional for the country and period. The abbreviations (e.g., *dho* for *dicho*) and symbols are frequent but conventional—as is their frequency, for that matter, and their variability: sometimes the modern *h* with upstroke is used, sometimes the old one with downstroke, resembling a *y*; '*que*' is usually '*q*' but is sometimes spelled out, mainly when there is a bit of space left at the end of a line. The abbreviations for '*officio*', '*beneficio*', and especially '*servicio*' would be initially illegible to anyone not familiar with the fantasies involved, but are quite routine when one is. The one exception, soon decyphered, is a figure that begins 'on the line', swings right and curves up and around counter-clockwise, then shoots in a south-west trajectory past the starting point until, well below the line, it loops up and to the right, clearing the rest of the figure, and joins the next word; it might be described as a very fanciful infinity sign, or perhaps a '*p*' gone badly awry. This (ours not to reason why) stands for the preposition '*en*', and usually, when there is such, includes the beginning letter '*e*' of the following word, so that '∞*Londres*' means '*en Londres*', '∞*l tratato*' means '*en el tratato*', '∞*ste*' means '*en este*', etc.

The paper is of rather medium quality which, fairly typically, means that its condition is still quite good, though some pages or passages are a bit faded and there has been some 'bleeding' through of the ink, in neither case with any serious loss of legibility. The sheets are about 12½ by 17½ inches, folded once (a usual procedure) to make two leaves (or, as all sides are written on, four pages) of about 8¾ by 12½ inches. These have been preassembled, the required number of sheets having been stacked and folded together so that instead of a series of separate four-page folio sheets one has a single sheaf comparable to a book signature.[1]

The text begins slightly to the left of the centre of the page, with a rigidly straight margin maintained, and runs all the way to the right-hand edge, both of which are traditional Spanish practices intended to preclude the addition of unauthorised words to official documents.[2] There are twenty-nine or thirty lines to the page (making a reference to ten lines in the following discussion equivalent to a third of a page). With the abbreviations spelled out, a page here is roughly equivalent to a page of double-spaced typescript. The public Instructions run to fourteen pages in twenty numbered sections, the Secret Instructions (to which the above description equally applies) to twenty pages in six numbered sections. Their contents, briefly summarised, are as follows:

[1] For a comparatively long manuscript to be in this preassembled 'booklet' form is a fairly sure sign of a copy, as distinct from a fresh composition, as the number of pages needed for the text must necessarily be known in advance. It is a less reliable indication, however, for shorter pieces: a person composing a draft or taking dictation might be fairly certain that he would need, say, more than four pages but not more than eight and so be able to preassemble the right number of sheets. (This *caveat* is confirmed by the evidence one finds of occasional bad guesses, an additional leaf or two tacked on at the end—though, conversely again, this type of miscalculation also sometimes occurred in mere copying, especially when from a markedly different format.)

[2] One will find this somewhat less strictly adhered to in the correspondence of Spanish ambassadors at the time as well. When a letter was to be folded, sealed, and addressed on the outside of the letter itself (i.e., serving as its own envelope) it was considered desirable to have no writing on the inside of that part of the page that was, after folding, to be the exposed outside of the letter, so that prying eyes could not read through the paper; this provided an additional motive for writing only on half the page (and of course only on one side), but it was not universally followed: English ambassadors at the time, for example, wrote over the whole surface of the page.

(1) (1¼ pages) Instructions regarding mode of travel, etc., and for arranging for his first audience with James. (Runs rather heavily to verbiage.) Indicates that further travel instructions will be given orally (which these vague and rambling ones certainly call for).

(2) (18 lines) Instructions for first audience with James.

(3) (10 lines) Ditto with Queen Anne.

(4) (23 lines) Re Villamediana's handover of embassy affairs to Zúñiga, briefing Zúñiga thoroughly before leaving, etc.

(5) (1 page) Because English Protestants are so quick to seize upon any 'vice and disorder among Catholics', thereby 'becoming more confirmed in the error of their way' [*sc.* gaining a propaganda advantage that aids their own cause by discrediting Catholics], Zúñiga is to be particularly careful in governing the conduct of his entire household to see that this does not happen.

(6) (20 lines) 'The end of greatest consideration with which I have made peace with England has been (after the service of God, as I have said) for the good and quietude of Christendom', an altruistic end which Zúñiga is to seek to promote at every opportunity. (Twenty fulsome lines of this, not necessarily insincere, but extremely suitable for reading by James, his ministers or his spies.)

(7) (2¼ pages) On the past and current attempt of the Dutch, especially through the efforts of their resident Caron, to divert English trade from the 'obedient states of Flanders' to the rebel provinces, the disadvantages of which, including political ones, Zúñiga is to persuade James of. (In fairly strong language for public Instructions, but anything less would have been suspect. The subject of the Dutch is considerably supplemented in Zúñiga's Secret Instructions, as noted below.)

(8) (1 page) If any English Catholics seek Zúñiga's aid or protection he is to take care to avoid all such offices whenever possible because of the risk of making James displeased with them; instead, he is to do everything possible to bring the King and his Catholic subjects together. (Again unexceptionable, but again considerably supplemented in Zúñiga's Secret Instructions, below.)

(9) (18 lines) The king of Denmark being a relative of the king of England, Zúñiga is to take whatever opportunity his embassy to England may offer in order to promote closer Spanish-Danish relations.

(10) (13 lines) The same regarding the duke of Holstein. (This whole paragraph—obviously an afterthought belatedly inspired by 9, into which it might as well have been incorporated—was added as a

marginal insert in this draft after the next paragraph had been written.)

(11) (16 lines) As the French ambassador to London works constantly against Spanish interests, Zúñiga has to be very cautious with him, take care to penetrate his designs, and do whatever is necessary to frustrate them. (The brevity of this section obviously does not reflect the importance attached to its subject, nor does that of item (17), nor the fact that neither Franco-Spanish relations nor French affairs in general are given any further attention in the Secret Instructions. The length here is sufficient since (a) matters such as this, to the considerable degree to which they are dependent upon *ad hoc* initiative, are not really susceptible to detailed instructions beforehand, (b) Zúñiga's briefing on the current situation, means of execution, etc., will come from having read recent diplomatic reports and orally from Villamediana [in this particular case there is of course no previous resident ambassador to London available in Spain to help in the briefing before departure, a role Zúñiga himself later performed in his turn], and (c) what remains to be said here, limited to the core of the matter, happens to be capable of succinct statement. Though its burden is clearly and bluntly stated it is so deftly worded that it would not have been compromising if seen by either English or French: although it orders anti-French activity it is not an aggressive Spanish initiative but merely necessary self-protection against the French ambassador's, and by implication France's, anti-Spanish activity, which this whole paragraph is neatly made to be primarily an accusation of.) (A special aspect of Franco-Spanish rivalry is dealt with in item [12].)

(12) (1⅔ pages) Regarding the French ambassador's claim to precedence over the Spanish ambassador, which Zúñiga is to counter. (A symbolic manifestation, in the area of protocol, of the two principal powers' competition for prestige and thus influence in the world at large, and thus not so frivolous a matter as it might seem at first glance. Gives a very useful summary of the legalistic and practical background of the argument, though, unfortunately for the interested historian, most of Zúñiga's briefing on the latter was to come orally from Villamediana. Since there was of course no Spanish ambassador to Spain nor French to France, London was the highest ranking court available at which this issue could be fought out: thus its special importance and particularly comprehensive coverage —far longer than any other item here—in the Instructions of a Spanish ambassador to that court, or of a French one.)

(13) (12 lines) Concerning Spanish complaints about English piracy. (This was to be a matter of first importance in Anglo-Spanish relations for years, but as Spain's attempt at resolving the problem through diplomacy was necessarily only beginning there was little in the way of either background information or experience-based guidelines that could be furnished to a new ambassador. Thus the brevity of the instruction—stating simply that Villamediana has begun pressing the matter and Zúñiga is to continue—reflects not a low priority, but the current nature of the problem: an example, in its way, of what a document can tell the historian by what it does *not* say.)

(14) (11 lines) 'It will be very appropriate to your office to see to it that the natives of my kingdoms who may be trading in England, Scotland and Ireland be given all good reception and keep the immunities usual and customary in all time of peace with the particularities that have been declared in the capitulation of it [i.e., the recent peace treaty].' (As of 1605 this reflects a perhaps reasonable hopefulness, but could be misleading regarding commercial fact: even a decade later the then Spanish ambassador could find at most two or three Spanish merchants in the whole of the British Isles: a convenient example of the need to confirm in subsequent ambassadorial correspondence the implications of *a priori* instructions, which on occasion can be quite inappropriate to the reality. This instruction may reflect the Spanish government's concern or their hopes—or even a picayune desire to be tit-for-tat, since the rights of English merchants in Spain gave them no end of headaches—but its direct implication that such a problem really existed is utterly false.)

(15) (8 lines) The same (somewhat more reality-based than [14]) with regard to the subjects of the Archdukes (the 'Spanish Netherlands' being then under their independent sovereignty, 1598–1621). An additional four lines, saying the same with regard to the duke of Savoy, have subsequently been deleted (which rather suggests a change of Spanish attitude between April and June).

(16) (8 lines) Zúñiga is to take care to report any development that could damage the interests of Philip or his allies, together with his recommendations on such matters. (During about this same period, with the English diplomatic machinery under the rather thin-skinned stewardship of Robert Cecil, English ambassadors were advising each other to confine themselves to reporting the facts; their advice was not wanted.)

(17) (13 lines) 'Although the King of France appears to desire the

continuation of my friendship, you are to proceed very vigilantly in penetrating whatever you can from England of his designs in matter of war and everything there may be against me and my kingdoms, making use for this of the best means you can, and you will advise me of what you learn of consideration.' (Although since 1598 Franco-Spanish relations were formally defined by the Treaty of Vervins, the condition of 'perpetual peace and friendship' that thereby existed between them would not be seriously compromised by Henry IV's learning of the contents of this instruction, for two significant reasons: this was widely understood as the natural thing to do—Henry being a most unlikely person to cast the first stone—which may serve as a contemporary definition of 'friendship'; and Henry himself was after all still giving aid to Philip's Dutch rebels, which gives a fairly realistic definition of 'peace'.)

(18) (19 lines) Zúñiga is to maintain two-way correspondence on all important matters with the Archdukes, and with Philip's own ministers in Flanders (in other times this would have been with his governor general there), his viceroys and governors in Italy, his ambassadors to Rome, the Emperor, France, Flanders, Savoy, Venice, and Genoa, and 'the viceroys and governors of the frontiers of these kingdoms', for which he will be given copies of the various cyphers currently used by them. (Any state with several permanent embassies abroad maintained a similar practice of information-swapping among them—some consequences of which for the historian are discussed elsewhere; Spain gained an advantage in Italy by including the viceroyalties of Naples and Sicily and the governorship of Milan, places where other states had no ambassadors and so perforce lacked effective, openly-maintained listening posts there. Especially the fact that after 1540 there were no regular embassies at Milan, which remained at the centre of successive crises, must have had a substantial effect upon the intelligence and the resulting foreign policy of the various powers.)

(19) (21 lines) Zúñiga is to send his despatches by way of Flanders via the ordinary and extraordinary posts that run from there (both London-Brussels and Brussels-Spain), except when the occasion obliges him to send a special courier (some instructions regarding this); he is to keep a record of postal and other embassy expenses and send a signed account to Spain for approval. (These accounts are discussed as sources later on.)

(20) (9 lines) That's all for now; anything left unsaid here or that may come up is remitted to Zúñiga's 'prudence and experience',

with which he will see to everything in appropriate fashion; further instructions will be sent later [in the course of his embassy] as required. (Both stylistic convention and the normal amenities require some such closing paragraph, but it is significant that in fulfilling that routine requirement the wording manages to preclude the existence of any other current written Instructions, an intentionally deceptive implication naturally meant to mask the existence of the Secret Instructions noted below.)

Since these were fairly typical instructions, some things about them warrant particular notice—not least how remarkably little substance they really contain. Twelve of the twenty sections (sixty per cent, comprising fifty per cent of the space) are unrelated to issues, or even to any aspect of specific foreign policy: eight of these (1–5, 18–20) deal with practical details, two (14–15) with standard consular protection, two (16–17) with the important but still routine matter of information gathering. Of the remaining eight, one (6) is a policy statement but largely for English consumption, while two (9–10, which could easily have been combined) deal with improving relations with third parties whose affairs are fairly remote from Anglo-Spanish relations, included here solely because of a potential opportunity provided by the accidents of English geography and James's marriage ties.[1]

Only five, totalling a shade over five pages (hardly more than a third of the space), can be called substantive, issue-oriented items. Two, totalling a little over two pages, involve France (11–12; 17 is really a matter of routine information gathering, given a separate paragraph because of France's special importance to Spanish affairs—but its inclusion here would not greatly

---

[1] In discussing the relative importance of these instructions one may characterise these two as minor if only because they would necessarily involve only a minuscule part of Zúñiga's activities, there being no opportunity for doing very much: but the positive implication of aggressive opportunistic diplomacy is just as significant. And the hoped-for opportunities did occur, including two visits by Christian IV of Denmark to his sister (Queen Anne) in London in 1606 and 1614. The latter is interestingly dealt with in Calvin F. Senning, 'The visit of Christian IV to England in 1614', *The Historian*, XXXI, No. 4 (August 1969), pp. 555–72.

affect the argument of brevity of treatment). These are quite self-contained, and the Secret Instructions conspicuously lack any section on France. (This does not, of course, reflect any lack of importance attached to France by Spanish policymakers, nor to such corollary matters as Anglo-French relations, but rather a comparative lack of complexity in dealing with Franco-Spanish affairs from London, France being neither the host country nor so involved in Anglo-Spanish affairs as both France and England were in Spanish-Dutch affairs. The Instructions of a Spanish ambassador to France at the time in fact present something of a mirror image of these, England figuring in them about as France does here, and with the substantial attention to Dutch affairs centring mainly on French involvement as it does on English involvement here.)

Only one item (7)—though one of the longest at two and a quarter pages—deals with the Dutch, and this only concerns their threat to the Southern Netherlands' English trade. But in the Secret Instructions drawn up separately at the same time, two of the six items, totalling over nine of the twenty pages, deal with more delicate Dutch matters involving England: the Dutch war, especially with regard to Englishmen serving in the rebel armies, etc. (3) (about 3 pages); and the possibility of using England as intermediary in the quest for negotiations for a truce or treaty, their strong desire for which the Spanish felt they could now avow publicly (4) ($6\frac{1}{3}$ pages), the latter a fascinating set of guidelines for manœuvre that could serve as a model for planned deviousness.

Only two items in the public Instructions, totalling only a bit over a page, deal with England herself: a conciliatory twenty-nine lines on how the ambassador is to conduct himself with English Catholics (8), and a necessary mention of the problem of English piracy (necessary because it would be missed if these public Instructions were shown, the ambassador for example showing James item (6) or item (8) to demonstrate Philip's good faith, but necessary also as specific authorisation to negotiate the matter officially). For Zúñiga's instructions on further matters regarding affairs with England, and for his real instructions regarding some of these, one must go to the remaining four of the six items in his Secret Instructions (1–2, 5–6), which total nearly eleven pages, almost as long as the entire public Instructions and over eight times as long as the 'English' content there.

These start off (1) with over seven pages on how Zúñiga is really to conduct himself with the English Catholics, the only really moderate aspect of which is a repeated warning to be careful not to get caught at it. (This is an unusually good example of the fact that a given policy outlined in instructions such as these cannot be assumed, on the basis of *this* evidence, to be in force at some later date, though one unfortunately frequently sees citation of such 'evidence' for policy at a substantially later time. In the present case, the secretly-instructed policy of heavy direct involvement with the English Catholic community proved so counterproductive that in a few years it was quite reversed, being replaced by what was essentially the falsely-pretended policy of earlier public Instructions.)

(2) ($1\frac{1}{3}$ pages) deals with what was to be a staple of Anglo-Spanish relations for two decades, and regarding the beginning date of which there has been a good deal of confusion: 'Among the discussions that the Count of Villamediana had with the Queen of England and the Secretary Cecil not many days after he arrived at that court they gave him to understand their desire that discussions of marriage of the Infanta my daughter with the Prince of Wales be moved, and . . . in respect of their young age and other difficulties [i.e., in effect: since nothing could come of the discussions very soon anyway] and it seeming advisable not to give disappointment at a time when peace and friendship were being negotiated, it was permitted to the said count that he should give good reception to the proposal to the end of bettering with this negotiation that of the Catholics, but giving to understand to the said Queen and to whoever might speak to her in this (as the count did, and afterwards the Constable) that the effecting of this had to be preceded by the Prince's being raised a Catholic and being [a Catholic], and having represented this difficulty of religion to them it was up to them to satisfy it, and

meanwhile [for however long] they did not do so, the negotiation was to be suspended [*se ha de dar silencio a la plática*].' Villamediana will fill Zúñiga in further, and there is to be enclosed here a copy of what at the time of the Constable's return to Spain he had written down for Villamediana on the matter, 'which is of the substance that you will see, but if they should speak to you about it you will give ear with good grace, especially going along in that of religion, and you will advise me of what they say'.

(5) (1 page) notes that Villamediana will brief him on the Spanish pensions that during the peace negotiations of 1603–4 were granted to 'certain ministers of that king and to other persons'; he is to familiarise himself with them and with the whole arrangement in order to make best use of them; this is followed by some specific directions regarding procedure.[1]

(6) (1 page) deals with what was really a routine embassy duty, understood as such by everyone, but tucked away out of sight in the Secret Instructions in order to preserve the decencies and fictions of friendly diplomacy. Zúñiga was to exert great care and effort in 'penetrating the state of [that] king's *cosas*, such as how fares his treasury, and *estimación* of his vassals, their relations with him and their intentions and those that English, Scots and Irish have among themselves and with their neighbours against the common good and [in] particular [that] of my kingdoms, and where their Intelligence is operating and in particular the friendships and correspondence that the said king currently has [*va tratando*] with [the king] of France and the bases on which it is founded and that which may be treated of between them, the which is very necessary to know, and for this the count of

---

[1] Since Zúñiga was the first resident to operate this pension system and so had a large hand in shaping it, there is some irony in the fact that when eight years later James got full evidence of it—in full detail—it was by the theft of a written pre-departure briefing on the matter that Zúñiga, who had since been replaced by Alonso de Velasco, himself had prepared for Velasco's replacement. Because it provides opportunity for simultaneous discussion of the use of diplomatic documents then, their archival disposal, and their specific later historiographical use, this affair has seemed an appropriate one for use in Chapter 7 to illustrate the problem of scattered documentation.

Villamediana will advise you of certain ways [*caminos*], and those and such others as you may discover you can follow and inform me particularly of all that you learn. . . .'

This, and items (16) and (17) of the public Instructions, aided by the pensioners of item (5) here, fairly well define the information gathering and report (and historical document) producing role of the ambassador.

In addition to the fourteen pages of public Instructions and twenty pages of Secret Instructions, the packet contains nine drafts of related letters, all less than a page in length, which conveniently illustrate the documentary by-product of a routine ambassadorial appointment.[1] All are 1605; all are from Philip III, though they were of course drawn up for him; unless otherwise noted, all are formally dated from Valladolid, which at the time was the regular seat of the Spanish government:

(1) To Zúñiga, 20 April; rubriqued[2] draft; Zúñiga's formal letter of appointment. The dating, in a different hand from the copyist's, suggests that this document, and by implication some of the others here, may have been drafted substantially earlier than even the 20 April date.

[1] As was customary in a well-run secretariat, the label bears a notation of still other documents that had been removed from the folder: 'There was taken from here the dispatch given to the Admiral of England [the Earl of Nottingham, who came in 1605 as extraordinary ambassador for the formal oath-taking that made binding the 1604 Treaty of London] and the Instruction that the Council of State sent and [sic] to the deputies [i.e., the Spanish peace delegation] that were in England, [taken out] to give to the Mr Secretary Andres de Rozas.' These had presumably previously been taken from elsewhere to be consulted in drafting Zúñiga's Instructions.

[2] By a secretary of state or similar official in charge of the papers of this department. In Spain (and some other cultures) a personalised rubrique was (and still is) adopted as an individual's regular short-form signature. As it normally consists of only one initial it often does not narrow the field down sufficiently for reliable identification, and just what letter it is is often hopelessly lost anyway in a riot of fanciful flourishes, whorls and squiggles. Thus the investigator working in documents where they occur frequently and their owners' identities are important has little choice but to make himself (as they are encountered and identified) a set of facsimiles for routine future reference.

(2) To James I, n.p., [blank] April 1605; rubriqued draft. A Spanish draft of the gist of Zúñiga's Letter of Credence. If other evidence were lacking, a passage stating that Zúñiga himself was to carry this to England provides clear indication of an intended April departure. The form of such a document is so radically altered in the process of its obligatory conversion into the conventional Latin formulae for sending that it is not at all obvious that this is really a draft of the official Letter of Credence and not just a friendly notice of the appointment; the key words here are the request that James give Zúñiga 'entero credito' ('fidem integram' in the subsequent Latin 'original') as his ambassador—the operative phrase that makes this document literally a 'credential', and of course gives it its conventional name, Letter of Credence. It is significant regarding Spain's still-uncertain official attitude towards James's legitimacy on the English throne that he is referred to three times with the cautiously noncommittal (and rather slighting) 'Your Serenity', never as 'Your Majesty' (true also of items [3] and [4] below; item [5] casts an interesting sidelight on this concern).

(3) Latin version of item (2) (larded with a long string of Philip's titles and other formulae conventional in Latin letters but not bothered with in the Spanish draft); date altered from Ventasilla, 27 April, to Valladolid, [blank] June 1605. Originally neat enough to serve as a fair copy, but with numerous subsequent alterations in wording. *See* item (4).

(4) Later copy of item (3): 15 June 1605: '[sent] with Don Pº de Çuñiga'. Probably intended as a fair copy but botched at the end when the copyist omitted the day of the month from the date, thus having to insert it between the lines and spoiling the document for sending, after which, presumably rattled, he made a further mess. Result: a second excellent file copy.

(5) To Queen Anne of England, n.p., n.d.; rubriqued rough draft, in Spanish, of item (6). A letter of introduction for Zúñiga, somewhat analogous to the more important Letter of Credence addressed to the King Regnant: strictly speaking only a standard courtesy (the one to the king was a technical necessity) but one considered unusually important in this case as the Spanish hoped to exercise special influence through the Queen Consort because she was Catholic. Drawn up with particular care on a matter that also governed the wording of items (2)-(3)-(4), there is added at the bottom of the page a brief 'example of how the Queen of France [Marie de' Medici] was written to', indicating how that other queen

consort had been addressed in the salutation and in the text: 'Señora. And four Majesties in the body of the letter and at the end of it Our Lord protect Your Majesty and keep you in his Holy Grace'; it was signed 'Good Brother of Your Majesty, *Yo el Rey*', with the *sobrescrito* reading 'To the Most Christian Queen my sister'. In this draft to Anne, 'Your Serenity' has twice been substituted for (apparently) 'Your Majesty', though one still stands (but see item [6]).

(6) Latin version of item (5) (with the same effect on its form as with items [2] and [3]): date altered from Ventasilla, 25 April, to 15 June 1605: signed by Philip[1] and countersigned by a secretary of state: obviously an intended fair copy that became available as a file copy when the altered date made it inappropriate for sending. Some subsequent additional fiddling with Latin style changed 'Britain' to 'Great Britain' (which conforms to the usage in the analogous letter to James), but like James the lady got three 'Your Serenities' and no 'Majesties' at all.

(7) To the Count of Villamediana, the working head of the peace delegation that had negotiated the Treaty of London the previous year, who had been kept there on an 'extraordinary' basis pending the arrival of a permanent resident; Valladolid, [blank] April 1605; draft. Notifies Zúñiga's appointment; charges him (routinely) with introducing the new ambassador to the king and queen and their ministers, and with briefing him on affairs both orally and in writing; gives permission then to return to Spain; and expresses satisfaction with Villamediana's performance. An undeleted statement that this letter is being sent with Zúñiga would, taken alone, force the researcher to choose between two possible secretarial oversights—either failure to delete the passage or failure to correct the date; actually, the latter choice is made obvious by the deletion of a reference to the Lord High Admiral of England which would have been applicable in April but not in June. An annotation indicates that Zúñiga received a copy.

(8) 'To the Viceroys and Ambassadors', Valladolid, 20 April 1605: rubriqued draft. Informs them of Zúñiga's appointment and instructs them to maintain '*buena Intelligencia*' with him—to corre-

---

[1] The traditional notion that the king of Spain never signed his name is a myth. Latin documents he signed, as here, Philippus (with the usual variant spellings). Spanish documents he did sign '*Yo el Rey*', but this ended in his personal rubric, a rather fanciful F that is not immediately recognisable as such.

spond with him and keep him informed of everything of importance, as he will with them. The subscription list (all duly checked off as sent): the viceroys of Naples and Sicily, the governor-general of Milan, and the Spanish ambassadors to Rome, the Emperor, France, Savoy, Venice, and Genoa. Presumably not sent until June (no specific indication).

(9) To the Archduke Albert, n.p., n.d.; draft. Normally the subscription list for item (8) would have included the governor-general of the Netherlands, but they had been ceded in 1598, as an ostensibly sovereign state, to the Archdukes Albert and Isabel; thus this letter carries the same burden as item (8), but in terms suitable to Albert's regal blood and sovereign status.

THE AMBASSADOR'S REPORTS HOME

For both symbolic and pragmatic reasons the ambassador's despatches to the home government may fairly be considered the principal type of diplomatic document. They originate with, and record the doings of, the central figure in diplomatic activity (if not in policymaking); and they are by far the most numerous —an imposing quantitative consideration—and the most comprehensive in coverage: far more so, for example, than his correspondence with others or his government's correspondence with him.

Inevitably, these despatches reflect all aspects of the ambassador's role, as described in some detail earlier, and as reflected in the Instructions discussed in the previous section; in brief: to perform the ritual necessities, represent his own government in specific negotiation and general liaison with the host government, and collect as much information (ranging from state secrets to routine technical data) as possible about this and other countries and any other matters that might be of interest to his own government either as specific intelligence or as general background for making policy decisions. His final duty—perhaps the most important, considered on an on-going basis, and certainly from the point of view of policymakers at home—was to report on all this.

This he did by sending regular despatches by 'regular' channels at fixed intervals (conditions permitting), their normal frequency varying usually from once or twice a week to once a month or more, supplemented, as need arose, by extraordinary despatches sent by special courier.[1]

These 'despatches', in the broader sense of a single mailing taken as a whole, consisted of the ambassador's official report plus (usually) a covering letter to the secretary through whose hands it would go and (often) enclosures of various kinds. The latter two are discussed in subsequent sections; the immediate concern here is with his report proper, his 'official despatch' in the narrower sense.

This was in the form of a letter. Its content may previously have been written down from time to time, as things happened, information was collected, etc., over the whole period since the last previous report (a week perhaps, or a month), in which case it would have something of the air—and the more evenly distributed contents—of a journal; or it may have been drafted at the last minute before sending, in which case, like a modern weekly newspaper, it would often be weighted most heavily with the more recent events, the freshest news (even though it might all be equally new to the home government).

Usually this various information was all contained in a single letter, its length ranging from a page or two to twenty pages or more, depending mainly upon how much there was to report. Since this usually involved a jumble of various topics this procedure inevitably complicated rational handling by the home government: if one wanted to consult a particular person only on what was reported at the bottom of page four and the top of

[1] This wide variety in the frequency of sending despatches had a considerable effect upon their contents, their ultimate role in decision making at home, and their nature as 'evidence' for the historian—a complex time-factor discussed in Chapter 7. When circumstances required and conditions permitted, as during a crucial phase of a peace congress and especially when distances were short, an ambassador might send off despatches as often as daily, while a resident in an out-of-the-way place who found little to report and where communications were bad (an English resident in Constantinople, for example) might do so as infrequently as once or twice a year, but these are fairly unusual extremes.

page five, one had either to abstract a copy of that especially for him or let him see the whole letter, which might not be desirable. Thus it is not surprising that occasionally a conscientious ambassador attempted to rationalise his reporting—but to little effect. Sarmiento (Gondomar), at the beginning of his London embassy in 1613, was one, taking it upon himself to report on separate topics in separate letters in the same despatch. As this seems a rather obvious thing to do, and since the practice of regular reporting had by then been around for a good while, a full century for the Spanish themselves, one is rather surprised to find the Spanish government elated at such a brilliant idea and ordering their other ambassadors to do the same. But the weight of practice, the extra burden this procedure put on the ambassador and his staff, and the bureaucratic tendency to stick to a single procedure that will work for all cases (sometimes necessary mention of a particular topic was too brief for a separate report to be worth while) were apparently all too much, and nothing came of it. Before long Sarmiento himself was usually stuffing everything into one omnibus letter. So much for reform.

This official report might be addressed either (but usually consistently) to the chief of state or the chief minister. In the case of monarchs who chose to direct foreign affairs themselves and so read most ambassadorial despatches themselves, the former would be true, but the reverse does not necessarily apply: just because a letter is formally addressed to a king it does not necessarily follow that he ever saw it, or wanted to. Most of the less active monarchs who delegated most of the despatch-reading and decision-making still usually read some from time to time (and made an occasional decision themselves), in matters of particular importance or particular interest, or touching whatever happened to be available during a conscientious spurt of royal participation between hunting trips, but the historian must have other evidence (marginal comments, conciliar documents, etc.) to be sure of this for any given document; its being addressed to him may be purely nominal—as his signature on a reply to it may also sometimes be.

Unlike correspondence between one official and another at

home and other types of domestic government document,[1] diplomatic correspondence was usually dated (some of the problems that are involved in dating are discussed in Chapter 7). In a well-ordered diplomatic corps an ambassador's official reports (and his other correspondence) have the additional merit of beginning by acknowledging receipt of the addressee's last letter to him, citing the letter's date and often the date on which it was received as well (in correspondence in general this may involve individual mention of several letters received since the writer last wrote, but here it was the ambassador who wrote more often than his government replied). He may also make specific mention of the date of his own last letter to the addressee or—not unusual— several letters still unanswered, all of which helps the historian not only to sort out which letter is in reply to which (sometimes not otherwise very clear) but, with the aid of matching references in letters to him, identify the whole body of correspondence that existed and know which pieces he lacks.

The comprehensive and detailed nature of ambassadors' reporting is illustrated later on, but it had less 'substantive' aspects that are worthy of mention. The ambassador was concerned not only with the various kinds of business within his charge but with any activities of others that might impinge upon his own functions, either favourably or unfavourably—though the latter was usually supposed, ambassadors being no less jealous of their purview than other public officials. When these things enter his reports one gets a glimpse not often available elsewhere of unofficial doings on the fringe of international affairs. A typical example comes from an English ambassador in Madrid:

> A certain Italian soldier that hath served this king called Jhon Baptista Adan Tallamar repaired to one Mr Lee Consul of Lisbon and signified unto him, that he knew many things much importing Your Majesty's service, desiring that he might be shipped for England, and he would discover them unto Your Majesty's Council, and

[1] This point has been made with regard to English State Papers in G. R. Elton's volume in this series, *England 1200–1640* (Ithaca and London, 1969), pp. 71–2.

accordingly the said Consul hath caused him to be imbarked in a ship of Bristol with direction unto the Mayor for the sending him up to London. He pretendeth to have gotten knowledge of some great entreprise intended against Your Majesty; I doubt not but when he shall be in England the truth will be gotten out of him; and if he prove an impostor (of which kind of people this place aboundeth) he shall be used accordingly; when I shall understand his Propositions and Discoveries, I hope I shall be able easily to conjecture of the probabilities of them.[1]

How much can be learned from ambassadors' despatches on matters beyond the purely diplomatic? As 'sources' they are as varied for the modern historian as they were for contemporary policymakers: typically they are practically unlimited since the reporting duties of the ambassador were practically so. The amount of data on international commerce, for example, is in the aggregate enormous. Most pertinent, however, is the ambassador's special task of comprehensive reporting about the host country—political developments, government structure, economic conditions, and anything else that seemed important or even remotely relevant. Yet the official reports of these official observers—obvious treasure-houses of information carefully collected about the local scene—have been remarkably little used as sources for domestic history. Some details have been added to the internal history of most European countries for the period from the Venetian Relations, but that is a special type of report, submitted on the ambassador's return home at the end of his embassy and so inevitably of a rather general summing-up nature, lacking in the immediate details of events, alteration, etc. A century ago S. R. Gardiner made enormous advances in the historiography of the reign of James I largely by comprehensive research in the despatches of Spanish ambassadors in what should have been a model to follow, but historians, willingly enough to adopt Gardiner's findings (especially those that confirmed earlier beliefs), have not been moved to adopt his procedure as well,

[1] John Digby to James I, Madrid, 20/30 March 1613, SP94/19/304-05v; 305 (spelling modernised).

though after Gardiner the fruitfulness of diplomatic sources for domestic history has hardly been open to doubt.

One might, however, offer an opposite example here from one's own research. It is well known that after Philip II's death his ministers were pushed aside and control of Spanish government and Spanish policy taken over by the Duke of Lerma and his hangers-on. In the records of the Council of State, whenever great matters are being discussed, the opinion expressed first, and usually concurred in by most of the rest, is that of the Comendador Mayor de Leon, identified only by this high-ranking title in one of the religious military orders. One automatically knows this to be Lerma, since one knows that his was the deciding voice in affairs. One knows it, that is, until one recalls that Lerma was the Comendador Mayor de Castilla, not Leon, and eventually encounters cases—surprisingly infrequent—where the conciliar documents record the presence not only of the Comendador Mayor de Leon but of the Duke of Lerma as well, with the latter's opinion on foreign affairs being given further down the list. It turns out that it is the former, not the latter, whose opinions are usually agreed to by most of the others, adopted as those of the council, sent to the king for formal approval, and thus become the policy of Spain. Though there still is no doubt that Lerma is the top man at court and—crucial matter—is in effective control of royal patronage, it becomes clear that most foreign policy matters are being decided in (and by) the Council of State, and that the dominant voice there is not the favourite's but someone else's. This of course leaves the question of whose voice it is, since he is consistently identified in the conciliar document only by his Comendador Mayor title, not by name, and it is not a title whose holder one is apt to know or very readily discover. After sufficient investigation, however, it proves to be Juan de Idiáquez—not one of the new crowd at all, but one of Philip II's old ministers. He retained this dominant position until his death in 1614, which is to say through sixteen of the twenty years of Lerma's *privanza*. If this does not completely reverse it very radically alters one of the best-known 'facts' of Spanish history, and by extension one of the most important facts of European history: who dominated Spanish policy at a time when Spain dominated Europe.

I have chosen this example, however, not only for the importance of the matter involved but as an illustration of what may be found specifically in an ambassador's report about the internal history of the host country: I muddled it all out in the conciliar documents, but as a matter of fact John Digby, who himself had seen many of those documents and had other contemporary sources of information available to him as well, figured it out and explained it in one of his first reports after taking over the English embassy there in 1611; the situation was clearly spelled out for any historian who wanted (or happened) to look in this collection of reports on that country at that time—and has been for three and a half centuries.

Versions Originating with the Ambassador

Draft Because an ambassador's reports to his home government were relatively straightforward—mainly narrative and descriptive—and involved little or no consultation with others, they required little of the thorough-going drafting process that the government's policy-stating and instruction-giving replies to them entailed. Thus writing them, in contrast to government letters, though often done by dictation to a secretary and usually the product of careful thought as to style and content, did not automatically produce fully fledged drafts usable as file copies. For simple or routine matters, especially if they ran heavily to formula phrasing and organisation, the first version produced might in fact well be the 'fair copy' actually sent, without any prior drafts having been written at all. 'File copies' therefore usually had to be specially made after the letter was written.

Sometimes this was done simply by making individual copies of individual letters, but not always. Here too the influence of the relative modesty of the embassy's needs is felt. Since it was comparatively a small-scale operation that did not share the government's need for a complex multi-category filing system nor one that would allow later individual retrieval of copies of letters sent, the ambassador was free to choose a more compact system, and quite frequently did: the letterbook—outgoing correspondence simply transcribed into a blank bound volume— was, for its compactness and its freedom from loss of individual copies, the most suitable and often the most widely used form of embassy file copy. Thus comparatively few full-fledged drafts of ambassadorial correspondence were actually produced, and, transcribed into an embassy letterbook, few of those produced were used as records and preserved as such; as those few— transcribed or not—were likelier to end up in family collections of personal papers than in official archives, after three or four centuries of private handling still fewer survive. As always, however, there are exceptions: some ambassadors made almost a fetish of assembling a full collection of copies of practically everything they wrote, and of copies (if not originals) of practically everything they received, and some of these collections have come down to the present almost intact. (Letterbooks are discussed below.)

Original From a bird's-eye view diplomacy appears as a matter of policy decided at home by rulers and executed abroad by ambassadors. Viewed from the ambassador's end it is a matter of instructions received and executed, followed by despatches sent home which eventually produce a feed-back of still more instructions, and so on. But if one views diplomacy as neither an equal partnership between master and servant (which it certainly was not) nor primarily the activity of diplomats (which is to mistake the sword for the swordsman) but as, in a profounder sense, a function of the state, whose eyes and ears (and of course negotiating agent) the ambassador is, then the ambassador's role seems even more crucial and his despatches even more vital, since they were in an age with no sophisticated communication—not only no radio or transatlantic television, but no home subscriptions to foreign newspapers—in fact the state's principal and almost only contact with the outside world, the world in which the state, through diplomacy, was seeking to act. The ambassador's despatches, and especially his formal reports, were that point of contact. As regards his reports, one may say that the fair copy actually sent and received was the exact point at which contact was made. Some characteristics of fair copies of documents are discussed above, under 'Instructions'; some problems involved in their use are discussed later in this book; some of the uses and variant versions made of the fair copy of the ambassador's report are discussed below.

Duplicate original Fairly frequently in troubled times, when regular channels became more uncertain—mail passing through south-western France was sometimes seized by Huguenot raiders, for example, and other couriers sometimes holed up for days or weeks along the way for fear of a similar fate—an ambassador would send a duplicate of his report to increase the chance of delivery, or improve its speed. This might happen in several ways. He might simply send it with a subsequent departure of the same mail service, hoping that if the original did not get through (with the slowness of even normal communications he could not afford to wait to find out) the duplicate would. He might send them both off simultaneously, or nearly so, the one by a fast but currently risky route (the regular mails), the other by slower but surer means (merchants from the ambassador's country who happened to be returning home were often used in this way). He might combine these two, a chance to send a duplicate by another route coming up unexpectedly later. He might send the original with another ambassador's courier and a duplicate later by his own (who may earlier have been indisposed) or by the regular mail. (Sometimes, in fact, he might send more than one duplicate, employing various routes.)

This obviously is a boon to researchers since it increases the chances of the letter's survival in one form or another, but it poses some serious problems. This version is simply a transcription of the original; when it is signed, as it usually is, it is in fact nothing more than a second 'fair copy', and thus often indistinguishable from the original unless the sender (by an explanatory note) or the recipient has deliberately made it so. (And the latter can be ambiguous: Spanish ambassadors, like any others, used this form, but the contemporary secretary's identifying annotation *'duplicado'* usually means a copy made after receipt.)

Instead of preserving on the duplicate the date of the original, the ambassador sometimes assigned to each the respective date of its sending. If they were sent on, and dated as, say, 10 and 20 April, and one encounters only the latter (knowing nothing of the former's existence), the possibilities for misreading are legion: the whole context of what he is reporting is shifted by ten days, perhaps a crucial difference; 'yesterday' becomes the 19th instead of the 9th, and 'last Tuesday' becomes a mess;[1] and of course if the letter would have taken a minimum of ten days to reach its destination it was obviously not the basis of a council decision taken on the 25th.

Even if the ambassador clearly states that this is a duplicate he is sending on the 20th of an original sent on the 10th, one has no way of knowing (without further evidence) whether the original ever arrived—that is, if a ten-day trip may be assumed for both, whether the government received this information ten days after the 10th or ten days after the 20th. If there is evidence that both did arrive but not which was used, then the ambassador's

---

[1] Depending upon what days the 10th and 20th fell on, either within the respective ranges (a) Wed.–Sat. and Sat.–Tues. or (b) Sun.–Tues. and Wed.–Fri., the date implied in the duplicate for 'last Tuesday' would be either (a) seven or (b) fourteen days too late. But this is not all. In terms of how many days ago it (and whatever occurred that day) was in relation to the letter's date—a difference in which can alter meaning considerably, quite apart from the correctness of the date itself—the available range in either case would be 1–7 days, but the respective ranges come out (a) 1–4 and 4–7, and (b) 5–7 and 1–3, so that the duplicate implies in (a) that it was three days *longer ago* than it was, and in (b) that it was four days *more recent*. For example, if the 10th was a Sunday, then Tuesday (and Tuesday's event) came five days ago, but the duplicate indicates yesterday, while if it really was yesterday (if the 10th were a Wednesday) the duplicate indicates it was four days ago. As the historian necessarily derives a good deal of the meaning of diplomatic correspondence in terms of date and of time relationships one need hardly labour the confusion and error that a wrong date such as this can cause.

explanation of which he sent by which route may at least make clear what the likelihood is: if the original was sent by a fast courier and the duplicate by slow merchant ship the former may have arrived by the time the latter was being dispatched; if the reverse, the latter may well have arrived first—i.e., the letter was originally sent on the 10th but, after a ten-day journey, cannot have arrived (in duplicate form) before the 30th. When both versions bear the same original date, similar conditions of course prevail. (When the date of arrival is important to the historian and the ambassador's covering note says only, 'I sent the original of this ten days ago with my secretary John Smith', one is properly grateful to the court gossip who, in one of his trivia-packed letters to a friend, mentions that 'John Smith arrived here on the 20th'.)

When no other versions exists, that a duplicate does is clearly a very good thing (as the crisis circumstances of their origin suggests, their contents are more than normally important to the historian), and even when the original has survived, the duplicate can tell him a good deal he would not otherwise know about those circumstances. But it can be very slippery evidence that the researcher has in his hands.

The Ambassador's letterbook When drafts and individual copies were not so employed, the ambassador's record of outgoing correspondence was in the form of a copybook, a blank volume (usually bound in advance) into which letters sent were transcribed. Letters sent were of four types: (a) his official reports; (b) the often substantial covering letters, addressed to a secretary of state or other minister through whom (a) was directed; (c) other official correspondence—letters to his government's other ambassadors and such; and (d) personal correspondence. Sometimes each of these may have its own letterbook; quite often (b) is included with (a), the letters of a given date or a given mailing (which might include letters of more than one date) usually grouped together; or (b) and (c) may share a letterbook, or (a), (b) and (c), and so on.

In principle this entailed a simple transcription in full of the

73

letter sent, but in practice this must be qualified regarding both completeness and fidelity to the version sent. From the researcher's point of view this version is actually superior to the originals in one regard: the letterbook itself surviving, the individual letters are not subject to separate loss. But it can be inferior in several ways. It lacks government notations regarding arrival and disposition—relevant to (b) as well as (a). It sometimes omits secret material that was coded in the fair copy (there is much variation in this). It usually lacks copies of enclosures (those included that were not authored by the ambassador himself tend to be rather special items, and rather short). And any holograph postscript the ambassador may have added is frequently lacking; as this may be either urgent last-minute news or mere personal pleasantry, the seriousness of the loss will vary. (The latter, though not hard evidence of 'events', can be vital to understanding the nature of the relationship between writer and addressee, which in turn is often essential to understanding the actual meaning of what is found in their correspondence.)

Usually the texts are reliably copied, with only insignificant variations in wording, but occasionally the variations are substantial. Sometimes this apparently resulted from a revision of the 'original' after the text had been copied into the letterbook and from not transferring the correction, or from the copy being made after the original had gone and thus having to be taken from a draft not precisely the same as the fair copy—either one no more than a clerical sin. Elsewhere, however, it is a clear case of tampering. Sometimes the text is considerably tidied up for the ambassador's permanent records (when the letterbook version is noticeably superior to the original stylistically one may be fairly certain which is a revision of which). If the ambassador is, for example, complaining about something he may do so discreetly in the version actually sent but speak more boldly for posterity's admiration in his own copy. In his narrative of some passage of diplomatic arms with a minister or a monarch (a staple of diplomatic reports) he sometimes speaks and acts far more boldly in the letterbook version than in the original (where presumably his responsibility for accuracy is stronger): since a proper ambassador must comport himself—be angry, pleased, strongwilled, etc.—as the interests of his sovereign (not his own personal feelings) require, he is largely engaged in showbiz, and it is therefore perhaps not surprising that in recounting the unscripted dramas he participates in he should often tend to improve his part in the telling.

Since such records were not routinely turned over to the government (except by the most conscientious), their rate of survival has been far less good than for the originals the government received and filed away: but by the same token their survival is far less important. What is *really* needed, in archives that have preserved only in-letters, is *government* letterbooks.

Versions Originating with the Home Government

An ambassador's reports (and the rest of his despatches) were of course written to be read, but the original sent and received was not always the most suitable form for this, which could vary considerably according to practical considerations—how much reading was involved, how many readers must be accommodated, the purpose of the reading, and so forth. Neither the range of variation nor the specific usual choices, however, were the same for every state. Generally speaking, the more fully developed the government structure in both size and complexity (which would normally also be true of the government business to be handled) the more variant applications were involved, either necessary or possible, and the greater the variety of versions actually employed. Though the larger states would naturally be more fully developed than smaller ones at any given time, the government structure of most states was more fully developed at a later date than at an earlier one, so that the requirements and usages would not be the same in 1500 as in 1600 or 1700. The versions discussed here cover the spectrum used by the most advanced states fairly thoroughly; some in fact tend to shade into others. Only some, of course, were employed by smaller states, and there was naturally some local variation with regard to particular usages.

Decyphers Some, much, or (infrequently) all of the original of an ambassador's report might be in cypher. (The normal procedure for encyphering a letter was to draft it in 'clear', underline everything that was to be put into cypher, and do so in making the fair copy.) When only occasional words or short passages were in cypher they were usually decyphered between the lines or in the margin. If the pages got very long, some secretaries (or some secretariats) would put the decyphered text on a separate slip of paper and glue that by one end to the original (usually at the appropriate place). If there was a great deal of cypher it would more normally be done on a separate sheet (both neater and easier), attached to the original; if almost all was in cypher the secretary would often also transcribe the parts in clear along with it—i.e., sensibly producing a clear copy of the entire letter while he was at it (conversely, non-secret passages were sometimes encyphered while at it when most of the letter was going to be anyway). A separate decypher of a letter entirely in cypher would similarly amount to a copy of the whole letter. (Some secretariats, however, would continue decyphering to any length between the lines.)

Over the centuries some of these have become separated from the originals (and some of the little stuck-on slips have come off and been lost), but it is still very rare not to have the decyphered text readily available. Most times it will be decyphered right on the face of the document, while separate decyphers are as apt to be encountered as any other type of 'copy'—if not next to the coded version then in some other relevant *liasse* one will be going through anyway. The few remaining other cases can usually be quickly resolved by resort to available keys, including published ones.[1] It is sad to report (since it is sometimes looked forward to as a romantic prospect) that the chances of a researcher's

---

[1] E.g., Jerome Devos, *Les chiffres de Philippe II, 1555–1598, et du Despacho universal durant le XVIIe siècle* (Brussels, 1950). Some archives—the Archives Générale du Royaume de Belgique, for example—have assembled special *liasses* of cypher keys.

having to decypher diplomatic reports is exceedingly slight.[1]

There is one special problem with decyphers: when one is long enough to be a letter itself and has become separated from the original it is often not possible to tell that it is not a copy of the full letter, which at times can be seriously misleading. (A simple excerpt from a letter is usually labelled as such; a decypher, intended to be kept with the original, is often merely labelled with the date of the letter, making it appear, in isolation, a copy of the whole letter.)

The following, a brief contemporary decypher from a report by the English ambassador in Madrid in early 1613, is a fair example of what they are apt to contain:

May it please yor most excellent Ma^{ty}. The Spanish Embassador there [Alonso de Velasco], hath lately advertized many pticulars hether concerning Ireland, as your Ma^{ty} will see by the Copie of his letter which goeth herewith, and the Irish Bisshop that liveth in this Court hath moved this King and State, that he would be pleased to give the Irishe some Ayd and assistance, but this King and State will by no meanes give eare unto this motion. But with much importunity the Irish have so farre prevayled, that it hath ben treated in this Counsell what Course was fittest to be held for their releife, and the resolution your Ma^{ty} will see by the Copie of a Speache made by Don Juan de Idiaques in the Counsell, which I send verbatim unto your Ma^{ty} with some small addition of the Duke of Lerma. And because I desire that your Ma^{ty} may with more confidence relye upon my advertisements, your Ma^{ty} may be the more assured of the truthe of them if the Spanish Embasdor there doe show unto you the Copie of the King of Spaines letter concerning the Bisinesses of Ireland (in conformity of Don Juan de Idiaques his speache) to his Embassador in Rome as I am informed he shall have order to doe.[2]

[1] Cypher and code are two distinct things, though the word 'code' is commonly used loosely to cover them both. A cypher is a set of symbols used in place of letters or combinations of letters to spell out words; a code is a set of symbols or words or names used in place of whole words or names, usually the latter. Thus to write 'The King of France left Paris yesterday' one would use a single code symbol each for the person and the place but spell out the rest of the message in cyphered 'alphabet'.

[2] John Digby to James I, [Madrid, ? March 1613], SP 94/19/312. I have

Copies and shortened versions In a government in which more than one person is involved in making foreign policy decisions (which means almost any government) the single original often will not suffice for everyone to be able to read it by the time the decision must be made or advice given. When the letter is short or the number needed is small the need can be answered simply by making the required number of full transcriptions. If an entire privy council or council of state has to read it, however, then labour-saving expedients have to be used to allow the clerks to finish the task in the available time; where ministers and councillors have a good deal of such correspondence to read, the same device is necessary to allow *them* to get through it all.

The two principal forms for this are excerpts and minutes. The former is simple, though administering it—deciding what should be excerpted and getting all the related excerpts together and to the right people at the right time—sometimes was not. The simplest case would be a letter from an ambassador in which part is about matters the council should consider and the rest merely personal, in which one would just copy the former part and not the latter. If the letter is on several matters and the council is considering only one of them on this occasion, then one would excerpt only the part dealing with that matter. By definition, an extract is a full (i.e., not summarised) transcription of only a part of a document; in practice it is usually not very long—if it were, minuting would be necessary.

Minutes of ambassadorial reports are designed to meet both needs: for efficient multiple reproduction and for efficient reading, the latter inseparable from the need for efficient handling of the business of state, whose subject matter was not only often massive but extremely varied as well. Such minutes thus took the form of a restatement, normally in the third person, of what the

spelled out most abbreviations on the double grounds that they are tiresome to the modern reader and are as likely the decypherer's as the author's anyway, but have retained variant spellings and one clear misspelling (of Embassador) for their relevance here: they have a chaotic effect on letter frequency and so make a code more difficult to crack.

ambassador has said in a given letter. This *may* be a paraphrase, shortening the relevant text considerably, thus reducing the wordage to be copied numerous times and to be read by councillors (who may have a good deal of such material to read), but not always. It might shorten the total wordage simply by abstracting certain relevant parts of a letter without actually abridging the text of these parts themselves. And the purpose is not only—often not even primarily—to *shorten* texts (though one took advantage of opportunities to drop irrelevant passages or abridge occasional digressive ones) but to reorganise them for more efficient handling in the government's consultative process. If an ambassador reports in topical fashion on commercial, military and other developments, mentioning those of several states under each heading, the needs of a council meeting being held to discuss one of these topics could be met by merely excerpting that part, but if the meeting were being held to discuss French affairs, one would abstract out of the letter all the references to France found under the various headings; if the ambassador's report were organised by country the converse would be true.

In practice, in a state with wide-ranging interests, multiple sources of information, and a highly developed machinery for processing the latter for use in handling the former, the minuting process was much more highly articulated than this. Spanish procedure by the middle of the period 1500–1700 can serve as a model. Although the Council of State met frequently, its sittings were planned on a specialised basis, dealing with some particular topic (e.g., defence of the Indies) or crisis or affairs with a particular state. Thus a *consulta* on French affairs—or any other —would normally come up only from time to time. Meanwhile, several despatches may have been received from the Spanish ambassador in Paris. All of these might be combined in one set of minutes, reorganised so that references to the same topic in the various letters are brought together.

This obviously facilitates councillors' consideration of these matters—not least in providing a more coherent briefing on the current status of the various aspects of French affairs—but it raises problems for the researcher. The document will normally be carefully labelled as 'minutes of despatches of such-and-such specific dates from the ambassador to France', and the date of the actual council meeting will also be noted. But (unless one has the original text as well) it is often impossible to tell which parts come from which letters, frequently an important consideration. If, for example, something potentially important for which one has no other evidence has purportedly happened 'just now' and the letters span perhaps six weeks or more, one needs to know when it happened not only for its own sake but in order to know whether the government considered it so unimportant as to let it go for weeks without calling a meeting, or conversely has called one immediately upon receipt of the news—or for that matter whether it might not have been handled in a previous meeting or even without the council, and included in these minutes for completeness or for merely follow-up consultation.

The greatest virtue of this minuting system is that it seldom left anything out that was of importance to the subject in hand, and if that subject were broad enough—affairs with the country reported from—it omitted very little from the whole despatches: it might well run to a dozen or two dozen itemised subjects. But if a fairly narrow subject matter was abstracted from a broader report, one not only loses the rest of the report both as a source on other matters and as the context of this report on this narrow one, but risks erroneously supposing that this is the entire report, often a very misleading assumption with regard to this matter's place and importance in the larger scheme of things.

A further characteristic, that of converting the writer's first-person text into third person, sometimes loses a bit of the flavour but seldom alters the document's meaning. The same, however, cannot be said of the tendency to shift the tense of verbs in the process of transforming the ambassador's own account into the secretary's statement of what that account says, a tendency no doubt strengthened by the fact that while the ambassador was writing in the present about events that had just happened, for the official engaged in minuting the ambassador's writing was done in the past, tending to push the events reported into the past perfect. The two examples most conspicuous in my own experience involve S. R. Gardiner's treatment of the occasion on which the Spanish ambassador Sarmiento (Gondomar) supposedly established his ascendancy over James I and the later one on which James demonstrated his dependency. In the former case in late 1613, the Privy Council had ordered the arrest of one Doña Luisa de Carvajal, a dependent of the Spanish embassy, for her religious activities; the ambassador sent a complaint to the king, who was away from London, which James rebuffed, but the ambassador threatened to leave the country if she were not released, and in apparent response to this threat she was. Gardiner had available to him only the minutes of the ambassador's report on this matter, which telescope the time involved badly and gave him the possible impression that this whole exchange was with James when in fact (as the original text makes clear) the latter passage—the threat and acquiescence to it—involved only the council and not James at all. In the second case the minutes (on which Gardiner based his much-quoted account) relate Sarmiento's report of the dissolution of the Addled Parliament in 1614 and of the audience on the subject he *had had* with James. If this audience is understood to have occurred before the dissolution, this account of it can, with a little willingness on the reader's part, be understood to show James getting the ambassador's reassurance of Spanish intentions before going through with the dissolution; such was Gardiner's understanding, which has been followed by historians of the reign since, but in the report upon which the minutes were based the audience clearly occurs *after* the dissolution, not before as the minutes' past perfect seems to imply.

Obviously, a document version that can seem to record a confrontation that never occurred (as in the first case) or can in effect reverse the meaning of the original (as in the second) is a very uncertain source to use by itself. Fortunately, they seldom need to be, since an archive that preserves minutes, a mere working document, will normally have preserved the original or copies of it. The minutes themselves are in fact better thought of not as just another version of ambassadorial correspondence but as a principal type of consultative conciliar document, not as a dependable record of what the ambassador wrote but as the actual version the councillors read—in sum, not as a reproduction of something else but as a functioning historical entity in its own right.

Minutes do, however, have a special usefulness in providing an overview of subjects, or aspects thereof, that an ambassador is currently reporting upon and the council is currently consulting about, and thus of the issues, problems and areas of concern at a given time. The archives may in fact possess (the Spanish ones do fairly often) a still more succinct version of this, a summary list of the 'points of the despatches' of given dates from a given ambassador. These sometimes consist of little more than subject headings, but even then they can provide a very informative overview of concerns at the time: a dozen topics touched upon is not unusual, and twice that not really rare. When they deal with matters capable of brief summary, the official drawing up the list may not only list the topics but characterise what is reported about them, in which case this ostensible outline can serve the researcher quite handily as a sort of skeletal equivalent of minutes.

Two further government-made versions of an ambassador's reports should be mentioned. When the original, or a decypher or transcript thereof, is filed away for safekeeping, it will be identified, so that it may be quickly located later, by a secretarial notation on the outside (sender, addressee, place and date of sending, and ideally date of receipt), normally along what would be the top edge when the despatch is standing with others in its place in vertical files, in the manner of modern file folders or bundles of them. But since an ambassador might have written more than one report with the same identifying date, and even if he did not a secretary may later be seeking a report on a particular matter whose date he knows only roughly—some time in the previous winter, for example—a really well-run secretariat will add to these bare data a capsule summary of contents. One would suppose that a secretariat highly enough developed to follow this procedure was also highly enough developed to do it reliably, neither distorting nor omitting mention of matters of importance, and this is in fact normally the case. The advantage of these summaries to a secretary looking for reports on given matters is obvious—as is the advantage it provides to the researcher trying to plough through as many documents as possible and grateful for any system that will tell him their contents at a glance.

One will only rarely find register books of despatches received, but this is no serious lack. Even when the form was used they rarely contain even a summary of the despatches' contents, and so serve mainly as a guide to what was written, a fairly limited usefulness. (The limitations of the form here are implicit in the name 'register', a simple record of documents sent or received, useful for documents of a consistent formula type but far less meaningful for a type of document so varied in nature and contents as diplomatic correspondence.)

The Ambassador's Covering Letter
The ambassador's report was normally accompanied by a covering letter to the official—a secretary of state or some other—within whose purview handling despatches from and to that embassy fell. Its purpose is first of all to refer to the letter or letters and perhaps other materials in the despatch (i.e., the whole packet mailed), and, where applicable, to recent letters received, to despatches sent earlier, and to similar practical details of the official correspondence. But the covering letter served other functions as well, for the ambassador and for the researcher.

As the ambassador was usually in some sense committed to a career in government service, or at least to profiting by government favour, and success in this was as much a matter of politics at home as of service abroad, relations with the official who handled his papers were extremely important, that official being the ambassador's principal contact with the court from whence all favours flowed but from which he was vulnerably separated. Keeping fences mended (while being careful not to become too committed to any one official in a mutable world) was thus a prime function of this second layer of 'official' correspondence. From it—especially on a cumulative scale—one gets a considerable amount of information about the actual handling of the despatches involved, about the activities of the ambassador, the movements of other embassy personnel, etc., and about the current working structure and power relationships in the home government.

For example, the English ambassador in Madrid writes to Robert Carr, Viscount Rochester (soon to become Earl of Somerset), on 8 August 1613:[1]

> My very good Lord: By Your Lordship's letter sent by my secretary I have perceived that testimony of Your Lordship's favour which I have ever much aimed at. The continuance and measure thereof I desire may be but according to the fidelity Your Lordship shall find in me to my master's service and the particular respect and observance towards yourself, for I hope (now His Majesty hath put me wholly and only into your[2] Lordship's hands) I shall not only acquit myself as a good and loyal servant towards His Majesty but shall be

[1] Digby to [Rochester], Madrid, 8 Aug. 1613os, P.R.O. SP94/20/21 & v; holograph. Spelling mostly modernised on the grounds that that is how it was then—modern, not quaintly archaic. One thing modernisation distorts, however, is the repetitious use of formal address, which is made to seem more laborious and even more obsequious than it was. In practice it was not only routine but made routinely simple by the use of extremely short abbreviations: for Your Lordship y^r Lo: or y^r Lo^p or (not very dignified sounding) y^r Lor^p, or for the king y^r Ma^{ty}; as also in the other languages.

[2] Here Digby has struck out what appears to be 'most', presumably having started to write 'your most capable hands' or some such, then for reasons of his own did not. Such minor alterations, sometimes quite suggestive, are frequently to be found in originals not previously drafted, as appears to be the case here, but infrequently in the fair copies of letters and other documents previously carefully drafted; such amendments, often quite revealing, are of course far more numerous in the drafts themselves.

found to serve Your Lordship as honestly as any gentleman that ever depended on your love.[1]

In my letter sent by Mr Cottington to Your Lordship I entreated that he might not be left loose, for that besides the fidelity to the King's service which hath been ever found in him, he hath so much knowledge of Spain, and such secrets have lately passed through his hands, that it is fit that some care be had of him; further, he is a right able and an understanding man for any kind of employment, therefore out of these regards let me move Your Lordship to oblige him to you by being the cause that some good may be done him.

All other things worthy Your Lordship's knowledge which the present affordeth and my knowledge attaineth to, Your Lordship will find in the despatches that come herewith. And therefore I will not unnecessarily give Your Lordship trouble but with my hearty wishes for the continuance of all honour and happiness unto Your Lordship I commend you to God's most holy protection, Resting.

Mad. the 3d of   Your Lordship's to be commanded
Aug[t] 1613 st[o] vet   [signed] Jhon Digbye

The covering letter is also somewhat of an elaborative appendix to the main report itself, touching upon items that are not thought sufficiently substantive, or adding details thought too trivial or otherwise inappropriate for the main report. whose contents were inevitably restricted by the mandatory tenor of seriousness and sobriety required in an official state paper and of deference and propriety required in addressing a king or chief minister, as • distinct from a mere secretary whose social rank may be no more than the ambassador's (in Spain it would be far lower) and who may be a personal friend as well. Thus one often gets not only a good deal of personal chatting between them and news and

[1] The conventions of 'patronage' in government service required this assurance if Digby was to work effectively with him; but although such an assurance might reflect a real patron-client relationship it was also a routine courtesy to be extended to any minister to whom one was functionally responsible. Here the order of priority given the pledge of fidelity and service to the king and to the minister is quite appropriate to the case: when Somerset's loyalty to James came into question two years later Digby began sending all his important despatches to James via other hands, especially Archbishop Abbot's.

comment about mutual acquaintances and gossip about all sorts of minor miscellany, but further comment upon things dealt with in the main report as well. Some of these additions are consigned to this covering letter because trivial, or tangential to the point of the main report, or of personal interest only to the secretary. Some are amusing anecdotes, too funny not to tell but necessarily told here because there is normally no room for levity in the main report which often allows for a limited amount of irony or other mildly humorous treatment of its contents, but seldom for outright jokes. But not least important for the researcher is the permissibility of greater candour here, where the writer not only need be less deferential but less circumspect, and not necessarily even convenable.

Sarmiento (Gondomar) provides a convenient example early in his embassy in London, when he was having trouble with a Treasury official who in earlier days had quite obsequiously sought his patronage but now, having become an enemy, was systematically blocking dispatch of the ambassador's long-overdue and badly needed expense money. The ambassador's 'official' complaints to the king and the chief minister, though increasingly desperate, were necessarily circumspect and proper, but to a secretary of state who was also a friend and ally he allowed himself an outburst of temper and a dash of vernacular, the ambassador grumbling, 'time was when he used to kiss my ass'.[1] It is an earthy bit of candour that would be sought in vain in the ambassador's main correspondence addressed to the king, but which gives an inkling of the realities—in this case intra-government squabbling—that lay behind diplomatic activity but can seldom be gained from the main correspondence.

A rather fuller example of the types and variety of contents may be had from the covering letter to Sir Thomas Lake that

[1] The original Spanish is '. . . *me besaba el culo*'. Although I am informed that the British reader may prefer the alternative spelling 'arse' to avoid confusion with the homonym that means 'donkey', I have opted for the American vernacular in translation on the grounds that the context precludes ambiguity, it seeming unlikely that the President of the Hacienda ever kissed Sarmiento's donkey.

went with Digby's first despatch after learning of the death of the Earl of Salisbury, who had been simultaneously Secretary of State and Lord Treasurer.[1]

Sir: By my last letters unto you, which were of the fifth of July, I advertised of the receipt of yours of the fourth of June. I now recommend unto your care the delivery of the enclosed Despatch, which according to your directions I am bold to address unto His Majesty. It chiefly concerneth a narration how the Treaty of Marriage for the Prince with the Infanta betwixt His Majesty and this king hath been hitherto carried, from the beginning of my employment to the issue unto which it is now brought. I have written it in nature of a Discourse unto the Secretary of State. If His Majesty shall be pleased to make any other use of it than thereby to receive what hath formerly passed, he may be pleased to make unto it whatsoever Introduction he liketh, and likewise cause such things to be added which have been omitted, or amended in which I have erred. I am certain they both here have and will cause this Negotiation to be divulged and spoken of, as shall suit most to their Honour and Advantage, which hath made me collect together all these particulars. His Majesty may make such use thereof as to his wisdom shall seem fittest.

That which here chiefly busieth us is the Reception of the Duke of Maine, who having perfectly recovered his health came unto this Court the seventh of July; and on the eleventh had his first audience, being himself and all his train in mourning. The next week we shall begin our Braveries and Triumphes: but I will refer all that concerning either him or his business unto another Despatch, by which, when all things are ended, you shall receive a perfect Relation of what hath passed.

By my former letters unto my Lord Treasurer, the which I conceive you have seen, I advertised the preparation of six Galleons at Lisbon, which should have been ready in the beginning of July to have gone forth under the conduct of Don Juan de Fajardo. But their want of money, provisions and mariners hath caused that they are not yet in a readiness, so that it will be August before that they can go to sea. And I assure myself, all the service they are like to do is to waft and guard home their West Indian Fleet, though it was

[1] Digby to Sir Thomas Lake, Madrid, 12 July 1612 o.s., P.R.O., SP94/19/ 121–2.

87

intended that they should first have done some service against the pirates who extremely infest these coasts.

The news I wrote that four of this king's Gallious[1] should be cast away upon the coast of Florida is again secondly confirmed from Seville; yet here in the court they absolutely deny it: But they may have many reasons to conceal it if it were so. I do advertise you hereof, only as a report yet doubtful.

I have seen letters both from Goa and Ormuz which advertise that the king of Persia sendeth this year in the East Indian Carracks of Portugal a quantity of silks to the value of four or five hundred thousand crowns, and with them an Ambassador or Deputado; which, if it be true (as we shall certainly know within few months) it will be a great testimony how much the Persian desireth to settle a Trade in these parts of the world. The which (for my part) I should be very sorry that we in England should absolutely neglect. I know they here do much apprehend His Majesty's entertaining of the business: And the Spanish Ambassador had order by money or any means whatsoever, both to discredit Sir Robert Sherly and to hinder His Majesty from proceeding with him. But hereof I have formerly so fully advertised my Lord Treasurer that I omit to write more.

What remaineth now is only in my particular, that I entreat you, in case my letters shall hereafter come more slowly or seldom then [i.e., than] may be expected, that you will favour me to let His Majesty know the true cause thereof. First for the subject of writing, the time and place will afford but little, for now entereth a vacation in which the king and the Duke of Lerma will be absent from Madrid until the end of October, living seven or eight days journey from this place. Then for the Conveyance of Letters: All Extraordinaries will be dispatched from the place where the Duke of Lerma is, so that there will be no means of sending but by the Ordinary, who goeth only once a month, unless I should dispatch a messenger of purpose, which is so chargeable that it were a great indiscretion to use it, but in matters of Consequence. I well know if these considerations be not represented unto His Majesty I may incur the censure of slackness in regard of the diligence which I conceive is used by his other Ministers that live not so far remote. And this is all wherewith for the present I will trouble you, more then the kind

[1] A spelling slip; conceivably a carelessly-written 'Galleasses', but almost certainly 'Gallions'.

remembrance of my love and service unto you. And so I rest

Madrid the 12th   Your assured friend to
of July 1612 st⁰ vet   do you service,
                                                              Jhon Digbye

Here likewise goeth enclosed a letter to my Lords of the Council
in answer of a late directions [sic, in a hasty postscript] from them,
which though they arrived after the business was dispatched, yet I
held it fit to advertise the receipt of their letters, with this short
answer. I pray you dispose thereof as you shall judge fitting.

Enclosures with Ambassadors' Despatches

Perhaps the most appropriate beginning sample of the range of
enclosures an ambassador sent with his main report is those John
Digby sent from Madrid in the same period as the reports that
are quoted several times in this volume. Limiting the example to
those items now in the Public Record Office 'State Papers Spain'
series for 1612: in early January he sent a memorandum on the
appointment of consuls; in early February a Spanish order for
the admission of an English consul at Seville, a note from Father
Creswell, a printed newsletter, and a list of Englishmen to be
released from Spanish galleys; other enclosures during the year
include data on the contents of the treasure fleet, copies of letters
from Philip III to his ambassadors to Rome and the Emperor
(with decyphers for both), the instructions of the imperial
ambassador to Spain, a letter from the Spanish ambassador in
Brussels and the opinion on it rendered by the Council of State,
and other Council documents, and copies of several reports from
Spanish ambassadors in London.[1] The fact that this is only a

[1] Public Record Office archivists have unfortunately seen fit to sort such
materials out by the dates they bear, filing them not with the reports they came
with but in the chronological slots their own dates indicate among (here) the
English ambassador's chronologically ordered reports. Filed here with his 1612
reports are copies of seven letters from Pedro de Zúñiga (on an extraordinary
embassy to England) to Philip III between 2 July and 22 September 1612;
though Digby enclosed the latter one with his report of 13/23 May 1613 (one
could not always get hold of such things immediately) it is now to be found filed
according to its own date, eight months earlier in Digby's correspondence,
with no relevance to the adjacent items and of course a potentially misleading

partial list of what happens to be currently found in one place out of the larger body of survivors from the still larger body of enclosures actually sent in a given year gives some indication of the variety and scope of this activity.[1]

With regard to types of enclosures, however, this particular group cannot be taken as typical in balance. Most of these items, it will be noted, are clandestinely acquired copies of documents belonging to the host government—correspondence, council records, etc.—all of which are important in allowing the researcher to know what information of this sort was available to the ambassador's government (and occasionally, though rarely, in filling lacunae in the host state's archives). This—as with any such partial group—is partly the result of 'selection' by use, filing procedures and time, but in this case largely because Digby was especially active and quite astonishingly successful at this sort of thing; though he was not unique in this, some ambassadors had very little of this sort of material to send, while, at the opposite extreme, in some cases a state's spies mailed such material directly, without its ever passing through the ambassador's hands or being enclosed in his despatches.

An ambassador also sent a good deal of other material that he

eight-months-plus earlier than it reached English hands (in sum, the archivists have treated these documents as though they were reposing in a Spanish archive, not an English one: from the point of view of their *greatest* relevance as historical documents they are English ones, not Spanish). Similarly, any 1611 letters from the Spanish resident in London that Digby sent copies of from Madrid in 1612 will be filed under 1611. Thus one may be confident that Digby sent several such items in 1612, but not necessarily including all of, or limited to, those filed in the archive under that year. With regard to archival practice, one can ascertain when Digby sent this particular document, but such is not always the case; since this is a matter of considerable importance in understanding the formation of English policy, the motives for changes made, action taken, etc., it is a strong argument for leaving entire despatches alone, at least so far as contemporaries did.

[1] This list, being only partial, is limited to items that appear in the 1612 part of the archival table of contents for SP94/19. That is in turn of course limited to things that are both extant and happen to be in *this* series in *this* archive; typically, some items regarding France, for example, will have been moved to State Papers France, while others will have ended up in private hands.

did not himself write that was perfectly legitimate—books, pamphlets, etc., of political import, of which there were a good many; memoranda of advice and such from local sympathisers; copies of letters received; etc.—or if of espionage nature, at least were not copies of stolen documents—the reports of local informants, for example. Digby himself sent a good deal of this material, though little of it is represented in this particular group of remains: the successive volumes of Francisco Suárez' *Defence of the Faith* which he made a special point of procuring and sending to James hot off their Coimbra press were not of course filed with his correspondence (though one does find a scattering of printed matter—mainly flysheets and very short pamphlets—still filed with many ambassadors' correspondence).

But the bulk of an ambassador's enclosures were usually authored by himself. Copies of memorials presented to the host government, and other similar formal representations, and of the ambassador's relevant letters, especially to local ministers but conceivably to anyone, were staple items in a typical diplomatic pouch. A regular one of special interest—and of particular usefulness in divining how the ambassador operated—is the account of embassy expenses which normally had to be submitted to the home government for approval at stated intervals (every six months was most common); in some cases, including John Digby's, his secret service account was calculated, reported and allocated for separately from the rest.

What might be called the 'basic' type of enclosure, however, was that which was merely an extension of his basic reporting duties, sending home statistics and other information regarding shipping movements, the state of the economy, government revenues, military preparedness, the host government's conduct towards a particular state, the background of an earlier treaty, a record of parliamentary proceedings and similar political developments, population estimates, and so forth. How large a place this occupied among separate enclosures, however, varied not only with the nature of the material but with the occasion and the ambassador's usual way of handling the task. Sometimes the material was rather special, as with the data on the treasure fleet mentioned above, and having come from an outside source and already undoubtedly written down separately, was fairly naturally apt to be sent along separately. If the home government had asked for a specific body of information—all of a country's changes in import tariffs since a particular date, for example—it amounted to a special research project, the results of which were often sent as a separate document. But aside from such special material and special occasions the amount of information sent in the form of special enclosures depended upon how long a treatment of any given subject a given ambassador was inclined still to include with his miscellaneous main report, and on whether he was inclined to send all information along in bits as he acquired it or, on non-urgent matters, to save it up for a single more coherent treatment. Digby, the running example used here, was inclined to send most information along as soon as he got it, and to include even the fairly lengthy results of special assignments in his regular reports with all the rest; while in some other hands almost anything even remotely capable of standing alone was apt to be made into a separate special 'relation' or '*avis*' on its subject.

Superficially the distinction seems to be a minor one, merely whether a given treatment of a subject was included in the main report or sent as a separate document, but it is of some importance to the impression given a potential researcher by a given set of despatches. A high number of those comprehensive separate essays is both very impressive (as they were clearly meant to be) and very welcome for the convenience they provide, but the lack of them does not necessarily mean a thing beyond a difference in format. An ambassador who writes few *separate* relations may have included many valuable ones, sometimes quite extensive, right in the body of his main report, and with the intention of attaching as much importance to them as if he had given them separate form complete with fancy titles.

The variety of subject matter that might be dealt with in a separate report enclosed with the main one was almost un-

limited, as may be seen from a brief but somewhat off beat one
sent by a Spanish ambassador to London:[1]

I was lately informed here that an English ship that came from the
East Indies loaded with merchandise, having arrived at a port of the
Turk in the Red Sea called Herben, the Moors agreed to trade with
them, making a show of giving them a good reception, but the
Captain with about twenty men having come ashore the Vaxã
ordered them seized and the merchandise they had brought embargoed, with the intention of taking all of it there was in the ship.
The Captain, feigning being ill, asked permission of the Vaxã
to send to his ship for a pipe of beer, saying that the water of that
area did not agree with him. They promptly brought him the pipe
of beer and he toasted the Vaxã and other Moors with it [who
joined him in the toasting], so that it was exhausted in a very brief
time, and the Captain, still pretending that it was very bad for him
to drink water, once again asked the Vaxã permission to send the
empty pipe to his ship so that they could fill it again with beer. The
Vaxã granted this permission very willingly, because he had found
beer to be much to his liking and wanted to go on drinking it.
But the Captain, who had different designs, had himself secretly
put in the barrel and carried to the ship in it, and as soon as he was
aboard opened up with his artillery, sending to tell the Vaxã to
turn over to him immediately the men he had left ashore because
otherwise he would level the place to the ground. The Vaxã,
thinking to put fear into him so that he would not fire any more
artillery, ordered the English to be taken to the Marina and the
heads of some cut off, threatening that he would have them all
killed if he did not stop firing his artillery, but the English Captain
paying no mind and persevering in his resolution, the Vaxã took it
for best to send him those he still had alive, with which the ship
promptly departed, and encountering some Turkish barks near that
port he seized the merchandise and supplies they carried, giving
letters of exchange on the Vaxã so that he should pay for the
merchandise on the account of the beer he had drunk, who promptly
advised Constantinople of this event, and they say that they have

[1] Diego Sarmiento de Acuña to Philip III, London, 16 November 1613;
the signed original and a signed duplicate original are some twenty folios
apart in Simancas, *Estado* 2590 (unfoliated); a letterbook copy is at *Est.* 7023/
63-4.

ordered embargoed all the merchandise of the English merchants who reside in that city and in the states of the Turk, with which some ships of this kingdom that were loaded with merchandise for the Levant do not dare depart until it is seen what the end of this will be, of which I have wanted to inform Your Majesty, whose Catholic person God protect as Christendom has need of.

London, 16 November 1613.

Don Diego Sarmiento de Acuña

CONCILIAR DOCUMENTS

The amount of documentation generated by the policymaking process depended not only on the amount of diplomatic business a given state had but the degree to which it was a consultative process. The autocrat of a small state might decide things in concert with only one or two advisers, producing almost nothing on paper between receiving a piece of diplomatic correspondence and responding to it (except perhaps for drafts of the reply). A middle case such as England was, under normal circumstances, a varying mixture of king-in-council, dealing with what might be called a middle-sized amount of business and developing only slowly its consultative machinery and the habit of keeping full records of the decision-making process. The extreme was perhaps reached in Spain in the quarter-century between the reign of Philip II and the ministry of Olivares, during which the broadest extent of both 'empire' and foreign involvement was combined with an unusually full resort to collegial government, with practically everything involving foreign affairs (and much else) getting extensive consultative and 'advisory' handling by the Council of State, a large-scale, highly articulated procedure that, from the point of view of document consumption, processing and production, including the documentary by-product that records the process itself, provides as comprehensive an example as one might wish of the spectrum of conciliar documents the principal types of which are to be found in local variations in other times and places.[1]

[1] For the English case, inadequacies in both production and preservation of conciliar sources are extensively described in G. R. Elton, *England 1200–1640*,

The conciliar procedure began with the intake of documents from outside, often (as already described) transformed for conciliar use.[1] For a Council session on English affairs, for example, this would be first of all the recent reports (received since the last such sitting) of the Spanish ambassador there, ordinarily in minute form, several copies of which might have been circulated among the councillors in advance of the meeting, plus whatever relevant enclosures there had been, some of which would have been circulated in copy, extract or summary form. To this may be added a lesser amount of similar material pertinent to the English affairs from Spanish ambassadors elsewhere—extracts from despatches, intelligence reports, etc.—and whatever else may have come up in the way of memorials from the English

pp. 75–81. To the degree that one here contrasts the English and Spanish examples as sources, however, it is appropriate to note that there is no Spanish published analogue to the *Acts of the Privy Council of England* (ed. J. R. Dasent and others, London, 1890 ff: 45 vols to date, covering 1542–1631) or the earlier (and less complete) *Proceedings and Ordinances of the Privy Council of England, 1386–1542* (ed. N. H. Nicholas, 7 vols, London, 1834–7).

[1] An ambassador's despatches would normally be delivered by the courier to the secretary in charge of the papers relating to the host country (Europe being usually divided between two secretaries with distinct purviews). He would take out letters addressed to himself and whatever private correspondence there might be (forwarding that to the addressees as a service to the ambassador), and send the formal report and relevant enclosures (which might, depending upon its contents, include the covering letter addressed to himself) to the king, to whom the report was formally addressed. In practice at the time this would usually be handled for the king by the Duke of Lerma, acting as his chief minister, who had his own secretariat; Lerma in turn would send the documents back to the secretary with orders for the calling of a council meeting for consultation on their contents and whatever other documents would be needed for that consultation as the subject matter required. For the role of the favourite in this process and in government in general in the period see John Lynch, *Spain under the Habsburgs, Volume II: Spain and America, 1598–1700* (Oxford, 1969), pp. 14–30, a realistic appraisal that admirably renounces the old notion of the *privanza* as a sort of ministerial dictatorship while recognising not only its areas of power but its important areas of specific function in the day-to-day governing process—precisely the sort of treatment one would expect from this excellent and much-awaited volume. See also Francisco Tomás Valiente, *Los Validos en la monarchía española del siglo XVII (estudio institucional)* (Madrid, 1963).

ambassador, correspondence directly from the English king (rare), Spanish-origin local reports on English complaints, whatever relevant earlier material may have been assembled from the Spanish archives as background, and the *avisos* of whatever specialists may have been consulted.

Individual councillors' opinions on these things may be recorded in a number of ways. Some may make annotations on a copy of the minutes of despatches. Some may circulate their opinions in memorandum (*aviso*) form in writing before the meeting, or at the meeting itself—a particular form of memorandum (*aviso*) formally referred to as a *parecer* (opinion). The discussion may be minuted in the record of the meeting itself (especially if final conclusion was reached by the council as a body) in the form of individual opinions offered orally; this may sometimes record some little debate and thrashing out of positions or working out of consensus. When the vote is ultimately taken on an issue, individual votes are accompanied by an explanation of the reasons for voting so, which are often recorded along with the vote. The result of this vote (assuming an agreement was reached), in the form of a formal council recommendation, would be sent to the king (or the favourite acting in his name) for approval, which was usually fairly automatic.

One might note parenthetically that the distinction between the consultative process under Philip II and here under Philip III was that the former referred matters to the council for consultation and advice to aid him in making the policy decisions, while the latter referred matters to it in effect for decision (naturally couched discreetly as recommendations), retaining only the right of approval: though in neither case did the decision become a reality without the king's participation, the task of sorting out what the right decision would be was largely the king's in the one case, the council's in the other. (The English council in the period may seem even more independent as it handled some business on its own without the monarch's participation, but the difference is mainly one of conciliar division of labour: lesser duties were similarly delegated in Spain, but to other councils.)

The terminology employed in the Spanish case provides a useful illustration of the inseparability of the policymaking and paper-making aspects of the consultative process. The council meeting was called a *consulta*. The group that met, especially when it was a fairly small fraction of the entire council, was itself called a *consulta*. The document recording the recommendations of the group, of individual members, or both, was called a *consulta*. And the entire record of the consultative meeting of the consultative group, including all the documents consulted about, was called a *consulta*. For the researcher the context usually makes clear what is meant when the term is used, but the distinction seems less important than its limited nature: if men make language, it is significant that the bureaucrats of the time saw no need for separate terms for the group, the process, the paper product and the policy product.

At this point in the process there intervenes covering correspondence (memoranda of explanation and instruction) in both directions between the council and the monarch or chief minister, and ultimately the royal verdict on the council's recommendations—usually literally on them, consisting of marginal notations of approval or (infrequently) disapproval or qualification, and sometimes of additional comment. The standard notation was 'let it be done so'—which left the Council of State with the task of doing it, especially the Secretary of State and his staff, as this, too, was paperwork: drawing up the order, letter in reply, or whatever document was called for in the recommendation. The general gist of this, the important specifics, and perhaps some of the precise terminology will have been prescribed there, but the text itself will usually still require writing; it will often require careful drafting and perhaps extensive redrafting, with the consequent advantages for the researcher already noted in connection with drafts in general and with Instructions. One result of this particular sort of draft's being essentially a council document—i.e., an integral part of the conciliar process as distinct from being merely 'correspondence' per se—is that while correspondence *from* ambassadors is usually filed as such (with occasional pieces left with the conciliar documents), the file copies—final drafts or botched fair copies—of correspondence *to* ambassadors (and similar diplomatic correspondence), though nominally from the monarch, were normally kept with the entire *consulta* they pertained to; the researcher may count himself lucky when, as in the Simancas case, modern archivists have left that integral arrangement alone, and not torn it apart to make pretty little series of 'drafts of correspondence to ambassadors'.

As the fair copy sent will normally have been retained by the ambassador as part of his 'personal' correspondence, the draft will usually be the only version of such out-letters to be found in the official archives and often—if they were saved at all—the only version surviving. (As noted earlier, registers of letters sent are uncommon, and not very useful anyway for diplomatic correspondence.) Unlike correspondence *from* ambassadors, the chances of survival are almost never enhanced by production of copies and other forms of duplication. This is particularly unfortunate since the disappearance of a single letter *to* an ambassador can be so much greater a loss than a single letter *from* him. The two sides of the correspondence are equally important—since both are indispensable, the question of relative value is rather meaningless—but quantitatively (as noted earlier) they are very unequal; the loss of one of half a dozen weekly despatches still leaves most of that side of the correspondence remaining, while the loss of the single response to those six—a fairly typical ratio— wipes out that indispensable side completely for the entire six weeks.

The indispensability of the policymaking side of foreign relations, and of the policymaking documents to research about that side, are both obvious. This documentation can also, however, be essential to a correct reading of the other side—the ambassador's reports. The affair of Doña Luisa de Carvajal in London in 1613, mentioned earlier with regard to minutes, is a fair example. Apart from the inaccuracies already noted, it supposedly illustrates a sort of proconsular status held by a forceful Spanish ambassador, not only acquiesced in by the host government but accorded him by his own. The fact is—as the *consultas* on his report of the incident show in some detail—that the Spanish government was furious at his high-handed handling of the matter: he had in effect threatened to desert his post without leave, and would have been in very hot water had he carried it out—a case where even an ambassador's actual report of the matter tells only a part of the story and, taken alone, has given a very misleading impression. If it is—or should be—axiomatic that no single document has an assured validity in isolation, this is equally true of any single *type* of document. As historical sources, conciliar documents are therefore not only complementary to ambassadorial despatches but supplementary as well.

THE AMBASSADOR'S CORRESPONDENCE WITH VARIOUS PERSONS

The ambassador's correspondence with the official who handled his despatches has been mentioned in connection with its role as a covering letter; its characteristics of informality, candour, and inclusion of trivia and personal matters—all priceless virtues for the researcher—are shared by his correspondence with other ministers, friends and so on at home. These are usually to be found in private collections or public repositories for such collections (the British Museum, for example, not the Public Record Office). When they survive at all they typically survive as a coherent group—essentially all such correspondence received by one person from one or several others over a given period (it is usually the recipient's private collection, not the sender's)— and one manageable in size: qualities which (apart from their virtues as manuscript sources) make them both appropriate and convenient for publication. It is thus not surprising that published documents run fairly heavily to collections such as *Hispania Illustrata* (London, 1703), which consists almost entirely of letters to Henry Bennet, Earl of Arlington, a former ambassador to Spain, from three of his successors, 1667-78. Neither is it surprising, unfortunately, that such ready availability of this *supplementary* type of diplomatic documentation—useful but oblique

—has led to its over-use in place of the more massive and thus less published *main* diplomatic correspondence—one of numerous biases that exist in the sources, some of the principal of which are discussed in Chapter 7.

Two less frequent types, both inherently important even when their contents are routine, are an ambassador's correspondence with ministers and other persons in the host country, and with his opposite number, the host government's ambassador to this resident's (the writer's) home government. As one would hardly engage in such correspondence without reporting it, copies of letters both sent and received were naturally enclosed with the ambassador's reports, making his state's main government archive (and of course that of his opposite number—the same thing viewed from the opposite end) the usual place to find such material now, though some will survive in the private papers of ministers and others.

For a variety of reasons, ranging from proximity to hostility, there was practically no written correspondence between the various ambassadors to the same court. Maintaining correspondence with other ambassadors from the same state who were resident at various other courts, however, was one of an ambassador's more important continuing functions. Among a set of colleagues collectively, this involved nothing less than a comprehensive network of information exchange among all of a state's diplomatic outposts. (In Spain's case it included the viceroys, governors, etc., of its own outlying domains as well—Milan, Naples, etc.)

Participating in this outer network, each party corresponding in bilateral fashion with each of the others, was not—except as a clerical task—as great an extra burden as one might suppose, since the bulk of the information sent to fellow ambassadors merely duplicated—mostly verbatim—what had been written to report to the home government anyway. Not everything the ambassador sent home was sent to his fellow ambassadors as well (normally, no secret material, for example), but almost everything he sent them, personal gossip aside, duty required him to report home not only 'as well' but first of all. Thus the examples of this type of correspondence which follow can readily serve a double function in the limited space of a volume such as this, illustrating not only the contents of inter-ambassadorial correspondence but the variety of information that was included in regular despatches home as well—not only the miscellany of the covering letter but much of the substantive matter of the main report.

The information exchanged was so varied and mixed that one might describe it simply as 'general', but one can distinguish particular characteristics. Special emphasis was given to matters pertaining to the addressee's host country or that region, and there was always a general inclusion of matters affecting the home country. Any ambassador needed to be kept informed of events of international importance in all regions and any writer would send all the news he could (and rumour if he must), but naturally could send fuller and more certain information about events at or near his own post. And quite apart from broad international matters, the ambassador was interested in, and assumed that his colleagues were interested in, developments both political and social within the various governments and courts. John Digby writes to a colleague in January of 1612, for example.[1]

> Our ordinary news is the *mercedes* which the king hath given this Christmas. He hath bestowed on the Duke of *Alva* ten thousand[2]

[1] John Digby to an English ambassador, Madrid, 5 January 1612 o.s., P.R.O. SP/94/19/5; original, but with no indication of addressee and no firm internal evidence. Spelling modernised. The Spanish words or names Digby intentionally wrote in a particularly large hand are italicised here.

[2] Digby is not necessarily meaning to convert for his reader into English currency; the Spanish *ducado* of ten *reales*, exchanging at four to the pound sterling, happened to be equivalent to the crown, and the English usually simply called it that. In crowns or ducats, 10,000—though only about one-tenth of the ordinary rents of the Alba estates—was a goodly sum, equal to the annual rents of the upper gentry and lower nobility. The king was then trying to woo the current duke back to court after a period of alienation: a strictly political gift. '*Merced*' might be translated as 'royal bounty', but it was both patronage and (often) the form in which normally expected subsequent reward for services rendered was given.

crowns a year for three lives and thirty thousand crowns *de ayuda de costa*.¹

The *Marques de Guadalcaçar* is made *Vice King de Nueva España*. The *Conde de Niebla*, son to the *Duke de Medina Sidonia* & son-in-law to the *Duke of Lerma, General of the Ocean*. And this is for the present all that is worth the advertising to you from hence. As for the books for which you write, your Lordship shall be sure of them, the Venetian ambassador having promised me conveyance for them by the way of *Alicante*.² I missed writing unto your Lordship by the last *Ordinary* for that he departed from hence before the other was arrived here, contrary to my expectations. Hereafter you shall find me very punctual. So with the rememberance of my love & service to yourself & your good Lady I commend you to God. And rest Madrid, January 5th st⁰ vet: 1611

> Your Lordship's assured friend
> to do you service
> Jhon Digbye

Since the concluding of this letter I received your Lordship's of the 8 [apparently] of December, and whereas you seem to tax me of not giving you perfect relation of my proceedings here there was no other cause of it but that I knew by another hand there was gone a relation to you of it beginning Experience having etc., or at least I conjecture it hath this passage. The Duke of Lerma delivered the same with his accustomed gravity and courtesy etc. But my Lordship [here Digby, come to the end of the page, starts writing sideways in the margin] you may rest assured that I shall hold all confident correspondency with you that may either concern the service of the King our Master in general, or that may respect the particular friendship, service and esteem I bear unto your person.³

> JD

¹ I.e., outright; equal to the annual rents of a quite wealthy Spanish noble at the time.

² This rather suggests that the addressee was Dudley Carleton, the English resident at Venice, but the conclusion should not be too readily jumped at.

³ Digby is obviously rattled by the reprimand, probably because he was still a 'new boy' in diplomatic service, having been on this, his first embassy, only a few months.

Inclusion of such detail about the local scene was quite usual, the lack of greater matters to recount as well was also usual, for the Christmas season: then as now, a great deal of the regular political news was man-made and so tended not to 'happen' on holidays or at other inconvenient times. A letter from Dudley Carleton to Digby in late March of the following year is rather more typical.[1]

My very good Lord: Since my last to Your Lordship of the 2 of March I have received one from you without date which brought with it a copy of that king's letter to his ambassador resident in the Empire, by which, as also by many other courses lately taken by that crown in conformity to that which that dispatch imports,[2] it seemeth apparent that with you they are resolved to withhold France from any longer swimming *entre deux eaux*. In these parts here is likely to be added shortly a new experiment tending to the same end, the issue whereof will make it appear to the world whether the amity betwixt those crowns is truly real or hath with it some mixture of jealousy in case of either of their growing in strength or greatness. There is among the Grisons as I understand from some of very good credit, a treaty beginning of a league betwixt that people[3] and the State of Milan[4] to begin shortly after the expiring of the confederation they have with this state which ends in August next. The continuance and renewing of it hath been proposed on

[1] [Dudley Carleton] to John Digby [Venice], 30 March 1613, P.R.O. SP/94/19/31&v.; copy (perhaps a decypher).

[2] Merely alluding to a subject where (as here) it is not necessary to specify it is of course a routine security precaution in case the letter comes into hostile hands. However, the stilted reference to 'this state' and 'this state of X', etc., are redolent of code-key formulae (in the code-list sequence: the State of X, the King of X, the Queen of X . . .), leaving little doubt that these names were in code in the original whether the text was in cypher or not.

[3] I.e., of the 'Grey League' of the eastern Swiss area.

[4] On this copy 'Milan' is a somewhat unsure reading here, but is confirmed below. Milan had of course since 1540 been not an independent state but a subject domain administered by a Spanish governor; such negotiations were usually handled by the governor, but they were with the Spanish, not Milanese, as one might suppose from the wording here. Carleton having been at the Venice embassy—which served as (usually) England's only diplomatic and espionage outpost in Italy—since November 1610, he here and below is apparently merely thinking and speaking loosely in 'Italian' terms.

this part but rejected by the Grisons through the urgent opposition of the French ministers who are present among them & seem to affect the having of that people wholly at the devotion of the crown of France without any dependence on any other. If that were their true intent then it may be judged in probability that they will soon discover the danger that would ensue their combination with Milan, which would lock up all the passes into Lombardy, and if they would not suffer this state to become partners with them in the service of that people they will apprehend more danger in the Spaniards with whom there is worse sharing. The Jesuits do with all diligence set forward this treaty betwixt Milan & the Grisons in hope to settle themselves in Valtellina, which they have long aimed at. The ambassador of Poland, being upon his return from Rome homeward, hath made a suit to this state for a safe conduct for five Jesuits which have accompanied him out of Poland, but the same answer is made him as was formerly to the Archduke Ferdinand for one he would have sent to Rome, that they would willingly gratify him but their people were so incensed against those of that order that they doubted a safe conduct would not serve their turn. I presume Your Honour hath heard enough of the revolutions in the State of Mantua, which are now settled by the young Cardinal's being received & acknowledged all over the state as their lawful Duke & Prince. The widow Duchess troubled him a while with a pretended *graccistanta* [*sc. grazistanza*] & the Duke of Savoy demanded first Monferrate for the daughter of the deceased Duke & then the greatest part of the *beni allodiali* for the . . . Dowager. [After about another folio page on the affairs of Milan, Savoy, the Duke of Modena, etc., Carleton continues:] The Bishop of Bamberg, the Emperor's ambassador at Rome, arrived here in this Town on Friday last, where he playeth least in sight & remaineth *sconosciuto* without accepting as yet any visits from any public ministers or going himself to see this prince,[1]

[1] This document bears no identification of the writer or the place of origin. As it is unlikely that an ambassador would refer to the doge of Venice, hardly a true ruler, as 'this prince', this rendering of the applicable designator in the ambassadors' common code (Digby, for example, would have used the same 'this prince' indicator to refer to Philip III) implies misleadingly that the letter would not have been written from there. Internal evidence makes it clear that it was, but only because every other possibility is referred to as somewhere else (otherwise it would perfectly well have been from, say, the English resident in Paris reporting on Italian affairs, or a copy of the Italian part abstracted from his despatch). A typical example of the minor ways in which a decypher can mislead the investigator.

but he cannot long continue this if it be true which is delivered me for a certainty that the Pope hath at this instant made an overture to this state to enter into a league with the Emperor against the Turk wherein this Bishop must needs have somewhat to do, he coming immediately from Rome and going directly to the Empire. It is not hard to imagine that these Signori will entertain that motion, as they use to do all of that nature, with thanking the Pope for his fatherly care of the common good but forbearing to engage themselves until some more urgent occasion force them to it.

News that directly affected the ambassadors' own country or countrymen was apt to get quite extensive treatment, as in this excerpt from a letter from Digby to Carleton later the same year:[1]

The English Merchants of St Sebastian in Biscay wrote unto me that divers ships being returned from Greeneland [i.e., Spitzbergen] which went thither to fish the whale were by the Moscovian Companie not permitted to fish and so were come back empty, and that the Spaniards pretended to recover their damages & hinderances out of the goods of the English Merchants residing there, and like wise that they much threatened their persons, whereupon many of the chief of them removed themselves to Bilbao, others that remained durst not stir out of their houses for fear they should be wronged and injured by the townsmen. Hereupon I went to the Secretary of State & told him what the Merchants had written desiring that the king's letters might be sent presently to St Sebastian for the preventing of such disorders as might happen. The secretary fell suddenly into a very great complaint of His Majesty's proceeding with this king, that he would (as he said) cause so great an innovation as that the Spaniards, which had for so many years fished in the Northern Seas over which hitherto no Prince had challenged any particular Dominion should now by His Majesty's Subjects be prohibited, and yet that His Majesty would give permission to his subjects to plant & inhabit in Viginia and the Islands of the Bermudos which had for many years been esteemed & known to belong unto the Conquest of Castile so that he thought [it] strange that His Majesty should at the same time suffer his people to possess themselves of what was rightly

[1] Digby to Carleton, Madrid, 3 November 1613os, P.R.O., SP94/19/151–154.

the King of Spain's & should forbid the Spaniards from that which they had long used & to which he knew not what particular claim His Majesty could pretend. I answered him, that concerning those Titles I never had instructions given me, & therefore he was to understand my reply only as by way of discourse & as of a private man. And so I told him, that first I conceived he had been misinformed that the Spaniards had divers years used to these parts now spoken of which had been of late discovered & the Spaniards were never there until the last Summer when an Englishman lead them thither. Secondly I could no way yield unto him that either Virginia or the Bermudos either were or [lacuna: had ever been] parts of the conquest of Castile but that the [lacuna: Spaniards declared them] selves the first Possidents, so that I supposed what is said of the whale fishing was to be debated & disputed in the same nature that the Indies were, which the Crown of Castile without controversy discovered & possessed, and that then he would see that His Majesty only followed their own footsteps. For that there were at the present divers of His Majesty's subjects in their Galleys for having offered to trade to the Indies being only taken in the way thither, and that I conceived the same reason of being the first Possident was equally to hold in both, and that as His Majesty had followed their example in reserving the trade of his discoveries unto his own subjects so he would willingly give free access unto them when they should hold it fit to permit the like unto theirs. Herewith he seemed to grow a little warm and told me there was great differences in the case, one being (beside the right of the first possident) a right established by the Pope's Donation & confirmed by a sufficient prescription. The other being a mere Innovation. I answered that for the Pope's Donation it was grown to be so slightly esteemed, that it was almost left to be alledged by them, and for their prescription, that no way altered the case for that before the kings of Castile could alledge any prescription, even from the very beginning of the Discovery (as would appear upon their Records) they permitted no other Nation to go thither, no not the subjects of their own king, save only those of the Crown of Castile, so that it appeareth they esteemed their Title good before any prescription could be alledged, and therefore the title would come merely to depend of the being the first Possident and that would be as favourable to His Majesty in this Case as to them in their Indies. But I said I had no intention at this present to enter into any argument of their Titles only I desired that he would provide that the English Merchants might not be wronged by way of fact, and that if anything were disputable in their Title they might by orderly & fair courses be decided betwixt their Majesties as they had often been betwixt this Crown & the Portugalls concerning the Mallucas & other discoveries.—Herewith the Secretary seemed to be somewhat in choller and told me that though this king esteemed the Peace with His Majesty as was fit & much desired it should be continued, yet he wanted not force nor power to defend his own without putting his undoubted & unquestionable right in disputation. I answered that His Majesty had so too, and what I had said herein was but by way of discourse, but in that I first moved him & whereupon this discourse had risen, which was, that he would take such order that the goods & persons of His Majesty's subjects might be secured, I would with confidence speak therein, for if any thing fell out to the contrary there should be strict account taken of it, and that I would adventure to say that if by their not preventing of these beginnings things should grow to ill terms betwixt their Majesties he should not see the English to come into Spain to intreat for the accommodating of them. Since [then] I have understood that the cause of the Secretary's [lacuna: hard] dealing with me was for that I moved h[lacuna: him to do this the] day after that it had been resolved in [lacuna: Council for] the removing of the new English Plantation in the Bermudos and likewise that those of Biscay had delivered their petition into the Council of State touching the wrongs which they had received by the English & demanded leave to recover their damages upon the English. But they have so well considered on the matter that there hath not been any way given hitherto to any proceeding against them, neither hear any more complaints from the said Merchants but that they live all quietly without disturbance.

For the researcher the documentary redundancy of sending the same material in various directions obviously improves chances of survival of at least one version. In the letter from Digby to Sir Thomas Lake quoted earlier as an example of an ambassador's correspondence with a secretary he announced a forthcoming relation of an extraordinary French embassy's recent coming to Spain. When the relation was subsequently sent one imagines that it was passed around from hand to hand a good bit instead of being filed properly and promptly. In any case, what one now finds among Digby's correspondence in the Public Record

Office immediately following that letter is not that document but the copy of it Digby sent to Dudley Carleton in Venice. This reader, at least, is grateful to Carleton for preserving it; it may not be a terribly substantive matter but it is rather fun (and a thoughtful analysis follows it, for those who prefer their history straight):[1]

My very good Lord: I have received yours of the 25 of May; and I hope that mine of the 25 of April, the 23 of May, and 20 of June are come safe unto your hands, whereof your lordship's last maketh no mention. I thank you very much for your particular advertisements from Constantinople, because I have some especial reason to hearken after that business, and therefore shall intreat your lordship to continue your favour unto me in that kind, still to let me know what cometh unto you concerning Sir Thomas Glover.

They here upon the receipt of the news of the election of the Emperor proclaimed a solemn feast day and made general fires of joy. The same *correo* brought with him to us the unfortunate tidings of my Lord Treasurer's death [i.e., Salisbury], but unto them the news which I am sure was very pleasing, both for that all our losses have a good relish unto them, and for that they very particularly ever esteemed him very adverse to them and their ends.

Our great French ambassador whom we have so long expected is at last arrived here with a thousand Frenchmen of all sorts in his train. He hitherto hath had but a very untoward beginning, for we hear that diverse of the company have fallen out among themselves, and that some of the principal men have forsaken him and gone back. Since his entrance into Spain, there happened unto him a very strange accident. There were a company or two of Spanish soldiers that were going out of Castile into Navarre, and near unto the city of Burgos they fell into the way by which the Duke came, where meeting with a great troop of *laquais*, they began to scoff & jest one at another. Presently there came diverse French gallants on horseback, and out of their French idle humour some of them cried *sa sa*

[1] Digby to Carleton, Madrid, 18 July 16120s, P.R.O., SP/94/19/124–126v. Spelling and punctuation mostly modernised; Digby's punctuation and capitalisation are unusually erratic here, making separation into sentences sometimes quite arbitrary. On this copy square brackets appear at the beginning and end of the long third paragraph, the standard indication of material to be extracted, as this presumably was.

cargons,[1] and so putting spurs to their mules, charged scornfully the soldiers with the *quita-soles* which they had in their hands to keep away the sun. The soldiers thinking this an indignity [i.e., being attacked with parasols], and taking it for a great *afrenta* offered unto them, struck diverse of them from their mules. Whereupon all the French betook them to their weapons, by which time the Duke of Maine, who was a little behind, came up, and himself and all the company assailed the soldiers, who defended themselves and hurt diverse of the French, but seeing the number of the French very many they retired themselves very orderly to a church not far off, in [i.e., during] which retreat I hear there was not one Spaniard hurt, and so resolving to make good the church they placed their banner on the church top. The Duke of Maine determined to have forced the church, and so I think he would have done, and cut all the Spaniards' throats, but that in the meantime the Governor and principal men of Burgos came and pacified the matter. This king hath dispatched Commissioners from hence to proceed against the soldiers, and it is thought diverse of them will be hanged if they be not saved by the D: de Maine his mediation. Since which time, they lying at a town called Barrajas,[2] three or four leagues from this place, have upon a falling out killed a Spanish hidalgo, which hath caused much heartburning, for diverse of his kindred being men of good sort and fashion, presently repaired to the king to demand that Justice might be done them, whereupon there was an Alcalde de la Corte sent thither to take true information of the business. The Duke de Maine was very forward himself to proceed in justice against those which committed the offence, the which the Alcalde hindereth, desiring that they may proceed by way of Process & Information. The which the Duke yielded unto, and caused his people to be delivered into the hands of the Justice, where they still remain imprisoned until their cause come to a trial.

All these [stout] and new alliances will not wear out the ancient antipathy that is between these two nations, for, though the Princes and States I conceive were never nearlier united both by alliance and resolution of running both one fortune, yet the people seem incompatible together. For notwithstanding Proclamations that are here every day, commanding upon great punishment that all men

[1] Digby has apparently transposed consonants, intending '*ça, ça, garçons*'; '*chargeons*' seems far too remote.

[2] Now the site of Madrid International Airport.

use the French with great courtesy & civility and that all officers here take great order and pains to see it observed, yet there passeth not one day without some remarkable accident betwixt them. I assure you that my Lord Admiral had never so much honour done him as he hath by this great troop of French, for they say here that in regard of them [i.e., in comparison with the French], *los Ingleses pareçian tantos Angeles*, and in truth, for the French, though they say there are very many of good account in the company, whom it may be we shall hereafter see brave (for yet they are in mourning), yet for the general I never saw such a band of tottered shagg-raggs. The Duke himself is (as you know) a goodly gentleman of his person, and liveth here with fitting magnificence. Hitherto, he hath only had an Audience of the king to give the *pesami*[1] for the death of the Queen.[2] His solemn visiting of the young Queen of France[3] *de gala* is deferred till the 15 of August, so that I conceive his departure from hence will not be so suddenly as was expected.

I find here, besides these public shows and outward alliances (which all the world may take notice of) that there is an extraordinary league of correspondency and conformity betwixt the principal Ministers of the French State and this, and that which maketh me most doubt of their intents is that contrary to what they publically make show of both to His Majesty and the United Provinces they juggle strangely underhand. But hereof, as His Majesty and they are not unadvertised, so I hope they will not be unprovided to countermine these labours.

I hear it, but will not write it unto you for certain, That besides many other *mercedes* which this king intendeth to do the Duke of

[1] Formal condolence. Digby has not here misspelled the Spanish *pesame* as first glance might suggest but, writing to a colleague in Venice, has used the Italian equivalent.

[2] Margaret of Austria, the recently (1611) deceased wife of Philip III.

[3] The Infanta Ana, daughter of Philip III, betrothed to Louis XIII; later better known to history as Anne of Austria. Though the marriage did not take place until 1615 she already was usually referred to as 'the Queen of France' by both the Spanish and the French—perhaps for psychological or propaganda reasons of reassurance, as it was still very uncertain that the marriage treaty (which also involved the marriage of the future Philip IV and Louis XIII's sister Elisabeth, and was what the French embassy had come about) would actually be completed; in any case, to interpret this premature usage as reflecting confidence that the treaty was as good as completed would be completely erroneous.

Maine, he meaneth to make him the offer of a Spanish wife, a daughter of the Duchess of Najara and sister of the Duke of Maqueda, who is both in regard of her person and her fortune the best marriage of a subject that I think can be found this day in Christendom, for she is a young lady of 16 or 17 years of age, extraordinarily handsome, and that shall have to her dowery seven or eight hundred thousand crowns in ready money, and it is said that her mother to match her to her full content will make her portion up a million. I believe this match may very well proceed, for that I think this king will be very glad to have some principal ladies to accompany the Queen his daughter into France. I am certain that this business is secretly working, and the Duke of Lerma being the man that undertaketh it you can well judge how great a probability there is of having it effected.

The day that this Duke had his Audience from the King, being fetched from his house by the Duke of Uceda and diverse other *Grandes*, and all the Nobility & Gentry of the Court at their return, there fell a quarrell between[1] two of our *Grandes*, the Conde de Saldaña, son to the Duke of Lerma, and the Adelantado of Castilla, who, by appointment, both stealing out of the troop, were perceived by some that had an eye on them, and presently all or most of the Spaniards leaving to accompany the Duke de Maine, followed presently to prevent their meeting. They were both taken, and remain yet with guards confining to their houses.[2]

Your Venetian ambassador, that should have been Don Rodrigo Calderon, who is now in Flanders, I conceive will avoid that employment, though it be yet given out that certainly after his return he shall put himself in order for that journey. He hath here very many enemies, & is generally detested & hated, but the Duke of Lerma standeth very firm and steadily unto him, and now in his absence

---

[1] As the virtues of familiarity are touted quite heavily in Chapter 7, it is perhaps well to note that violations detected in the norm do not always have an important significance, of which this provides a usable minor example. For Digby to use 'between' instead of 'betwixt' is actually startling to a reader accustomed to his style, but that he did so here has no implication with regard to authenticity of authorship.

[2] That Digby does not need to explain to a contemporary what they were up to (which may not be all that clear to a modern reader) is a measure of the seriousness of the problem of duelling among the nobility at the time, a practice which both the Spanish and English courts were taking fairly harsh measures to suppress.

worketh with all earnestness to reconcile men's affections unto him, and laboureth by all means possible that those which have formerly been his opposites, which are the Duke of Uceda [Lerma's elder son and eventual though brief successor as chief minister], the King's Confessor, and the Condessa de Lemos & indeed almost all men else, [1] but the Duke will be contented that he may be again admitted to the dispatch of business. But I have heard that one of the chief of them should make this answer to the Duke of Lerma when he importuned for him, *Quando entrara aquel vellaco en palaçio yo me saldre fuera* ['When that lout comes into the palace, I go out']. Yet the Duke of Lerma undertaking it *de veras* (as certainly he doth) I am apt to apprehend he will overcome all other difficulties. For in the Court of Spain, he needeth not to fear much who hath the Duke of Lerma for his *Angel de guardia*.

My Lord, These barren times and place afford little else worthy of so long a journey. And therefore with my kind remembrance of my love & service to Your Lordship & my Lady Carleton, I commit you both to the blessed protection of the Almighty. From Madrid July 18 st⁰ vet: 1612./.

Your Lordship's affectionate friend
to serve you,
Jhon Digbye

This system was not, however, an unmixed good. Its advantage was of course that ambassadors in the field were kept more fully informed of affairs in general for the better performance of their duties. Its disadvantage (though I have seen no evidence of any-one's recognising it) was a dangerous inbreeding of information. A state's policy decisions were based upon intelligence received at the centre from the outside world, almost all of which came from or via their embassies abroad. Theoretically the multiplicity of reports and the diversity of sources of them provided the essential element of 'control' of information by separate confirmation. In practice, however, a system wherein ambassadors were important sources of information for each other tended to homogenise the information available to them, and to the degree

---

[1] Comma added to avoid confusion (numerous superfluous commas have been dropped).

that information from that inter-embassy network was fed into the embassy-to-government network the input at the centre became homogenised as well, with consequent loss of that degree of 'control'. The dependability of a given piece of news reported by A was largely measured by its being reported also by B, C and D; if they themselves had heard it from A, however, their apparent confirmation of it was unintentionally specious, the report coming not from four separate sources but ultimately from only one. At worst the result could be for a totally false rumour, initially reported as rumour, to acquire the status of apparently solid information.

MISCELLANEOUS DIPLOMATIC DOCUMENTS

Memorials presented by foreign ambassadors to the host government have already been mentioned. These may involve matters of any sort, but were mainly useful for detailing the specifics of a complaint being registered and so run heavily to mundane problems of a 'consular' sort. They are thus naturally more frequent in situations involving substantial commerce, off-shore fishing, the nationals of one state living in another, and other such sources of complaint. The copies sent home with the ambassador's despatches usually survive more reliably than the originals actually presented and considered.

In discussing its function, mention has also been made of intra-government correspondence, the administrative memoranda dealing with the disposition of diplomatic documents, the consultative handling of their subject matter, the implementation of decisions, etc. When found they can provide very useful evidence of the governmental processes involved, but they are unfortunately rare. As most such memos had no anticipated value as permanent records they were seldom intentionally preserved as such, and when they did get into the permanent files (by accident or intent) they have deteriorated much more rapidly than the documents they dealt with because the cheapest sort of paper was usually used for them. Survival of such instructions and other details is naturally much greater when they were written on the document itself. Naturally, these administrative documents survive (when they do at all) only in the home government's archive.

Since the whole idea of the diplomatic system was one of representation through ambassadorial agents, it is natural that direct communications between governments should be quite rare. Aside from an ambassador's credentials, which are technically (as the ambassador himself is) from one chief of state to another, direct written communication between rulers was mainly limited to courtesies—congratulations, condolences and so forth—that served mainly to foster friendly relations and to support the underlying notion (valid from a counter-revolutionary point of view) that all legitimate monarchs are brothers and have a common interest derived from their status. Though such correspondence seldom has substantive content it is useful for tracing out the niceties of this formal relationship, and alterations that may occur in it.

Numerous copies of treaties can be found in the archives of the states that were parties to them, but treaties have been so extensively published—for Europe as a whole and for individual countries (some are discussed in Chapter 4)—that one hardly need resort to manuscript versions to obtain the final text. Two other manuscript forms, however, can be most revealing: the various drafts of terms to be proposed by a given state, draft comments on protocols proposed by another, etc., prior to arriving at the final text, and later translations made for subsequent consultations, etc. (e.g., in preparing to negotiate a similar treaty at some later date)—sometimes quite faulty, and significant in being so.

Well along in the seventeenth century the government itself (England's for example) sometimes tried to meet its ambassadors' need to be well informed by sending out regular newsletters, but whatever may be said for them with regard to their purpose, they naturally do not provide the researcher with a source comparable to the many-faceted body of correspondence provided by the inter-ambassadorial network for information exchange.

Newsletters of course already existed in various forms—public and private, some sending news abroad, some sending it home—many of them well known, such as those of Salvetti, John Chamberlain and others. Among miscellaneous reports home from abroad not of diplomatic origin, one must especially note those of the resident factors of trading companies, often useful for details on the local setting.

DIPLOMATIC DOCUMENTS AND NON-DIPLOMATIC HISTORY

An ambassador who is not only a thoughtful observer and a thorough reporter but happens also to be interested in the same specific problem as the historian is an obvious boon. S. R. Gardiner was concerned with describing the nature and causes of the difficulty English merchants encountered in Spain after trade was restored under the 1604 peace treaty. He was able to do so—in one of the most important specific historical statements in the work—without even any need for synthesis (as distinct, of course, from independent confirmation); much of his passage is in fact simply a paraphrase (sometimes so close that it almost requires quotation marks) of a single ambassadorial report on the matter:[1]

> I have likewise (finding the principal cause of wronging our merchants to be by the inferior ministers in the ports) taken the best order that I could imagine for the preventing of the like injuries hereafter. The chief motives of trouble unto them in all places were that certain *Denunciadores* (as they term them which are promoters and informers) have a third part of all such confiscations whereof they give information. The judge likewise who is to give sentence in the cause is to have another third part if he adjudge it for the King. So that those that are judges are the party that prosecute and are chiefly interested whereby it falleth out that in all pretences and informations made against the English, instantly their goods are seized, sentenced and confiscated. It is true that they then have the remedy of appellation to the courts of Madrid, which are tribunals of much delay but great sincerity and justice, for I have scarcely

[1] John Digby to the Lords of the Council, Madrid, 19/29 January 1612, P.R.O., SP94/19/7–9 (excerpt: 7v–8v).

heard of the appellation of any one Englishman that hath not passed for him, which showeth the strange injustice of those inferior ministers, that in so many causes as have been sentenced against the English since the peace, scarcely any one hath been confirmed here, but all repealed. But this, though it carry a fair colour of righting the English, in effect it proveth to them of little advantage, for the charge of following of the law, the loss that the merchant suffereth in neglecting his trade, and being most of them such as deal for other men, if they come to follow their business here they lose their employments. Besides, things proceed so slowly here that it is commonly two or three years before they can procure sentence, which when they are obtained, they are often little the better off for it, for commonly their *Denunciadores* are poor shifting fellows from whom there is no restitution to be had. And those that gave sentence being officers that are appointed for some[th] years only, are commonly removed to some other governments, or if they do remain upon the place their persons cannot be touched and it is not easy for a poor factor to seize the household stuff or goods of a judge or chief governor. The king's part is likewise as hard to come by for the giving order to such as received the money for restitution, they always give accounts of disbursing it in the king's service, in which reckoning there is commonly a year spent. And when the king giveth order for satisfaction elsewhere, it is usually two or three years before such warrants be paid. Of this I can give Your Lordships divers instances. I will trouble Your Lordships with only one of Sir John Watts, Alderman his goods were seized at Lisbon by the suggestion of an informer. Sentence passed against him, he appealed to the Council of War here, where the sentence given against him at Lisbon was revoked, and restitution awarded him, and power given him to this effect, which when he cometh to execute, the conde de Aguilar, who at the time of the doing of the wrong was the king's Captain General in Portugal and had two parts of the goods, who is now removed and made governor of Oran in Africa, the king's part he alledgeth he disbursed in the king's service. The king's officer will have this appear. The *Denunciador* is a beggarly fellow worth nothing, who being laid in prison is set free under colour of being a officer of the Castle of Lisbon. So that how Sir John Watts or any other in this or the like case after four or five years suit in law shall come by recompense, His Majesty or Your Lordships in your wisdom may be pleased to provide, for here I see little hope of helping him. . . .

This is obviously a useful document for both diplomatic and English economic history; what is more obvious is its relevance to the domestic history of Spain. To give all the available examples of such applicability of foreign observers' reports would require printing half the ambassadors' despatches that exist in all the archives of Europe. Yet aside from the Venetian relations that happen to be in print and a few national calendars of Venetian ambassadors' reports—both of which have by now exhausted most of their usefulness—and Gardiner's extensive use (a century ago) of Spanish dispatches from London for English political history, hardly anyone has taken advantage of this almost limitless source—sometimes supplementary, sometimes basic—for social, political and other kinds of domestic history. Somebody should.

This is particularly true when domestic documentation has already been exhaustively exploited, which is hardly true in the case of, for example, Carlos Riba y García, *El Consejo Supremo de Aragón en el Reinado de Felipe II. Estudio y transcripción de los documentos originales e inéditos de este Consejo existentes en el Museo Británico* (Valencia, 1914). This is not only one of the few examples of the use of a foreign archive for one's own domestic history but a too-rare example of a Spanish scholar consulting a foreign archive for any purpose, making it doubly unfortunate that the effort was expended on Spanish documents abroad, and on a subject for which still-unexploited documentation abounds in Spain; how much better if he had devoted that effort to English documents (including the reports of English ambassadors), and to a subject to which foreign documentation, not just foreign archives, could make a substantial contribution to knowledge.

CHAPTER 3

*Archives and Archival Collections:
Central Repositories*

What might be termed the standard (if not precisely the universal) pattern of a country's principal repositories is the dual one of a central state archive devoted exclusively to manuscripts, and a central state library devoted primarily to books but with a substantial manuscript section as well. The two are quite distinct in origin, purpose and function, and therefore in the types of documents they possess; happily they are also complementary. One might say that the former is pure but incomplete and in its 'purity' lacking in useful trivia and other miscellany, while the latter fills some of the gaps in the former and contains great quantities of useful miscellany as well.

The distinction in origin is that the former was a government archive in the working sense in the early modern period (or several, later brought together) and has since become an historical archive only with the passage of time, turning government records in the immediate sense into historical ones (though this role also was anticipated by contemporaries), while the latter has been established later as a repository for previously scattered historical documents accumulated for deposit there by purchase, donation and so forth. Functionally, it is the difference between production and preservation on the one hand and collection and preservation on the other, between the survival of a collection and the collection of survivals.

The distinction in terms of documentary holdings is therefore substantial. Those in the former consist almost entirely of government records; some of these may at one time have fallen into private or foreign hands and been later restored and their continuity as government records thus temporarily broken, but the overwhelming 'government' nature of the holdings is reflected not only in the fact that there is comparatively little from 'outside', but that what there is is most likely to be transcripts of comparable government documents from similar foreign state archives. Those of the central library, having been acquired by all-embracing collection rather than specialised production, will be potentially as miscellaneous as the institution's book section, accumulated in similarly broad fashion.

A 'working' archive was in its own time both the government's 'current' files and its reference files to be consulted for the handling of current affairs. The latter need was not limited to documents of the very recent past but instead might go back several centuries, a long-lived relevance that can be especially attributed to the fact that international affairs ran very heavily to disputes over and settlement of the rightful possession of domains, and that these rights were understood in terms of proprietary rule, which made testaments, cessions, renunciations, and other documents regarding transfers or recognition of rights to specific domains diplomatic documents of the first order of importance. Since no right was too old to claim if one could produce some shred of evidence for it, such documents were always potentially current in the sense of evidentiary basis for potential claims, and since domains already held were constantly subject to challenge they were actually current records in the sense of continuing proof of the rightfulness of one's current holdings. In this regard a government's 'diplomatic' archives necessarily resembled a modern land registry office, designed to accommodate the need for thorough 'title searches' that periodically arose in what was essentially a large-scale real estate competition between private owners—often decided by arms, but argued in terms of legalities which not only provided justification but could also affect the military decision by influencing support for one side or the other.

Thus the working archives reorganised early or late in the early modern period were intentionally made to include as much material as possible from as far back as possible, and in fact included (and include) a good deal; the Spanish archives Charles V established in the 1540s, for example, had (and have) quite substantial records from the mid-thirteenth century on; if this does not compare in quantity with what there is beginning with the late fifteenth century on, the difference is as much one of production as of preservation. By the same token, documents produced in the sixteenth and seventeenth centuries continued to be relevant for consultation in the eighteenth, a fact not only of some importance in understanding the nature of these government collections but important also to their organisation, which perforce continued rather longer to be that suitable for government use rather than a redesigned one for the presumed convenience of scholarly research, which may be one reason why some government archives have maintained their integral organisation, their organisational integrity, to the present, and as such should be blessed by historians.

But a good deal of a country's state papers may be lacking from its 'state paper office'—many of these may be found in the manuscript section of the country's main library. Whatever documents ministers or ambassadors kept as their private property may still remain in that family's (or some other's) private collection, but if they have been sold or donated to a public repository it will almost always be to the central library, rarely to the central archive. As a result, such special items as ambassadors' letterbooks or correspondence among ambassadors are more apt to be found deposited in the central library than in the main diplomatic archive. (Private papers will occasionally be deposited in a local archive, but often with a degree of control retained that makes the collection still in effect 'private'.) For centuries there has been a good deal of transcribing of historical documents in private collections, foreign archives, and even one's own central archive to make them more readily available for research; these too are normally deposited in the central library. Of the four countries given most of the specific focus in this volume, France perhaps fits this pattern the least well. There is neither a central government archive surviving from earlier centuries, as in Spain, nor one later consolidated, as in England. The solid blocks of government documents ordinarily found in the 'standard' single repository are divided, especially between the Archive du Ministère des Affaires Etrangères and the Bibliothèque Nationale. The former has the expectable solid blocks, but shares them with the latter, which unifies its share with the usual miscellany of a central library.

Belgium—for this period, for the records of the 'Spanish Netherlands' and the earlier Burgundian state—fits the pattern much better, with the Archives Générale du Royaume de Belgique holding the official collections and the Bibliothèque Royale (now Albert Ier) the miscellany; the Archive du Ministère des Affaires Etrangères, a modern establishment, holds little for earlier periods. England and Spain conform best of all. The latter two countries in fact provide an excellent basis for comparison not only of these two types of repository but of two examples of each which differ in a number of significant and usefully illustrative ways.

The peripatetic royal court of medieval tradition was increasingly an impediment to orderly government as the need grew for more permanent records than could be trundled about from one royal residence to another, to a degree that the development of a modern bureaucracy and that of a fixed seat of government go hand in hand. Since Spain's permanent capital was not fixed at Madrid until the 1560s, and since between 1516 and 1556 the king of Spain was the most peripatetic monarch on record, the Spanish example seems an exception to this rule, but the case is deceptive. Though the king was not in the peninsula most of the time, there was still a 'royal' court there to provide a focus, and since it was only a surrogate one, under a succession of viceroys and governors from Adrian to the future Philip II, it was even more geographically stable than it would have been had the king spent his entire reign in the country, as a viceregal court did not do so much progressing about. Although there was some shifting of temporary seats the court stayed mainly in and around two principal centres—Valladolid in Old Castile, and Toledo in New Castile. Thus it was quite consistent with the context for Charles to order the concentration of all past and future government records in a single convenient place, the one chosen as most suitable being the old castle of Simancas, not far from Valladolid; this was accomplished in 1543–5.

The Public Record Office has a similar origin, a drawing together of earlier government documents that were currently stored in some fifty-odd separate places—but not until the late 1830s, almost exactly three centuries later, and over a century after the end of the period in question.

The result is twofold. Except for Napoleon's pillaging, there was little subsequent loss of Simancas documents, but inevitably a considerable loss of English documents in government 'repositories' that ran heavily to dank cellars and leaky garrets.

And the Simancas archives, already having a rational overall organisation, were sensibly left pretty much as they were, generally preserving their relationship to one another and thus the evidence of their actual use and of the government operation that used them, while this was largely obliterated by the Public Record Office archivists' misplaced rationalising of documents according to their own notion of logical order as distinct from the natural order the documents possessed as historical entities.

Simancas was established at a time of rapidly developing departmentalisation of the Spanish government, with the old Royal Council of the kings of Castile increasingly limited to the internal affairs of that kingdom, while there developed analogous separate councils for Aragon, Italy (originally an appendage of the Council of Aragon), Flanders, the Indies, and (after 1580) Portugal, and specialised councils of the treasury (*hacienda*), Inquisition, military orders, war, etc. Most important was the newest of all, the Council of State. This was originally intended for handling foreign affairs, but the necessary inclusion of Italy and Flanders in its deliberations soon absorbed the major business of those councils into its purview; by a similar process the Council of War became largely an appendage of it; and the paramount importance of its business—and no doubt the concentration of the most powerful of the great nobility in this particular council—gave it increasing pre-eminence over the whole conciliar system (in practice; in protocol it ranked last because newest), with a sort of oversight over the whole, and with its foreign affairs business handled by means of specialised *ad hoc* juntas (sub-committees) for Italy, Germany, France, etc., and specially scheduled sittings of the whole council to deal separately with those various areas of business. The archive established in the 1540s reflected this working structure, with documents of foreign affairs filed in a special 'secretariat of state' section, separated by subject matter: *asuntos* (or *negocios*) *de Francia, de Inglaterra*, etc.

Within these areas particular kinds of materials were often specially filed, either as they were produced or when later brought together as needed for consultation: not only special classes of documents, such as treaties with a given state, royal renunciations, the Instructions of two or three successive ambassadors to a given court, etc., but by an almost endless range of topical foci such as the negotiation of a particular treaty or the history of a particular issue over an extended period. Where no such specialised categories were involved the files consisted of accumulations of ambassadors' dispatches from a given court over a period of time and, normally separately filed, of the records of council deliberations on them, including drafts of replies. In practice, however, ambassadors' reports and/or enclosures with them were often never placed in their proper *legajo* but left with the conciliar documents, a breakdown in clerical procedure which is a slight inconvenience but a great boon to the investigator as it retains the full evidentiary nature of the despatches, not only as reports to be read now but as working entities as read and acted upon then.

So enormous, active and flexible an operation naturally went somewhat awry at times, and there were many documents that went astray, later to be bundled together in a single *legajo* that might cover a century or more, often in little patches from here and there within the long nominal span, rather than finding their proper places in the various appropriate *legajos*, but this was done in conformity with the archive's division by area of business, resulting in *legajos* that are not totally miscellaneous but so only with regard to a single area. Fortunately, when the general movement towards inventorying European archives and making them accessible to scholars flowered in the nineteenth and early twentieth centuries, during which many over-eager archivists were mucking about obliterating all working relationships between documents, the documents at Simancas were as far as possible left as they were, and what organisation of scattered pieces was necessary was done in conformity with the archive's original working organisation—an admirable (and unfortunately rare) procedure resulting from a happy combination of the force of existing organisation (this is the only example of such a collection continuing from such an early date to the present as a single integrated archive) and a series of sensible archivists more concerned with archival integrity than with disruptive displays of clerical virtuosity—most notably Julián Paz and the current director, Ricardo Magdaleno.

In contrast, the documents brought together to form the Public Record Office, being in such great disarray, demanded some sort of immediate reorganisation. The diplomatic documents among them were sensibly classed as 'State Papers' (from 1509), separated from domestic papers from 1547, and from 1577 rationally sub-divided into individual series for Spain, France, Germany (Empire), Germany (States), and so on.[1] So much is to the good, at least approximating the rational organisation of the original working files. Within these series, however, the documents were unfortunately subjected to over-rationalisation, their original groupings obliterated in order to place all in their 'proper' places in a strict chronological order, with a destruction of documentary

[1] Professor Elton's description is about as succinctly comprehensive as possible: 'In the strictly technical sense, the class of documents known as State Papers are the office archives of the secretaries of state. That office did not exist before the sixteenth century, and indeed the archive (State Paper Office) was not created until the reign of James I when partially successful efforts were made to collect the materials of the previous reign at least. At present, the series called by this name begins in 1509; from 1547 it is divided into domestic and foreign sections, and from 1577 the foreign part is classified under the countries to which the correspondence refers.' *England 1200–1640*, p. 66; see pp. 66–75 for a detailed description of English State Papers, and pp. 33–89 for the broad spectrum of records of the State.

integrity that has already been mentioned with regard to enclo-sures with ambassadors' reports. The degree of blame for this, however, is limited by the fact that many (but not all) of these documents had already lost their original organisation during their centuries-long diaspora, scattered around several dozen storage places, most of them unsatisfactory; and one must con-cede that restoring the old associations by means of internal evidence would have been an impossibly Herculean task.

In any case one ironically must lament that the bad results were necessarily limited by the limitations of the collection itself: aside from enclosures with despatches there is very little to be out of place anyway, most of the records of consultation and decision and copies of government out-letters simply not having been preserved. Here lies a further distinction between the two repositories. While Simancas contains the broad spectrum of relevant types of documentation (though with varying degrees of completeness for the lesser types), including not only conciliar documents but drafts ('file copies') of out-letters to ambassadors, the Public Record Office is limited almost entirely to in-letters from ambassadors, with a scattering of enclosures sent with them. An ambassador's own records will sometimes be found (though more often at the British Museum), but these will usually be letterbooks, mainly duplicating the in-letters, or an occasional journal, largely repeating their contents in another form. The fact that all of the letters between English ambassadors quoted in Chapter 2 are from the Public Record Office might seem to con-tradict this, but in fact serves only to illustrate the occasional exception (just as the fact that Carleton's letters from Venice to his colleague in Madrid about Italian affairs are among the State Papers *Spain*, not Venice, illustrates the occasional aberration in segregating these documents according to origin and/or subject matter).

In sum, the researcher in diplomatic history at the Public Record Office can find the reports of the English ambassador to a given state at a given time immediately by going directly to the appropriate chronological place in the relevant series, but the few surviving enclosures will likely be separated from the despatches to which they belong, and he will unfortunately find little else. By contrast he will at Simancas find no such neat organisation, but will find many despatches largely intact (and often, when only scattered copies survive, secretarial notations of what pieces the despatch consisted of), and great quantities of conciliar and related documents.

One result of this difference is a further distinction between the two archives; there are published catalogues for Simancas but none for the Public Record Office.[1] With the straightforward organisation of the latter's State Papers Foreign they are hardly necessary: the typescript listings of contents—usually bare citations—that preface each volume (with a full set kept in the reading room) are useful for their identifications of unspecified senders or addressees, and little more could be usefully done short of calendaring the texts (calendars of many State Papers Foreign have of course been published), which would not be much to the point as a *guide* to (not a substitute for) archival research—a report on the contents of the volumes, not of the individual documents. The researcher hardly needs a published catalogue to tell him that the reports of the English ambassador to France for January 1600 are in the front part of the volume for that year in the State Papers France. At Simancas, on the other hand, even within a section known to deal with, say, affairs with France, research in the wide variety of types of document in all possible

---

[1] Publication of archival data comes on three levels of detail: (1) a broad outline of what the *archive* contains, usually entitled a 'guide' to that archive; (2) a catalogue of what the individual *volumes* contain (which may be a mere notation of the type of document and period covered in each volume, or some description of individual documents therein, or—quite commonly—a mixture of both); and (3) abstracts, excerpts and/or paraphrases of what the *documents* themselves contain, a form that varies considerably in practice but goes under the generic name of 'calendar' (or '*analyses*'). The concern here is with the second type. The third type is dealt with in Chapter 4 (and commented upon in Chapter 7). Regarding the first type, previous Public Record Office guides have been superseded by *Guide to the Public Records* (3 vols, London, 1963, 1969). The various guides to Simancas are of less use than direct resort to the relevant catalogues themselves.

combinations, and with even a single type such as ambassadorial reports for a single year turning up in numerous different scattered *legajos*—in sum, a vast treasure trove *and* a great mishmash—would be (and was) very largely a hit-or-miss affair without fairly thorough cataloguing; the most rudimentary advance planning—at least to the point of having some notion of what is there and where to look—would be impossible without the catalogues being in print.

In many ways these would serve as models for cataloguing any large miscellaneous archive; in others they illustrate characteristics that one is apt or bound to find in this basic research tool. There are by now twenty-odd Simancas catalogues (depending on how one counts them), a large part of them of papers of the Secretaría de Estado. Since the project began at the very beginning of this century there has been a remarkable continuity of approach under the long tenures of Julián Paz and Ricardo Magdaleno as directors of the Archivo General. The actual publication, however, has been quite diverse. Of the first five catalogues, for example, the two that were domestic in nature—covering *Diversos de Castilla* and the *Patronato Real*—and that for *Francia* (1914) were published in Madrid by the *Revista de Archivos, Bibliotecas y Museos* (the latter under the aegis of the *Centro de estudios históricos*), but that for *Capitulaciones con la Casa de Austria y papeles de las negociaciones de Alemania, Sajonia, Polonia, Prusia y Hamburgo, 1493–1796* was published in Vienna (1913) by the *Kaiserliche Akademie der Wissenschaften*, and that for *Las negociaciones de Flandes, Holanda y Bruselas, 1506–1795* in Paris by the *Revue de Bibliothèques* (in serial publication beginning in 1912, as a book in 1915).

The publishing of catalogues, making a fairly detailed knowledge of an archive's contents widely available to potential researchers (without providing a usable substitute for the documents themselves, as calendars do), naturally leads to a great increase in research in the materials thus publicly listed. In terms of before-and-after for the archive as a whole it amounts to opening up the archive for large-scale exploitation of its contents by historians. As between archives, this has the effect of channelling research to those that are publicly catalogued and away from those that are not. As regards a given archive, a comparable internal bias is created during the period of cataloguing itself in favour of those documents that have already been catalogued as of a given moment and against those that have not.

The shape this effect takes depends upon the order in which the cataloguing is done. In a completely miscellaneous repository the standard procedure is simply to catalogue the volumes or *legajos* in numerical order—the order of the numbers already assigned to them or assigned in the course of continuing acquisition. When, as in the case of Simancas (and the Public Record Office) the archive is organised on an historically relevant topical basis, and when (as at Simancas) the numbers assigned to *legajos* within these divisions do not conform to straight numerical sequence, the only sensible approach is section-by-section—in the case of diplomatic documents organised that way, country-by-country. In the archives of a state with less general international involvement one would deal with the various countries or areas in the order of their importance to that state's international affairs; but for the greatest part of the period in question (few Simancas documents go beyond the eighteenth century) Spain's involvement was so widespread that such an ordering would be almost completely arbitrary.

This being the case, the approach taken was probably the most sensible: simple alphabetical order. This at least made selection *objectively* arbitrary, and the inevitable bias in availability caused by lag in cataloguing a random one. And if one has to make the choice it is probably better at a given point to have historians working in all an archive's documentation for half the countries rather than in half the documentation for all. In any case, the bias is an extreme one in the case of Simancas because of the extraordinary delay in getting through all the principal countries and areas, especially from the disruption before and during the Civil War. Thus the catalogues for *Alemania*, *Flandes*, and *Francia* came off the presses in 1913–14, but *Inglaterra* was not reached until 1947

—Volume XVII in the Simancas catalogue series. This naturally gave archival research at Simancas a particular shape during those thirty-odd intervening years—an entirely different shape from what it would have had in a country that spells England *Angleterre*.

What does this involve in the way of quantity? The catalogues themselves can be a bit misleading. For example, the one for *Documentos relativos a Inglaterra* (*1254–1834*) lists some 583 *legajos*, of which almost exactly one-third—a shade under 200—pertain to the period 1500–1700, while of the 326 listed in Volume I (1265–1714) of the France catalogue, a little over 300 pertain to that period. In the first place, the fact that this averages, respectively, just one and $1\frac{1}{2}$ *legajos* per year is meaningless. Documentation naturally tends to be heavier for periods of more important crises, treaty negotiations, and so forth (which is where most historians would want it to be). Conversely, it is inevitably light for the early years when diplomatic reporting had not yet reached its later scale and for periods during which diplomatic relations were broken. Thus for the former reason the England section totals only about three *legajos* for the first dozen years of the sixteenth century, and for the latter reason perhaps half that for the last sixteen years. This leaves a good deal for other periods: for chronological spans such as the 1570s, 1604–24 (between two periods of broken relations), or the last four decades of the seventeenth century (a period of intermittent struggle against Louis XIV) the documentation is substantial. (There is again practically nothing between 1700 and 1713.)[1]

[1] Conversely, after the Public Record Office begins separate series of State Papers Foreign for individual states in 1577, the series for Spain, S.P. 94, has 43 volumes for the 82 years 1578–1659 which start slowly and are later bunched. The first five volumes cover 1578–81, ca. 1583–7, 1589–90, 1591–4, and 1595–7; the more than five years from 1598 to Elizabeth's death in March 1603 require only three volumes (6–8), while the less than two years from that date through 1604, covering the negotiation of peace and the restoration of diplomatic relations, require two (9–10), the subsequent twenty years 1605–24 require 23 (11–32), the three years 1625–7 (with relations broken again) only one (33), the next eight years 1628–35 only four (34–7), etc. By contrast, the series for England's ally France, S.P. 78, reaches 43 volumes by the end of the sixteenth century—only 28 per cent as long as Spain required.

The fact that there is half again as much French documentation listed as English is also misleading. As one would expect, for the reign of Charles V, a great part of which he spent outside the peninsula, the documents of 'Spain's' foreign affairs, like those of all the Emperor's affairs, are scattered in many European archives, especially at Vienna (with some in the *Alemania* section at Simancas). It is thus not surprising that at the Archivo General, which he himself founded for Spain, documents relative to his reign—which covers nearly twenty per cent of the period 1500–1700—comprise hardly two per cent of the 'documents relative to England' for those two centuries. Yet, largely because of the continuing frontier rivalry along the Pyrenees, which had to be handled on the scene in Spain, the same does not hold true for papers relating to Spain, which comprise thirteen or fourteen per cent of those for the two centuries, not nearly as far off the time fraction as one would expect (and finds in the case of other states as well as England). This frontier concern inflates the 'French' documentation in other periods as well, leading in fact to a special catalogue section for '*Aragon y Franco-Condado*', eleven *legajos* of which pertain just to Perpiñan, and much of which really has more to do with the governing of those areas than with international affairs. Another twenty *legajos* of '*Documentos diplomaticos diversos*' definitely concern international affairs, but are not noticeably French, most of them being correspondence from Spanish ambassadors to Venice and Rome in the late-sixteenth and early-seventeenth centuries and from Milan and Naples 1536–7, but including four volumes on the imprisonment in Spain of the Duke of Lorraine, and ranging from an edict of Alfonso the Wise in 1279 to a 541-folio (and folio size) bound volume containing Latin and French copies and minutes of 120 documents pertaining to the Council of Basel (1435–44), to a volume of personal papers for 1703 of Don Pedro de Ayala, the then *Archivero de Simancas*, branded in the catalogue by his modern successor as 'of no interest'.

In sum, when all of these and similar things are taken into account it turns out that the Simancas documentation, for the times that warrant it and when practical considerations do not preclude it, is substantial for both England and France, and for times of comparable importance is, in spite of a seeming disparity, about equal for the two countries.

The question of superiority between Simancas and the Public Record Office (a serious matter of comparative research potential with regard to any archives, but one in which chauvinism, insularity and lack of information often interfere) comes out about even on balance—but it is a balancing out of uneven elements. The Public Record Office has a higher concentration of English medieval documents than Simancas has of Spanish ones, and is superior in some types of domestic documentation (law court records, for example). The domestic and colonial State Papers are rich sources (as are the comparable Spanish series, though not all at Simancas) for matters impinging upon international affairs; so are the comparable Spanish series, but for fuller documentation of the colonial type one must resort to the Archive of the Indies at Sevilla. But as the Public Record Office is almost totally lacking in government policy-making and administrative records, and since its specifically diplomatic correspondence is almost totally limited to in-letters, as a source for the external life of the State in this period it does not compare to the Archivo General.

Simancas does, however, lack one type of document that the Public Record Office has in substantial numbers: modern transcripts made of diplomatic documents in foreign archives— mainly those directly relative to one's own country, but sometimes others as well. Perhaps the best known of these are the *Venetian Transcripts*, P.R.O. 31/14, in 212 bundles. The first fifty-five are for England, nominally covering 1505–1668 but with gaps, most conspicuously 1508–53 and 1560–1610. To these are added twenty-two volumes (56–75) of Venetian Transcripts concerning France (to 1612), two (76–7) for Milan (1494–5), thirteen (78–90) for Rome (to 1609), some other spotty small groups (91–106) for Spain, Brussels, and Turkey, and a wide variety (107–212: 106 volumes) of Venetian *Relazioni*, diaries, newsletters, etc.; much of this material has been calendared or published in full text. Among other series are the Spanish Transcripts, P.R.O. 31/11 (14 volumes, 1488–1555) and 31/12 (44 volumes, 1594–1627); Rome, 31/9 (11 volumes, 1589–1636) and 31/10 (newsletters, 7 volumes, 1554–1625); Vienna, 31/18 (5 volumes, 1513–45); Milan, 31/2 (2 volumes, 1425–1786); and France, 31/3, usually called 'Baschet's Transcripts' (203 volumes, 1501–1714 [Volume I reaches 1521]), which are largely English diplomatic reports from France, not the reverse.

If, when one compares the two central state archives, especially for this type of history in the period in question, the Archivo General is superior to the Public Record Office in most respects, the reverse is true of the two countries' central state libraries: the British Museum is far superior to the Biblioteca Nacional. As regards book sections there are few libraries anywhere that can begin to compete with the British Museum,[1] though for practically any subject that touches upon Spanish affairs there are at least some works—contemporary and early ones, and fugitive journal and institutional publications—for which the Biblioteca Nacional is indispensable. But in its manuscript section as well the British Museum is superior in quantity, far ahead in cataloguing, and better endowed in most of the basic types of document, though the Biblioteca Nacional does have superiority in some very valuable special types.

The British Museum started off with some very important manuscript acquisitions, most notably—in 1753, the very year of the Museum's founding—the old collection of Robert Cotton

---

[1] Except in service. It seldom takes longer than twenty minutes for an order of books to be delivered to one's desk at the Biblioteca Nacional, while the standard wait at the British Museum is more apt to be measured in hours; even in non-rush seasons I have had routine orders placed at opening time actually fail to arrive the same day. The same is true in the central archives: ten minutes is fairly standard at Simancas, thirty minutes an optimistic minimum at the Public Record Office. The practical effect of this is made more severe by the limited open hours available for research at the two archives (about even) and —outlandishly—at the British Museum, as against the serious library hours of the Biblioteca Nacional (10 p.m. closing, which seems a fairly universal practice).

(1571–1631), very famous and extremely valuable though comparatively modest in size (under 1,000 volumes), and the more recent one of Edward Harley, second Earl of Oxford (1689–1741), totalling 7,639 volumes plus 14,236 original rolls, charters, deeds and other legal documents.[1] And in the two centuries since, most of the private collections sold or donated to the public have gone to the same repository, leaving it (cause and consequence are no doubt mixed) with no real competitor as the most important general historical archive in England. There are valuable lesser ones elsewhere, such as at Trinity College, Cambridge, and the Ashmolean collection at Oxford, and specialised repositories such as Lambeth Palace, but nothing to compare with such substantial Spanish alternatives as the Archivo del Palacio, the Casa de Alba, or the collection of the Royal Academy of History.

That dispersal of documentation among several important archives requires a similar dispersal of researchers' efforts is itself

[1] The Cotton MSS include not only those that he collected himself, which run heavily to medieval and then-recent constitutional and political English history; in 1615 he had inherited most of Arthur Agard's papers and in 1623 those of William Camden. The Cotton Library (which in the interim had had a very erratic history) was opened to the public in 1700, sold (along with its dilapidated housing) to the crown for £4,500 in 1707, and subsequently moved from place to place before being installed in the British Museum in 1753. The famous fire damage of 1731 was much exaggerated by contemporary rumour and subsequent tradition: originally involving about a fifth of the 958 volumes, all but 15 eventually were wholly or largely restored. Some 170 volumes of state papers and contemporary tracts are specifically relevant here.

The manuscript part of Harley's collection was kept intact by his widow's selling it 'to the nation' for a nominal (in context) £10,000, thus providing one of the major components of the British Museum's manuscript holdings. Harley's collections of coins, medals, portraits, etc., were sold at auction. His 50,000 printed books, 41,000 prints and 350,000 pamphlets were sold to Thomas Osborne, the bookseller, for £13,000, reputed to be less than Harley had spent on binding them. The much cited *Harleian Miscellany* (ed. William Oldys, 8 vols, London, 1744–6; best edition: ed. Thomas Park, 10 vols, London, 1808–13)—not to be confused with the Museum's Harleian MSS—is a selection of scarce pamphlets and tracts made before the collection was broken up for resale. Osborne's sale catalogue for the library (5 vols, London, 1743–5), partly compiled by Oldys and with an introduction by Samuel Johnson, is itself a bibliographical gem.

only a matter of inconvenience (though, as noted in Chapter 7, this can create what might be called a 'convenience bias' in the use of documents, governing which shall have been exhausted and which published and the shape of extant scholarship). That access to some is more limited than to the Biblioteca Nacional is more serious. Perhaps most serious of all is the lag in cataloguing manuscript holdings—and thus making the existence of specific materials known to potential researchers—that greater size seems to make more conspicuously necessary and thus sooner and more effectively done (and which, parenthetically, convenient subdivisions in the form of acquired collections already established as coherent units make easier).

For the British Museum there not only are satisfactory catalogues, ranging from adequate to excellent, for various individual collections—the Cotton, Harleian, Lansdowne, Royal, Sloane, and Stowe MSS—but have been for some time. The Harleian MSS were in fact catalogued over two centuries ago, shortly after their acquisition (2 volumes folio, London, 1759–63), and then re-catalogued forty years later (4 volumes folio, London, 1808–12). The policy of cataloguing further acquisitions, including 'named' collections, under the single omnibus title of *Additions to the Manuscripts in the British Museum* (an exception was made for the Egerton MSS, which are listed separately in the Additional MSS catalogues)[1] was under way in 1843 with the publication of the catalogue of the 1,836 archival volumes (nos. 9,913–11,748) acquired in the period 1836–40. By 1959, 32,269 volumes (9,913–42,181) had been catalogued (in 17 catalogue volumes), but this is somewhat misleading. The 1959 catalogue covers acquisitions of 1926–30, a three-decade lag (which is increasing: this continuing catalogue has to date reached only 1935), and twentieth-century acquisitions in fact comprise only 18 per cent of those catalogued.

[1] The collection, bequeathed (along with £12,000 for its keep and augmentation) by Francis Henry Egerton, eighth and last Earl of Bridgewater (1756–1829) descendant of the Jacobean Chancellor Thomas Egerton, baron Ellesmere, deals mainly with French and Italian history and literature; 1,978 volumes (1071–3048) are catalogued separately as 'Egerton MSS' in the first seventeen Additional MSS catalogues discussed here.

Eighty-two per cent (26,385 volumes, coming in at a rate of more than 400 per year, against fewer than 200 during 1900–30) were acquired by 1899 and catalogued in print by 1903 (it is pertinent to note that this was in fact the only catalogue since 1880 to appear more than two years after the period covered), and fully 62 per cent in the first forty years, 1836–75, catalogued by 1880. Further, the amount of older material coming in has declined even more sharply than quantity as a whole, so that almost all Additional MSS for the period 1500–1700 were acquired and publicly advertised to researchers generations ago, most of them a century or more. (Similarly, nearly nine-tenths of the 1,978 Egerton volumes had been listed by 1903.)

As these collections total millions of folios of documents, the consequence of such early cataloguing of them is not (as it can be in the case of smaller numbers thus opened up to exploitation) the adverse one of exhausting the archive itself by now through researchers' increased activity but the desirable one of spreading that activity more widely, minimising over-concentration on favoured parts of it. But in avoiding this imbalance *within* the archive one has created (hardly a cause for blame) an imbalance *of* the archive vis-à-vis others, a self-nourishing factor of convenience-of-use further abetted by numerous 'outside' listings such as Ernest Van Bruyssel, 'Première liste des lettres, instructions et autres documents relatifs au règne de Philippe II, que renferme le Musée Britannique', *Compte-rendu des séances de la Commission Royale d'Histoire* (Brussels), 2nd ser., XII (1858–9), pp. 71–82.

The case of the Biblioteca Nacional is in considerable contrast. Until very recently the only guides to the contents of its manuscript section were some partial published listings[1] and a very

[1] Principally an 'Indice de manuscritos de la Biblioteca Nacional' by Bartolomé José Gallardo appended to Vol. II of *Ensayo de una biblioteca española de libros raros y curiosos* (Madrid, Rivadeneyra, 1866), a *Catálogo de los manuscritos que pertenecieron a don Pascual de Gayangos existentes hoy en la Biblioteca Nacional* (ed. Pedro Roca, Madrid, 1904; 401 pp.), and specialised listings of Catalan manuscripts (one ed. Jaime Massó Torrents, Barcelona, 1896, 216 pp.; another ed. Jesús Domínguez Bordona, Madrid, 1933, 724 pp.) and such other special

unsatisfactory card file. As a result, most research was either hit-or-miss, or focused on specific items known to be there, or was channelled by the scattered references in Sánchez Alonso (numerous, but incomplete and of course arbitrarily chosen from the point of view of other researchers' needs) and occasional journal reports of what someone had stumbled on to, or, worst of all, simply back-tracked on the footnote citations in the works of earlier researchers, recombing the same documents instead of going to new ones. Other researchers, of course, lacking advertisement of what was to be found there, simply went elsewhere.

In 1938 Julián Paz published Volume I of what was intended to be a multi-volume *Catálogo de 'Tomos de Varios'*; as the Biblioteca Nacional has a great many volumes of miscellaneous content this appears to be a very good idea, but in fact what Paz produced was merely a table of contents for forty-nine volumes of the already well-known 'Sucesos del año' series, and the project in any case foundered.

Not until 1953 did an *Inventario General de Manuscritos de la Biblioteca Nacional* begin appearing. It is an excellent catalogue, mentioning every document in every volume, but this is achieved at the price of slower progress through the collection—one, alas, must always in such things choose between incompatible desiderata. Volume I (Madrid, 1953) covers only 500 archival volumes (1–500), II (1956) only 396 (501–896), III (1957) 204 (897–1100). Volume VII (1963) is the most extreme example. Eighteen substantial volumes (averaging 520 folios—a total of 9,367) on the 'Govierno de el Duque de Villahermosa en Flandes' in the 1670s (8 volumes: 2,408–15) and '. . . en Cataluña' in the 1680s (10 volumes: 2,398–2,407) contain 3,211 individual documents— about 180 per volume. These are all itemised, including the subject and often the gist of each individual letter, at a rate of thirteen items per page and nearly fourteen pages per volume, with

categories as Greek, Latin, rabbinical, theatrical, and musical manuscripts. For other Madrid archives see for example Luis Sánchez Belda, *Guía de Archivo Histórico Nacional* (Madrid, 1958) and Vicente Vignau y Ballester, *El Archivo Histórico Nacional* (Madrid, 1898).

appended lists of all items that are autograph, bear marginal notations by the writer, etc.

One could hardly ask for better, but this does take up 249 pages, over half the 454 catalogue pages. Many other archival volumes are not susceptible to such detailed treatment: an example pertinent here is 2,416, a 66-folio 'Memoria de los accidentes más notables sucedidas en la guerra pasada durante el gobierno del Duque de Villahermosa: Año 1675', which requires only the title and a few items of the inventory's basic data, such as a notation that it is printed in *Colección de Documentos Inéditos para la Historia de España*, XCV, pp. 1–43. But many others are given extensive treatment—and the volume is also blessed with a thorough 156-page index—with the result that only 100 archival volumes are covered (2,375–2,474), including nineteen of those catalogued by Julián Paz, here given new summaries, as are the first thirty in the preceding *Inventario* volume. The first eight volumes (1953–65) are fairly substantial; half have about 500 pages of catalogue text, the rest somewhat less, with an average of more than 100 pages of subject-and-person index, plus substantial indexes of first lines for poetry and Latin documents and tables of equivalence of old and new archival numbers; in the most extreme example, Volume VI, there are 211 pages of indexes for 480 pages of catalogue text. But they manage to cover only 2,924 archival volumes, an average of only 350 and a rate at which it would take some years yet to complete the cataloguing of the whole manuscript section.

Once the *Inventario General* is completed, however, researchers will have the benefit of a far better tool than the British Museum catalogues are. Sheer quantity, of course, has precluded such extensive detailing of contents (by my calculations, at the Biblioteca Nacional rate the British Museum's Additional MSS acquired by 1930 would not have been catalogued until the year 2003), but one still must note the shortcomings with which the researcher inevitably works. In typical British Museum catalogues each archival volume's original title is given, or (if none) usually a made-up heading (often quite specific, sometimes uselessly vague) and perhaps some further indication of the general nature of its contents, plus some basic data about its length, format, etc. The treatment of individual documents is selective rather than uniform: a good many specific items are noted, sometimes in fairly full detail, while many others are not mentioned at all.

This naturally leads to a bias in the listings toward the interests, values, etc., of the individual cataloguers and their times. That these do not always match current ones is hardly surprising at this remove, though they do sometimes seem rather excessively C. of E.: until the most recent volumes, in the Additional MSS catalogues one found popes indexed not under 'P' but under 'Rome, bishops of'. But the Victorian interest in statesmen and 'diplomatists' at least makes these century-old selections more appropriate for the needs of present-day researchers in political and diplomatic history than for some other fields. The difficulty is that other interests as well are served, and the items noted may tell one nothing of the contents of the rest of the volume, or be misleading about it. The uniform nature of the few that happen to be listed may suggest a whole volume of diplomatic documents when in fact all the rest is irrelevant to the subject; more seriously, mention may be made only of some atypical miscellany, failing to make known that the bulk of the volume is relevant and perhaps even essential to one's subject. As a result one must investigate the slightest glimmer of relevance—mention of a single isolated item that itself is of no importance can be a sufficient hint to put one on the track of valuable but unlisted documentation—and hope that too much else has not gone undetected.

The holdings of a general archive of course differ markedly from those of a central 'state paper office' such as the Public Record Office or Simancas. The general one may contain substantial quantities of original state papers (or contemporary copies, etc.), including coherent sets of diplomatic correspondence, but in isolated blocks, not the continuous series of a record office. As these often originate as an ambassador's own collection of (or including) letters he received they can be an invaluable complement to the official archive, especially one such as the Public Record Office that has few or none of the government's own out-letters itself—making it fortunate that the British Museum is well endowed with such sets, some quite extensive. Other types include an ambassador's own collection of historical documents and transcripts, early collectors' general accumulations, and modern transcriptions (the British Museum has a good number of nineteenth-century ones, typically in copybook form), the last, unlike most earlier ones, not only from private collections but often from foreign archives (though the British Museum has some rather pointless transcripts of Public Record Office documents).

The British Museum is strong in all of these; the Biblioteca Nacional's greatest strength, or at least a special one, lies in some other types, of particular origin. By around 1600 the royal *cronistas*—literally, court chroniclers—had developed much broader responsibilities, not only for the writing of history (past and contemporary) but for the promotion of the writing of history by others, including the provision of the necessary research materials, and for providing background resources for the government itself. To these ends they pursued three rather distinct lines of activity: the keeping of a running account, usually called *annales*, of current events, written by themselves or others or both (sometimes involving a sort of anthology of several historians' accounts, including published ones); the collection of original documents or specially-made transcripts, usually organised either by subject or by year in *annales* fashion (though often rather confusingly called *relaciones*); and the compilation of data either relevant to a particular subject or generally to the 'history' of given years in sequence (sometimes well in the past—a good deal on the seventeenth century was done in the eighteenth) or thought to be potentially useful to the government then or later, ranging from copies of all sorts of treaties to statistical compilations to institutional analyses of Spanish government structure. Sometimes the results of all three of these kinds of activity are to be found in a single collection. Other government officials were also conscripted for this work, and interested amateurs and later archivists contributed to it.

The 'Sucesos del año' series mentioned earlier is the most impressive example—four dozen volumes[1] covering 1598-1666, after 1617 almost all at the rate of one volume per year—but the Biblioteca Nacional is rich in others as well. In 1715, for example, Joachín de Casas Fernández de Heredía put together seven excellent volumes of documents—letters, minutes, etc., with many accounts of troop strength, food and ammunition supply and other detailed technical matters, strategic proposals, and a good deal else—on the war with France in Catalonia in 1647 (MSS 2,330-6); MS 2,329 is a similar collection for 1643-4; MS 2,337 is a 389-folio 'diary' of that war by Antonio Pellicer y Tovar, commander of the Spanish Dragoons and brother of José Pellicer y Tovar, perhaps the most productive of all *cronistas*, for 1640-2 (the entry for 10 June 1641 is inserted, with obvious chronological error, into the 'Sucesos del año 1639', MS 2,370/ 285-87); MS 2,338 is a rather different sort of 'diario', not contemporaneously kept but made by Ramón Rubi de Marymon in 1628 covering events in Catalonia since 1577, in 165 folios.

---

[1] The series is actually 51 volumes (2,343-93). The first three (2,343-44, and the first 101 folios of 2,345), as the *Inventario General* notes, 'pertain to a collection that don Jerónimo Mascareñas, bishop of Segovia, ordered made of copies and extracts from the works of Father Román de la Higuera, especially from his *Ecclesiastical History of the Imperial City of Toledo*' (of which there is a 9-vol. MS copy at MSS 1,285-93; the material used here comes from MSS 1,286-7), attempting in *annales* fashion to cover the period A.D. 1-704; the remaining 108 folios of 2,345 consist of 13 miscellaneous items on both church history and other matters, some from Mascareñas' own writings, spottily embracing the period 1222-1496; the remaining 48 vols, after another quantum leap chronologically, cover 1598-1666 and are more typical of the type collection I have described. One might reasonably catalogue all 51 of these, or only the last 48 (even though all 51 come from the Colección Mascareñas); Paz rather oddly chose to catalogue the last 49, beginning with 2,345, part way through the initial coherent 3-vol. group; Sánchez Alonso cites the collection correctly (I/p. 24/109) but does not note the anomaly in citing Paz's catalogue (II/p. 9/22540).

Other principal types are represented by: two volumes containing 167 extremely varied documents—some originals, some copied as late as the eighteenth century—on both domestic and foreign affairs entitled 'Sucesos políticos del reinado de Felipe II' (MSS 1,749–50; of the nominal 954 folios some 70 are now missing); a 300-folio register (made by various copyists) of the letters to Philip IV from the Marquis de Aytona, Spanish ambassador to the Emperor, 1624–9 (MS 1,929; seventeenth-century MS); a 315-folio collection of 'Testamentos de Reyes y tratados varios' (MS 6,916; seventeenth- and eighteenth-century hands); and so forth. The Biblioteca Nacional is extremely rich not only in the compilations of collectors such as José Pellicer but in manuscript copies—sometimes numerous, sometimes the original revised by the author or copies annotated by later scholars—of their historical writings and those of others, both the well-known historians and works and the lesser known ones, some of which have been published, such as Pietro di Nores, *Guerra trà Filippo Secondo Rè di Spagna e Papa Paolo Quatro* (702 pages, MS 1,824; under a variant title, 403 folios, MS 1,392; published by Luciano Scarabelli as Volume XII (1847) of *Archivio Storico Italiano*, 512 pages), and some of which have not, such as a 370-folio *Relatione historica e politica delle differenze trà Papa Paolo V et i Venetiani l'anno 1605* (MS 1,825).

The type most characteristic of a miscellaneous archive, however, is the volume that is miscellaneous in contents—somewhat more typical of the British Museum than of the Biblioteca Nacional, but numerous in almost any general archive of the sort—ranging from important state papers to snippets of bad poetry. Perhaps even more than the great variety of kinds of more uniform volumes, these individual grab-bags of documentary riches and chaff—in contrast to compact series of basic materials—require an added measure of effort from the researcher. But the returns are well worth the effort: compared to solid runs of correspondence the amount of treasure found may not be great, but it is valuable none the less, and some of it almost bound to be essential. No matter how big the basic solid blocks they are not apt to be sufficient by themselves. A thorough search through large amounts of miscellany make the treatment of almost any subject better—surer, clearer, more complete—and often is indispensable just to get the subject right.

CHAPTER 4

Published Documents

The relevant published documents are extremely varied both in nature and in archival origin. They may be strictly one ambassador's diplomatic correspondence, perhaps only to or from a single person, or two or three, or between or among two or three, perhaps including both ambassadors and ministers at home; they may include other 'public' papers as well—e.g., from one man's career both as ambassador and later as secretary of state; they might include private correspondence and even poems or essays. Among the motives for publishing a public figure's collected papers, especially in or near his own time, is the claim to some literary merit—not, of course, a sound criterion for their worth as historical documents. They may be 'state papers' in the strict sense, those from the archives of a secretariat of state—a usage which (like the office) embraces both foreign and domestic affairs, though publication might be from specialised archival series—or in the broader sense of papers of that mixed affairs-of-state nature even if in private, not state-paper-office, hands. Or they might be in a more general collection of 'historical documents' that includes these more relevant types but others as well—those dealing with the personal affairs of the royal family, economic matters, etc.

They may come from a specialised or miscellaneous public archive, or a large or small private one, or have been assembled from several. The matter of archival origin in fact has a considerable bearing on the published result. At one extreme, a researcher working in a miscellaneous collection may encounter one or two isolated documents of apparent importance and publish them alone in some journal or society publication. At the other extreme are the homogenous bodies of documents too vast for full publication: to print the solid runs of 'State Papers, Foreign',

'State Papers, Spain', etc., in the Public Record Office in full
would be out of the question (without doubling the national
debt); the practicable choices available (aside from doing neither)
are to publish full texts of a few select segments, or calendars of
as long a run as possible—the Public Record Office chose the
latter as the least unsatisfactory alternative. In between these
extremes, a Thomas Birch may encounter a comparatively compact body of papers left by one ambassador (Thomas Edmondes)
who had served at two courts and, with some selection and the
addition of a few more country house relics, fit *An historical view
of the negotiations between the Courts of England, France, and Brussels,
1592-1617* into one moderate-sized volume (London, 1749);
alternatively, one may handle in one volume a small fraction of
an important figure's papers that happen to be in one particular
archive—e.g., *Il carteggio intimo di Margherita d'Austria, duchessa di
Parma e Piacenza. Studio critico di documenti farnesiani* (ed. Ines
d'Onofrio, Naples, 1919; 276 pages)—a rationale for publication
within the available practicable scope that would not exist if all
that person's papers were housed in one place.

Two further general considerations should be noted. Different
types of document publication are alternatives to each other, and
to a less mutually exclusive degree so are the various outlets for
a given type. If when large-scale publication got under way in the
nineteenth century the authorities opted, as the English did, for
extensive calendaring of government-held documents one will
not also find a large systematic collection of printed sources as in
France, and vice-versa. In Belgium, which has neither, large-
scale publication is spread over various somewhat general series
put out by groups of savants, either publicly or privately sponsored. (This would also have been true of Spain, but largely for
lack of financial support the numerous comparable series seldom
lasted very long.) If one has a large printed collection taking care
of the basic part of that task, as in France, the major 'society' and
other alternative series can run heavily to other things such as
memoirs—of which France has three major series and a number
of lesser ones. Of the four states dealt with mainly in this volume,

only in Spain does none of these forms predominate, but the lack is largely offset by a great amount of small-scale separate publication; in addition, Spain being particularly heavily involved with others in the period, the researcher can fall back on foreign-published documents for Spanish foreign affairs much better than for any other country.

In transalpine Europe the techniques of document making and record keeping were usually comparatively rudimentary early and much better developed later in the sixteenth century; by 1600 or shortly thereafter most countries' state papers were being kept in a very orderly fashion: a factor not only of production and preservation, but of archival accessibility. This is perhaps at least a partial explanation of why the tendency is for document publication, both contemporary and modern, to be comparatively slight for the early and increasing for the later sixteenth century and to proceed at a high level for the seventeenth. The fact that early document publication, which followed a very similar timetable, also followed that pattern of content is probably due both to those factors and to a greater interest in what were then contemporary or recent events; this early pattern of publication may also have influenced the modern one.

The greatest of the large systematic (as distinct from miscellaneous) general collections is the *Collection de documents inédits relatifs à l'histoire de France* (Paris, 1835 ff), set on foot by François Guizot in 1834 when he was Minister of Public Instruction and carried on since 1881 under the aegis of the *Comité des Travaux Historiques et Scientifiques*. It passed the 300-volume mark some years ago (the first 177 of which are described in Franklin, *Les sources de l'histoire de France*). It is divided into six series, of obviously unequal relevance here: (1) chronicles, memoirs and journals; (2) charters; (3) correspondence and other political and administrative documents; (4) Revolutionary period; (5) philology, philosophy, etc.; and (6) archaeology. It is not a straight run of 'state papers' in archival order but (the parts relevant here) groups of documents of a certain reign, minister, etc., with individual titles in the series. For diplomatic history its principal contents are not ambassadors' correspondence but that of government top people at home, such as the *Recueil des lettres missives* of Henry IV (ed. J. Berger Xivrey and Joseph Gaudet, 9 vols, Paris, 1843–76), Richelieu's *Lettres, instructions diplomatiques et papiers d'état* (ed. Denis M. L. Avenel, 8 vols, Paris, 1853–77), and Mazarin, *Lettres pendant son ministère* (ed. Pierre Adolph Chèruel and Comte Georges d'Avenel, 9 vols, Paris, 1872–1926), etc. Nothing else in western Europe compares with this in scope. Subsequent expansion of French borders has even made it occasionally international in content: e.g., the *Papiers d'Etat du Cardinal de Granvelle, d'après les manuscrits de la bibliothèque de Besançon* (ed. Charles Weiss, 9 vols, Paris, 1841–52).

The largest and best known Spanish collection is the *Colección de documentos inéditos para la historia de España* (113 vols, Madrid 1842–95; *Catálogo de la . . . by* Julián Paz, 2 vols, Madrid, 1930–1),[1] roughly divided among the reigns of Charles V, of Philip II, and the seventeenth century, with a good deal of attention to the Indies. As with any general collection (this one including manuscripts from several archives) it is inevitably very miscellaneous, but it is far too unsystematic, too fragmented and too poorly planned. There is a great deal of valuable material but very little that fits with very much else in any useful way; much, though important, is too minuscule to justify publication by itself; and when this is not true the choice of inclusions is sometimes remarkably bad. Much of its limited space is taken up with self-contained but overly-large and non-documentary items—Novoa's history of the reigns of Philip III and IV, for example, which occupies nearly six volumes—more appropriate for series such as the *Biblioteca de Autores Españoles*, the *Nueva Biblioteca de Autores Españoles*, the *Colección de libros españoles raros y curiosos*, some of which were already getting under way during the *Colección de documentos inéditos para la historia de España*'s period of publication. It has some solid blocks of diplomatic correspondence—five volumes (87, 89–92) of *Correspondencia de Felipe II con sus Embaja-*

---

[1] Usually cited incorrectly as 112 volumes because the last volume had limited distribution and is not widely known.

dores en la Corte de Inglaterra, 1558–1584, for example—but given the great amount of diplomatic *correspondence* published elsewhere, the *Colección de documentos inéditos para la historia de España*'s greatest value to diplomatic history may be in its occasional inclusion of more rarely published types of documents such as *consultas*. Its greatest shortcoming now, of course, is an acquired one, that of any venerable, useful, and therefore long-used collection: much of it has by now become terribly shopworn.

The *Memorial Historico español: colección de documentos, opusculos y antigüedades* (50 vols to date, Madrid, 1851 ff; published by the *Real Academia de la Historia*) is still in progress, but slowly in the past fifty years (vol. 40, 1900; vol. 45, 1912; vol. 49, 1948); its usefulness to historians of any period is weakened by its spreading its few volumes from the Middle Ages through the eighteenth century. There are also other collections, of which the *Nueva colección de documentos inéditos para la historia de España y de sus Indias* (6 vols, Madrid, 1892–6) is fairly typical in the disconformity between its ambitious title and the scale of its accomplishment: many such series have begun well but failed to sustain publication. Since 1936 (a bad year to start) or more properly since 1942 (Vol. II) a new series of *Documentos inéditos para la historia de España* has been coming out with encouraging frequency, but the bulk of Spain's published documents, including those for diplomatic history, are to be found published separately.

Among this there is surprisingly little full-scale publication of the correspondence of individual ambassadors. There is of course some, but publication of even one man's correspondence more typically focuses on a particular issue or problem, as in the *Correspondencia inédita de Guillén de San Clemente, Embajador en Alemania de . . . Felipe II y III sobre la intervención de España en los sucesos de Polonia y Hungría, 1581–1608* (Zaragoza, 1892). There is a certain amount of other conventional types, such as *Correspondencia entre embajadores: Don Pedro Ronquillo y el marqués de Cogolludo* (Madrid, 1951), but what is perhaps the most valuable feature of this body of published materials is the unusually high emphasis on the papers of foreign ambassadors *to* Spain, such as

La correspondencia diplomatica entre los duques de Parma y sus agentes y embajadores en la corte de Madrid (ed. C. Pérez Bustamente, Madrid, 1934), or E. Pacheco y Leyva, 'Relaciones vaticanas de Hacienda española del siglo XVI (PEEAHR, IV, pp. 45-124).[1] Although there is a fair supply of specialised projects of the scope of Luciano Serrano's edition of *Correspondencia diplomatica entre España y la Santa Sede* (4 vols, Madrid, 1914) and of more general ones such as Antonio de la Torre's *Documentos sobre relaciones internationales de los Reyes Católicos* (6 vols, Barcelona, 1949-66), which manages in 3,350 pages to embrace 3,846 documents, covering 1479-1504, mostly after 1492, perhaps in Spain more than elsewhere historical documents are frequently served up in small helpings in numerous and sometimes rather obscure journals.

Unlike states whose affairs were less widespread, Spanish monarchs in the sixteenth century maintained quite a substantial correspondence with a large number of people; thus instead of publishing omnibus 'Letters of the Kings of' collections one has collections of one monarch's correspondence with (perhaps only from or to) one particular person, such as *Maximiliano de Austria, gobernador de Carlos V en España. Cartas al emperador* (ed. R. Rodríguez, Madrid, 1963). The historical 'star' status of Charles V and Philip II, in contrast to Francis I or Henry III, say, undoubtedly accounts also for the more frequent publication of such important but unglamorous material as the *Correspondencia privada de Felipe II con su secretario Matéo Vásquez* (Madrid, 1959).

Spain's bureaucracy reached a high level of development earlier than other western states, and so left full and orderly records convenient for publication from an earlier date than others; this, coupled with the fact that her involvement in extrapeninsular affairs was greatest under Charles V, has had an atypical result: if one counts foreign archives and foreign publication, the available documentation and publication of 'Spanish' foreign affairs is greater for the first half of the sixteenth century

[1] *Publicaciones de la Escuela Española de Arqueología e Historia en Roma. Cuadernos de trabajos* (Madrid; *Junta para ampliación de Estudios*).

than it is later—just the opposite of the more general rule. (It is also of course more widely scattered for that period.) Conversely, although Spain's diplomatic activity continued to be widespread and intensive throughout the period 1500-1700, historians' interest has been enormous in the sixteenth century, a time of great power and great monarchs, and slight in the seventeenth, a time of troubles and decline; modern document publication has followed the same pattern as modern secondary work (or vice versa); the bulk of it on the period to 1598, far less for half a century, and practically nil after that.

One further peculiarity is that for the reign of Charles V a great part of the 'home side' documentation for 'Spanish' foreign affairs is widely scattered abroad, while throughout the period 1500-1700 much of the most important material on given aspects, handled on the scene in extra-peninsular Spanish domains, remains in archives in those now-independent states—true of Milan and other places, but especially of the Belgian archives, most importantly for the period of international focus on the 'Eighty Years' War' in the Netherlands.

A corollary asset, however, is that, since the subject usually involves a most important aspect of that other country's history as well, and at times European history as a whole, enormous amounts of relevant material have been published for and in various countries and on various scales, such as the *Correspondance de Marguerite d'Autriche, Duchesse de Parme, avec Philippe II* (6 vols: 3 vols, Brussels, 1867-81, ed. L. P. Gachard; 3 vols supplement, Utrecht, 1925-42, ed. J. S. Theissen and others) and *Correspondance de Philippe II sur les affaires des Pays-Bas* (9 vols: 5 vols, Brussels, 1848-79, ed. L. P. Gachard; 4 vols supplement, Brussels, 1940-53, ed. Joseph Lefèvre), or 'Extraits de la correspondance diplomatique de Jean Thomas de Langosco, comte de Stroppiani, et Claude Malopera, ambassadeurs du duc de Savoie à la cour de Charles-Quint, 1546-59' (ed. Giusseppe Greppi, *Compte-rendu des séances de la Commission Royale d'Histoire*, 2nd series, 1858-9, XII, pp. 117-270).

Belgian publication, both of the vast documentation that exists in Belgian archives and of large documentation in foreign archives pertinent to the history of the Netherlandish area, has been very extensive and of extremely high quality in both selection and editorial handling. As noted earlier, this activity has been spread over several large series of a fairly broad historical nature. Most important are those of the *Commission Royale d'Histoire*, whose *Bulletin* has appeared—somewhat irregularly and under various titles—since 1834, and its *Publications* since 1836, in separate octavo, grand octavo, and quarto series. These series are able to devote their space to correspondence, chronicles and such because of the large specialised slice of the publication task that has been borne by the separate *Commission Royale pour la Publication des Anciennes Lois et Ordonnances de la Belgique*. On the other hand, their contents are not as specialised as their series titles sometimes suggest. Joseph Kervyn de Lettenhove's highly-regarded *Relations politiques des Pays-Bas et de l'Angleterre sous le règne de Philippe II* (8 vols, Brussels, 1882–8), for example, which includes such things as an extensive list of Thomas Gresham's letters and transcripts of or extracts from some of them, is a part of the 'Collection de Chroniques belges inédites'.

It is a measure of the scope and quality of Belgian document publication that in discussing the output of individual major editors below, the list—or any representative one—is inevitably dominated by Belgians.

As the archives of the Netherlands as a whole stayed in the south when the northern provinces split off, plus of course the records of the official government during the revolt, the documentary resources and publication of them in the Kingdom of the Netherlands are necessarily mainly limited to the period from the revolt on,[1] and of course during and after the revolt to the rebel United Provinces side of things. This more restricted need is well served by the usual separate publication and there are several excellent middle-sized series and collections, the most important

---

[1] As is reflected also in e.g., George Willem Vreede, *Inleiding tot eene geschiedenis der nederlandsche diplomatie* (6 vols, Utrecht, 1856–65): Vols 1–3 deal with 1572–1650, Vols 4–6 with 1650–1810.

of which for this period is the *Archives ou correspondance inédite de la maison d'Orange-Nassau, 1552–1789* (ed. G. Groen van Prinsterer and others, 26 vols, Utrecht and Leiden, 1835–1917).[1] A peculiar characteristic of document publication is reflected by such collections as the *Lettres et négotiations de Paul Choart, Seigneur de Buzanval, ambassadeur ordinaire de Henri IV en Hollande et de François d'Aerssen, agent des Provinces-Unies en France (1598–1599) suivies de quelques pièces diplomatiques concernant les années 1593–1596 et 1602–1606* (ed. G. G. Vreede, Leiden, 1846; 495 pages). Whether it involves the egotism of larger states, the enforced humility of smaller ones, or merely objectivity and good sense as a geographical accident, it is an observable fact that most nationally bilateral diplomatic documentation has been published elsewhere than in Paris, London or Madrid.

EARLY PUBLISHED DOCUMENTS

Diplomatic correspondence began to be published in substantial quantity at a fairly early date. In the early sixteenth century the diplomatic machinery itself was still being developed, and in the bitter decades of the later sixteenth publication of any sort relative to international affairs consisted mainly of partisan polemics, government propaganda, etc., but what might be described— relatively, at least—as 'straight' publication was well under way in the early seventeenth century and reached quite remarkable proportions by the later seventeenth and early eighteenth. Just as with more recent publication, it varied considerably in quality, scope, and occasion for publication.

Some, such as Arnauld d'Ossat's *Lettres au Roy Henry le Grand et à Monsieur de Villeroy* (Paris, 1624), were published so soon after the writing as to be almost contemporary; others, such as the

[1] The greater continuing Belgian concern with both sides during the revolt may be seen in the publication there of such crucial 'rebel' items as the *Correspondance de Guillaume le Taciturne, prince d'Orange, publiée pour la première fois . . .* (ed. L. P. Gachard, 6 vols, Brussels, 1847–66). The term 'Belgian' is of course appropriate only to the place, not the spirit, of such publication, since Gachard and his fellows considered this to be a *Netherlands* matter, at least until 1609.

Lettres Latines de Monsieur [Jacques] de Bongars, Resident et Ambassadeur sous le Roi Henri IV . . . (Berlin, 1694) sufficiently later to be clearly 'historical' in nature. Some, inevitably, were rather hit-and-miss, but others were not: *Les Negotiations de Monsieur le Président [Pierre] Jeannin* (2 vols, Amsterdam, 1695), for example, devote their thousand-plus pages to just two years (1607–8) of this influential figure's very active diplomatic career. An ambassador's correspondence, memoirs, relations, etc., in fact might run through numerous editions in a fairly short time, if he were sufficiently famous—as was the case with the ubiquitous letters, relations, etc., of Cardinal Guido Bentivoglio—even when (perhaps especially when) that fame was gained in non-diplomatic fields, as in the case of the *Ambassades et Négotiations* (4th ed., augmented, in 903 quarto pages, Paris, 1633) of Cardinal Jacques Davy Du Perron (1556–1618), best known as a churchman, controversialist, and writer of 'Ana' literature.

Publication on this scale was clearly answering a need that went beyond that of historians for documentary raw material; it was, rather, filling a public demand (from the publisher's point of view a commercial demand) for historical literature that was not yet being satisfied by a rapidly developing historical literature, as well as serving an authentic public taste for reading sources as well as secondary works. By the turn of the eighteenth century such efforts had often become truly major projects, reaching a sort of climax with the establishment of *Le Theatre du Monde, ou les Nouveaux Travaux de Mars et de Neptune ou l'on traite exactement de tout ce qui passe dans les Pais et Cours de l'Europe. On y a joint les Traitez de Paix, d'Alliances, de Commerce, etc.* . . . (Amsterdam, 1701 et seq.)—a sort of early *Annual Register*.

Indeed, it is here, from roughly the mid-seventeenth to mid-eighteenth centuries, and not in the nineteenth as is the case with most other European countries, that one finds England's great age of publication of documents pertaining to state affairs. A tradition of rationalised, large-scale publication of collected materials of a given coherent type with a fairly wide audience in mind was already established in other fields by such as Richard

Hakluyt and his continuator Samuel Purchas.[1] Its shift to an emphasis on state papers may be said to be marked, at least symbolically, by the simultaneous publication in 1654 of the *Cabala, sive Scrinia sacra. Mysteries of State & Government: in letters of illustrious persons and great agents, in the reigns of Henry the Eighth, Queen Elizabeth, K. James, and the late King Charles,* and a supplement, *Cabala. Scrinia Sacra; Secrets of Empire* . . . , in the same year; and the continuing demand for such publications to be typified by the issuance of combined, augmented editions under slightly variant titles in 1663 and 1691, plus a more specialised 'further additional supplement', *Cabala. Scrinia Ceciliana: Mysteries of State and Government: In letters of . . . Lord Burghley and . . . other Ministers of State in the reigns of Queen Elizabeth and King James (1663).*

This activity flourished through the second half of the seventeenth century, then reached its apex in the first half of the eighteenth. Greatest and best known of all such efforts is Thomas Rymer's *Foedera, conventiones, litterae, et cujuscunque generis acta publica inter regis Angliae et alios quosvis imperatores, reges, pontifices, vel communitates,* covering from 1101 to the mid-seventeenth century (20 vols, London, 1704–35), completed (Vols 16–20) by Rymer's assistant Robert Sanderson. Volumes 1–17 were given a 2nd edition by George Holmes (1727–9; the last three volumes are the same in both editions); and a ten-volume 3rd edition appeared as early as 1739–45.[2]

In addition to Rymer, the period saw such various other projects as a *Collection of state tracts, published . . . in 1688 and during the reign of William III* (3 vols, London, 1705); John Rushworth's

[1] See Richard Hakluyt's publications, especially *The principal navigations . . . and discoveries of the English nation* (London, 1589; 2nd ed., 4 vols, London, 1598–1600; reprint of 2nd ed., 12 vols, Glasgow, 1903–5 [Hakluyt Society, extra series, vols 1–12], and full and partial editions since), and their continuation in Samuel Purchas's *Purchas his Pilgrimage* (London, 1613; 2nd ed. 1614; 3rd ed. 1617; 4th ed. 1626) and *Hakluytus Posthumus, or Pruchas his Pilgrimes, contayning a History of the World in Sea Voyages and Land-Travels by Englishmen and others . . .* (4 vols, London, 1625); Purchas's *Pilgrimage* and his *Pilgrimes,* two distinct collections, are often confused because of their similar titles.

[2] The contents of the various editions vary considerably; see T. D. Hardy, *Syllabus of documents in Rymer's Foedera* (3 vols, London, 1869–85).

Historical Collections of private passages of State, weighty matters in Law, remarkable proceedings in five parliaments [etc.] 1618–1648 (London, 1721); and publication of parts of the enormous private collections of manuscripts, transcripts, printed tracts, etc., of Robert Harley, Earl of Oxford, and of John Lord Somers: the *Harleian Miscellany* (ed. William Oldys, 8 vols, London, 1744) and the *Somers Tracts* (16 vols, London, 1748–52). An impressive number of editors such as Oldys were active in mid-century, perhaps the most prominent being Thomas Birch, whose publications include *A collection of the state papers of John Thurloe* (7 vols, London, 1742) and *Memoirs of the reign of Queen Elizabeth from the Year 1581 to her death* (2 vols, London, 1754).

But by the early nineteenth century, when continental states were about to launch the great modern projects that now form the backbone of their published sources, England changed her approach. Though new documents continued to be published, that an end to exploratory enthusiasm had been reached seems to be signalled by—instead of fresh new efforts—the republication of the *Harleian Miscellany* in ten volumes (ed. Thomas Park, 1808–13), the *Somers Tracts* in thirteen (ed. Sir Walter Scott, 1809–15), and even yet another edition of Rymer's *Foedera* (4 vols in 7, 1816–69, covering only 1069–1383, published by the Record Commission). The most creative accomplishment for the Tudor–Stuart period was perhaps the publication of *The Court and Times of James the First* and *The Court and Times of Charles the First* (each 2 vols, London, 1849)—not a new project at all but a series of transcripts that Thomas Birch had left, supposedly ready for publication, at the time of his death in 1766, which had since reposed among the Additional Manuscripts of the British Museum (to which he had bequeathed all his books and manuscripts); the material in fact had to wait another ninety years before receiving properly edited publication.[1]

[1] Much of the 'Birch' edition has been superseded by the superior one by Norman Egbert McClure of *The Letters of John Chamberlain* (2 vols, Philadelphia, 1939; American Philosophical Society, Memoirs, XII, Parts 1–2), which goes behind Birch's transcripts, but the 1849 edition of the latter is still useful (with care) for non-Chamberlain material.

England did participate in the nineteenth-century flourishing of learned societies that issued their own regular series of publications, but most of these were either specialised, such as the Selden Society, or local or regional, or too distantly antiquarian to be very pertinent to international affairs, though the Hakluyt Society certainly dealt with a subject—overseas expansion—at the centre of international dispute. The only one directly pertinent, and it only partly so, was the Camden Society, whose publications (1836 ff; since 1897 under the sponsorship of the Royal Historical Society), almost entirely documentary, cover English history more or less in general—political, diplomatic, social, etc. Naturally, only a fraction of its contents pertain to a particular type of history in a particular period, though there is perhaps more than one should expect (in so general a series) of *Letters from George Lord Carew to Sir Thomas Roe, ambassador at the Court of the Mogul, 1615–1617* (Vol. 76, 1860) and Robert Cecil's *Letters to Sir George Carew* (Vol. 82, 1864), both edited by John Maclean, and other such material.[1] And there has been a small amount of separate publication. But compared to other countries England has printed very few historical documents in the nineteenth and twentieth centuries. The reason for the lack, however, is not far to seek. With the reorganisation of the public records in the 1830s the English authorities opted for calendaring as their chosen form of publishing state papers, and the Royal Commission on Historical Manuscripts subsequently made the same choice as the

[1] See Hubert Hall, *List and Index of the publications of the Royal Historical Society 1871–1924 and of the Camden Society 1840–1897* (London, 1925). Camden has also published numerous volumes of Instructions to ambassadors but has now ceased to do so, a reversal of policy one vigorously applauds for the reasons stated in discussing Instructions (Chapter 2) and the inherent biases of documentation (Chapter 7). This particular bias even occurs to some degree in D. B. Horn's *British Diplomatic Representatives, 1689–1789* (Camden 3rd ser., London, 1932), a very useful reference tool for its subject; I attempt to suppress it somewhat in my companion volume, *British Diplomatic Representatives, 1509–1689* (in preparation). There is perhaps no better example than the Camden Society's of a willingness and ability to adapt to changing historical interests, standards and audience, in contrast to those numerous publications that have failed to do so and (usually) simply died on the vine.

way to publish the results of the comprehensive inventory planned of the extensive documentary holdings that remained (and remain) in private hands. The Historical Manuscripts Commission *Reports* (1870 ff) now run to well over a hundred volumes,[1] the various series of the *Calendar of State Papers* (1856 ff) to three or four times that.[2]

This is a very impressive accomplishment that has performed a substantial service in making sources available to researchers if not in the full text at least (it being a choice of compromises) in quantity. Indeed, English historians have tended to speak of it as the major watershed in modern English historiography. The *Dictionary of National Biography* article on Gresham, for example, notes with some awe that 'Burgon's *Life and Times of Sir Thomas Gresham* (2 vols, 1839) . . . practically exhausts the information to be found in the State Papers, although it was published before the printed calendars appeared'. This undoubted boon is most appropriately valued, however, as a temporary compromise only, one that has allowed researchers to deal with greater quantities of documentation than they otherwise could have, though more shallowly and tenuously than they should have, but whose time as a fundamental 'source' is now past. They indeed remain valuable for smatterings of this and that, filling peripheral gaps that do not require or merit exhaustive research in the manuscripts themselves, but they can no longer be counted more than supplementary.

FRANCE: A SPECIAL CASE

As noted before, in most transmontane states the development of adequate government machinery (including the diplomatic

[1] See Elton, *England 1200–1640*, p. 157, and Chapter 5 *passim* on English private papers.

[2] As only a part are pertinent to both the period and the subject, and for some it is not obvious how many 'volumes' are entailed (Professor Elton, *op. cit.*, p. 74 n, concludes with some exasperation that the *State Papers Spanish* total 24 volumes) I have not attempted a precise figure; in the old American Historical Association *Guide* (1931; p. 485) A. L. Cross reported 317 volumes to date.

machinery) for the orderly production of documentary records and the archival apparatus for keeping them was a generally progressive matter throughout the period: markedly improved early in the period, better developed in the late than the early sixteenth century and still better after about 1600. In the English example, the essential administrative reforms of Thomas Cromwell came in the 1530s; after some disruptive turmoil under the middle Tudors, the expanded, departmentalised, professionalised machinery functioned actively and well during the forty-five years of Elizabeth's reign; then to the high level of professionalisation and established administrative procedure reached by then was added the sweeping reorganisation of government archives under James I: the rest of the period may be said to be one of consolidation and refinement of gains already made. But such was not the case in France.

In the early sixteenth century France differed from England in lacking the tradition-shattering developments that made reform of any kind that much more feasible; the sudden need for special new administrative machinery (especially for the monastic property 'augmentations'); and sufficient internal control, including domestic tranquillity, for making such reforms. The French government differed from that of Charles V not only in the level of development already reached but in lacking the impetus of imperative need for further development, having only France to administer, not a multi-state empire strung over much of Europe and the Indies besides.

France not only started at a low level and developed quite slowly through the early sixteenth century, but continued to develop only slowly in the second half, under the disruptive repeated impact of political, religious and politico-religious civil war and ultimately foreign invasion. But France did not of course exist in a vacuum, and as soon as those inhibiting conditions were past, the advanced administrative techniques that had been developed elsewhere, which the French government had had no opportunity to develop itself or adopt from abroad on any appreciable scale, were rapidly adopted, or adapted, and the

native French growth (it was naturally a mixture of both) suddenly flowered. Thus it is not too much to say that 1598, being
the year of both the Edict of Nantes and of the Treaty of Vervins,
is also the crucial watershed in the history of French government
administration in these two centuries, for there is a more radical
change around that date in the orderly production and keeping
of diplomatic (and other government) documents than one finds
in the case of any major state.

While French diplomatic documents were of course being
produced in fair numbers at any time, and preserved perhaps
better than one has a right to expect, there is a vast difference
between the periods before and after about 1598, and it is perhaps
not surprising that document publication reflects this reality.

Reflecting both the early stage of development and the dis-
ruptions of war (including invasion) and of internal strife, printed
diplomatic sources are especially sparse for the early sixteenth
century.[1] There are some publications such as the *Ambassades en
Angleterre de Jean du Bellay. La première ambassade (1527–1529).
Correspondance diplomatique* (ed. V. L. Bourrilly and P. de
Vaissière, Paris, 1905; 604 pages), but they are comparatively
scarce for the period up to 1559.

After that, with the restoration of peace and a few years of
tranquillity before the religious civil wars, there is something of
a bulge noticeable in the *Documents inédits* and quite marked in
separate publication. One has, for example, the *Négotiations,
lettres et pièces diverses relatives au règne de François II, tirées du
portefeuille de Sébastien de l'Aubespine, évêque de Limoges* (ed. L.
Paris, Paris, 1841; 'Collection de documents inédits sur l'histoire
de France'), a 1,032-page volume traditionally cited as *Négotiations de François II* (there is also a 261-page edition of the same
year); the 'Dépêches de Sébastien de l'Aubespine, ambassadeur de
France en Espagne sous Philippe II, 1560' (*Revue d'histoire diplo-*

[1] An indispensable general source for the immediately preceding centuries
(tenth–fifteenth) is the *Collection des meilleures dissertations, notices et traités
particuliers relatifs à l'histoire de France composée en grande partie de pièces rares,
ou qui n'ont jamais été publiées séparément* (ed. C. Leber, 20 vols, Paris, 1838).

matique, 1899, No 4); the *Ambassade en Espagne de Jean Ebrard ... de 1562 à 1566, et mission ... en 1566* (ed. Edmond Cabié, Paris, 1903); the *Dépêches de M. Raymond de Beccarie de Pavie, baron de Fourquévaux, ambassadeur du roi Charles IX en Espagne, 1565–1572* (2 vols, Paris, 1896–1900); and so forth, but nothing comparable in quantity to what is available, after something of a slump for the civil war years, for the late 1590s and beyond.[1]

As the diplomatic machinery (at the centre and abroad) was a part of the overall machinery of government, this effect is, as one would expect, present in the documents of government in general as well, as witness the solid stretches of letters and papers of Henry IV, Richelieu, Mazarin, *et seq.* Diplomatic documents are to be found mainly in separate publication, usually only one volume of the papers of a particular ambassador and perhaps only one mission, but they are far greater in number than for the previous period, and extremely varied in type, from simple collections of one-way letters to or from a conventional ambassador such as the *Lettres inédites du roi Henri IV à Monsieur de Sillery, ambassadeur à Rome, du 1er avril au 27 juin 1600* (ed. Eugen Halphen, Paris, 1866) to such wide-ranging affairs as *L'expédition du duc de Guise à Naples. Lettres et instructions diplomatiques de la cour de France, 1647–1648. Documents inédits . . .* (ed. J. Loiseleur and G. Baguenault de Puchesse, Paris, 1875).

This sudden upsurge in document publication, and a comparable one in the quantity of scholarly research, ranging from such specialised works as J. Valfrey's *Hugue de Lionne. Ses ambassades en Italie, 1642–1656, d'après sa correspondance conservée aux archives du Ministère des Affaires Etrangères* (Paris, 1877) to the comprehensive output of Gaston Zeller, reflects however not just the condition of the archival sources but historians' greater interest

[1] This relatively sparse documentation has not, however, prevented some first-rate historical work based on it. Among several one may cite two first-rate monographs: J. Zeller, *La diplomatie française vers le milieu du XVIe siècle d'après la correspondance de Guillaume Pellicier, ambassadeur de François I à Venise (1539–42)* (Paris, 1881), and P. de Vaissière, *Charles de Marillac, ambassadeur et homme politique sous les règnes de François Ier, Henry II et François II, 1510–1560* (Paris, 1896).

in the personages of the time, and in its subject matter: the resurgence of France under Henri IV, state-building by Richelieu, the Thirty Years' War and so forth. And, as is reflected in the modern editions of, for example, the *Mémoires du comte Leveneur de Tillières* (Paris, 1862) or, in translation, *A journal of all that was accomplished by Monsieur de Maisse, ambassadeur in England from King Henry to Queen Elizabeth, 1597* (London, 1931), this was an interest shared by contemporaries. Not only does contemporary document publication on any substantial scale begin at this time, but the principal period covered does as well.

Perhaps most significant, when one has made allowance for any period's normal concern with itself, and some figures' not-disinterested publication of their own papers in their own lifetime, there remains a substantial interest in the post-1598 period for its own sake, a fact which is increasingly verified as the publishers of documents (and the writers of histories) become less and less contemporary to the period involved: a volume such as *L'ambassade extraordinaire de MM. le duc de Angoulême, comte de Béthune, de Préaux-Chateauneuf, envoyés par le roi Louis XIII vers l'Empereur Ferdinand II et les princes et potentats d'Allemagne, en l'année MDCXX, avec les observations de M. de Béthune, employé à cette ambassade* (Paris, 1667), at 572 folio pages nearly half a century after the event, is no more than a random typical example of an extensive, historically-oriented early publication of documents that extends far beyond the nominal 1700 limit of the period dealt with here. One naturally has to go to the early eighteenth century for the soon-after publication on the late seventeenth, but this 'early' publication continued on practically to the fall of the Bastille, often reaching back a century and a half or more.

One result has been an opportunity for modern editors to direct their efforts to gaps left by earlier ones, creating solid blocks of published documentation that looks almost the result of planned teamwork on both sides. An excellent example is P. Laffleur de Kermingant's four-volume *L'ambassade de France en Angleterre sous Henri IV, 1598-1605*, under two subtitles, *Mission de Jean de Thumery, sieur de Boissie, 1598-1602* (2 vols, Paris, 1886) and *Mission de Christophe de Harlay, comte de Beaumont, 1602–1605* (2 vols, Paris, 1895), which is neatly 'followed' by the *Lettres d'Henri IV et de Mess de Villeroy & de Puiseux a Monsr Antoine de Fevre de la Boderie, ambassadeur de France en Angleterre, depuis 1606 jusqu'en 1611* (2 vols, Amsterdam, 1733) and the *Ambassades de M. de la Boderie en Angleterre depuis les années 1606 jusqu'en 1611* (5 vols, Paris, 1750). It is unfortunate that many researchers isolate themselves in early sources (including printed) because 'purer' or in modern ones because 'better edited': the two together provide a combination often worth taking advantage of.

MEMOIRS

France is by far the best served of any Western European state in the systematic publication of contemporary memoirs, having major series covering all periods from the Middle Ages (Guizot, to the thirteenth century) to the eighteenth century (Barrière and Lescure) and the French Revolution (Berville and Barrière), and for this period 'Petitot' and 'Michaud'.[1] Both the *Collection complète des mémoires relatifs à l'histoire de France depuis le règne de Philippe-Auguste jusqu'à la paix de Paris* (ed. Claude B. Petitot, Alexandre Petitot, Bernard L. J. Monmerqué and others, 131 vols [series 1, 52 vols; series 2, 79 vols], Paris, 1819–29) and the *Nouvelle collection des mémoires pour servir à l'histoire de France depuis le XIIIᵉ siècle jusqu'à la fin du XVIIIᵉ* (ed. Joseph F. Michaud and Jean J. F. Poujoulat, 32 vols, 1836–9) have with some justification been criticised as being editorially weak, but their extensiveness inevitably dominates the field. Editorially Michaud is somewhat better than Petitot, and in fact some of its volumes are merely improved editions of some in Petitot, an improvement bought at the price of redundancy and of sacrifice of space hardly sufficient for covering the remaining important memoirs *not* included in Petitot. This redundancy is unfortunately extended to other series as well, and to separate publication: the ground is

[1] Plus the earlier *Collection universelle des mémoires particuliers relatifs à l'histoire de France* (72 vols, London and Paris, 1785ff).

covered with editions of the memoirs of such commanding figures as Richelieu, such highly regarded observers as Pierre de l'Estoile (the twelve-volume edition by Brunet, Halphen, Read, *et al.* [Paris, 1879–96] is still best, though for the Mornay memoirs it is hard not to prefer the two-volume La Forest edition of 1624–5), and such hardy perennials as Sully's. Obviously not all of these are superior editions: it is a wasteful duplication—perhaps more excusable for commercial houses and well-intentioned amateur editors than for supposedly serious historical societies—that seems an oddly inefficient way to satisfy quantitative demands that could be better met by longer press runs and later reprints, while unfortunately strewing the researcher's path with bad or incomplete editions through which he must pick his way with great care.

The extensive publications of the *Société de l'Histoire de France* (1835 ff; since 1927 absorbed into the *Société d'Histoire Contemporaine*, which by that date—1892 ff—had itself published 63 volumes) also duplicate much that is in Petitot and Michaud, but to much better purpose as they are usually far better edited critical editions. (As this series includes other types of historical documents as well, it manages to duplicate important material in the *Collection de documents inédits*, in that case usually quite redundantly.) But the series' greatest value is in the publication of more untrammelled items such as N. Goulas, *Gentilhomme ordinaire de la chambre du duc d'Orléans: mémoires publiés pour la première fois d'après le ms. original de la Bibliothèque Nationale* (ed. Charles Constant, 3 vols, Paris, 1879–82), which Hauser correctly says 'merits the title of historical annals rather than that of memoirs' (*Sources*, Vol. II, p. 730), and the *Sommaire mémorial (souvenirs) de Jules Gassot, secrétaire du roi, 1555–1623* (ed. Pierre Champion, Paris, 1934: *Sér. anter. à 1789*, Vol. 433). Other general series as well are rich in good modern editions of literature of the memoir-journal type, especially valuable when they cover a period for which sources are more difficult, such as V. L. Bourrilly's edition of *Le journal d'un bourgeois sous le règne de François Ier* (Paris, 1910: *Collection de textes pour servir à l'étude de l'histoire*, Vol. 43), which supersedes the earlier one published by the *Société de l'Histoire de France* (ed. Ludovic Lalanne, Paris, 1854). Memoirs, journals and so forth, unlike most other types of historical sources, were usually written to be published, and so often were, either soon after writing, or later, such as the *Mémoires de Madame de Motteville* (Amsterdam, 1723), which have had several modern editions, or the *Mémoires concernant les Affaires de France sous la Régence de Marie de Médicis* (The Hague, 1720), often in numerous editions, such as [G. de Sandras de Courtilz], *Mémoires de Mr L. C. D. R. contenant ce qui s'est passé de plus particulier sous le ministère du Cardinal de Richelieu et du Mazarin* (5th ed., The Hague, 1713). Much of this literature is important, some is available only in contemporary or early editions—some only in manuscript—and can often be consulted with profit (and pleasure) in its earliest forms even when superior modern editions exist, but the latter are often essential as well. Martin du Bellay de Langey, *Mémoires contenans le discours de plusieurs choses advenües du Royaume de France, depuis l'an 1513 jusques au trespas du Roy François premier, ausquels l'autheur a inseré trois livres, et quelques fragmens des Ogdoades de G. du Bellay son frère. Mis nouvellement en lumière . . . par R. du Bellay* (Paris, 1572) is the *only* single source that covers the entire reign, and should be seen in the early edition by the historian working in that period, but the same historian should equally take advantage of the modern edition of the *Mémoires* of both Martin and Guillaume du Bellay (eds. V. L. Bourrilly and F. Vindry, 4 vols, Paris, 1908–19; *Société de l'Histoire de France*), as well as Bourrilly's *Guillaume du Bellay, Seigneur de Langey, 1491–1543* (Paris, 1904).

The memoirs of Charles V are an excellent (though somewhat extreme) example of the problem of authenticity of text, and of sudden faddishness, and of the facile treatment sometimes given publication.

Wanting to leave his own account of his long career, Charles found an opportunity for doing so during his trip along the Rhine in 1550. Starting at 1515, he dictated his recollections in French to his Flemish secretary Van Male, who thereupon translated his notes into Latin—the proper vehicle for an Emperor's memoirs. But somewhere along the line both the French notes and the Latin manuscript became lost. The closest thing to it ever found was a Portuguese manuscript version written in 1620, attributed to Manuel de Mora, son of Philip II's minister Cristóbal de Mora; what it was translated from is unknown. Even this did not see print in any form for another 242 years; though it was consulted and commented upon extensively in the scholarly press as early as 1845[1] no one bothered to publish this manuscript for another seventeen years, when Joseph Kervyn de Lettenhove published it in French translation under the title *Commentaires* (Brussels, 1862) whereupon it appeared in Spanish and English translations before that year was out, and in German within a year. Not in translations of the *manuscript*, however, but in translations of the French translation of it. And that apparently satisfied the sudden but apparently superficial interest. It was another half century before Alfred Morel-Fatio appended the Portuguese text of the manuscript to his *Historiographie de Charles-Quint* (Paris, 1913), along with a new translation in French—the only language that it had earlier been translated directly into.[2] Comment hardly seems required.

ROUTES TO THE PUBLISHED SOURCES:
MODERN REFERENCE WORKS

As guides to research materials tend to overlap, and in very irregular fashion, the different types of materials discussed here and elsewhere (published documents, contemporary narratives, etc.), it seems best to mention some of the principal ones and some individual examples of particularly useful special types,

[1] L. P. Gachard, 'Notes sur les Commentaires', *Académie Royale de Belgique. Bulletin de la classe des Lettres et de Sciences Morales et Politiques*, XII (1845). On his and others' further published comments see Sánchez Alonso, *Fuentes*, II, 44, No. 4806, where some detail about the manuscript's origin is also given. Much of this comment was also circulated in reprint form.

[2] There has more recently been, for example, a new critical edition in Spanish: Carlos V, *Memorias* (ed. and trans. Manuel Fernández Alvarez, Madrid, 1960).

here in one place. Some biographical reference tools—eventually essential for any kind of historical research in the period—have been included. (Guides specifically to manuscript sources have been mentioned in connection with that subject.)

General

The second edition of the American Historical Association's *Guide to historical literature* (ed. G. F. Howe and others, New York, 1961) is perhaps the most convenient recent general listing, especially for further bibliographical aids beyond the few one can mention here. The first edition (ed. G. M. Dutcher and others, New York, 1931) remains valuable for its sometimes fuller annotation and for titles necessarily dropped in the later edition. Edith M. Coulter and Melanie Gerstenfeld, *Historical bibliographies* (Berkeley, 1935) and Pierre Caron and Marc Jaryc, *World lists of historical periodicals and bibliographies* (Oxford, 1939) contain fuller national listings of bibliographical aids, which is the special purpose of Olga Pinto, *Le bibliografie nazionali* (2nd ed., Florence, 1951; Biblioteca di bibliografia italiana, Vol. 20), covering seventy-odd countries.

Many bibliographies that are narrower topically are not specialised nationally, such as Edward G. Cox, *A reference guide to the literature of travel, including voyages, geographical descriptions, adventures, shipwrecks and expeditions* (3 vols, Seattle, 1935–49; University of Washington Publications in Language and Literature, Vols 9, 10, 12).

Compilations oriented towards the bibliophile, as distinct from the historian, are particularly useful for what they deal with as 'rare' books but which to the historian are fugitive contemporary sources. Though many are ostensibly international in scope they usually possess a national bias that can be as much an advantage as a shortcoming. Jacques C. Brunet, *Manuel du librarie et de l'amateur de livres* (5th ed., 9 vols, Paris, 1860–90) and Johann G. T. Grässe, *Trésor de livres rares et précieux* (7 vols, Dresden, 1859–69), for example, two of the best, are heavily weighted towards (and thus particularly strong on) French and German materials, respectively; perhaps lopsided when taken in isolation, together they complement each other in admirable fashion. (Volume 9 of the former is an additional asset, an extremely useful *Dictionnaire de géographie ancienne et moderne* by P. Deschamps, particularly helpful with regard to confusing changes in place names.)

National biographies

Among general biographical references, the *Biographie universelle ancienne et moderne* (new ed., 45 vols, Paris, 1854–65) and the *Nouvelle biographie générale depuis les temps les plus reculés jusqu'à nos jours, avec les renseignements bibliographiques et l'indication des sources à consulter* (ed. Jean C. F. Hoefer, 46 vols, Paris, 1853–66) conveniently complement each other, the articles in the former ('Michaud') being fewer but longer, in the latter shorter but including a good many more persons. The latter priceless quality is carried nearly to the ultimate in the three-or-four line sketches of Eduard M. Oettinger's *Moniteur des dates: Biographisch-genealogisch-historisches Welt-Register enthaltend de Personal-Akten der Menschheit . . . von mehr als 100,000 geschichtlichen Persönlich-keiten aller Zeiten und Nationen von Erschaffung der Welt bis auf den heutigen Tag* (9 vols, Leipzig, 1869–82). (Perhaps inevitably, most 'general' biographies tend to emphasise their own country of origin.)

On the national level the pacesetter was England's *Dictionary of National Biography* (eds. Leslie Stephen and Sidney Lee, 63 vols, London, 1885–1900; *Supplement*, 3 vols, 1901; *Index and epitome*, 1903; *Errata*, 1904; a slightly revised edition, including the 1901 supplement, in 22 large volumes, 1908–9; decennial supplements since, for persons subsequently deceased—i.e., the format does not provide for further additions for earlier periods).

For the purposes of diplomatic and political history, Belgium's *Biographie nationale* (28 vols, Brussels, 1866–1944; supplements 1957 ff) runs unfortunately too heavily to belles lettristes and such, but it is nevertheless reasonably useful for certain aspects and periods. France and Spain have nothing comparable—the *Dictionnaire de biographie française* (ed. Michel Prévost and others,

8 vols, Paris, 1933–56) is hardly in the same league—though
Spain has a fairly satisfactory substitute in the *Enciclopedia universal
ilustrada* (70 vols in 72, Barcelona, 1907–30; 10 volume appendix
1930–3; irregular annual supplements 1934 ff). For other states
one has, for example, the *Nieuw Nederlandsch biografisch woorden-
boek* (ed. P. C. Molhuysen and P. J. Blok, 10 vols, Leiden, 1911–
37) and the Ranke-inspired *Allgemeine deutsche Biographie* (ed.
Rochus von Liliencron and others, 56 vols, Leipzig, 1875–1912).

Spain
The basic Spanish bibliographical tool, indispensable not only for
Spanish diplomatic (and other) history but for the diplomatic
relations of any other country with Spain (which in this period,
at one time or another, means practically all of Europe) is Benito
Sánchez Alonso, *Fuentes de la historia española e hispanoamericana:
ensayo de bibliografía sistemática de impresos y manuscritos que ilustran
la historia política de España y sus antiguas provincias de ultramar*
(1st ed., Madrid, 1919; 2nd ed., 2 vols, 1927; *Apéndice*, 1946; 3rd
ed., 3 vols, 1952). As the 13,172 articles of the 2nd edition, the
4,842 of the appendix volume, and the 3,994 new ones added in
the 3rd edition each have been given separate series of numbers,
applicable segments of all three of which appear under any one
of the many specific headings, locating a given article number
cited in the index can be a great nuisance, but this and the fact
that after two decades it is time for someone of equal dedication
to add another four or five thousand articles are really the only
'complaints' one can reasonably make about this monumental
effort. Contemporary and modern books, contemporary pamphlets, modern articles, published documents (everything from the
large collections to individual fugitive items printed in obscure
journals), and even a very substantial amount of manuscript
materials (mainly at the Biblioteca Nacional, but also the Escorial,
the Bibliothèque Nationale in Paris, etc.) are included, often
several in one article, so that the 22,000 articles probably include
something like twice that many items. A quite unusual feature is
the extensive listing of locations of reviews of works mentioned.

Where a book has been previously published as separate articles, or a single article (usually later) is essentially a précis of it, or it derives from (is essentially a summary of) a volume of documents published by the author, all the relevant citations are frequently given. And, unlike similar works that run through multiple editions that are not allowed to increase in size, the 3rd edition has dropped only some forty-six of the roughly 18,000 earlier articles (though some have been combined with others) while adding about 4,000 (and adding to many previous articles).

On a lesser scale but nevertheless useful as supplement are Rafael Ballester y Castell, *Bigliografía de la historia de España: catálogo metódico y cronológico de las fuentes y obras principales relativos a la historia de España desde los origines hasta nuestros dias* (Barcelona, 1921) and *Las fuentes narrativas de la historia de España durante la Edad Moderna (1474–1808)* (Valladolid, 1927: *fasículo* I covers 1474–1598).

There is no published general catalogue of printed works in the Biblioteca Nacional such as those of the British Museum and the Bibliothèque Nationale in Paris, but some of that genre's role as bibliography is filled by C. L. Penney, *List of books printed before 1601 in the Library of the Hispanic Society of America* (New York, 1955) and . . . *1601–1700* . . . (New York, 1929–38). The usual variety of useful specialised works exists as well, such as Tomás Muñoz y Romero, *Diccionario bibliográfico-historico de los antiguos reinos, provincias, ciudades, villas, iglesias y santuarios de España* (Madrid, 1858).

The Low Countries

The basic historical reference is Henri Pirenne, *Bibliographie de l'histoire de Belgique: catalogue méthodique et chronologique des sources et des ouvrages principaux relatifs à l'histoire de tous les Pays-Bas jusqu'en 1598 et à l'histoire de Belgique jusqu'en 1914* (3rd ed., Brussels, 1931). The third edition, much enlarged, lists some 5,000 works and sources (encompassed in 440 pages, evaluation is mainly limited to asterisks for the more important). For the period after 1598 there is no analogue for the northern provinces.

S. de Wind, *Bibliotheek der Nederlandsche Geschiedschrijvers* (3 parts totalling 673 pages, Middleburg, 1831–35–40) is a 'bio-bibliographical' treatment of about 200 Dutch historical writers (and about 400 works) in the period 970–1648; extant copies frequently lack the 31-page index issued separately in 1840. The lack of a general historical bibliography is largely offset by richness in specialised ones. W. P. C. Knuttel, *Nederlandsche Bibliographie van Kerkgeschiedenis* (Amsterdam, 1889), for example, lists some 2,500 works in 427 quarto pages. P. A. Tiele, *Mémoire bibliographique sur les journaux des navigateurs néerlandais . . . et sur les anciennes éditions hollandaises de navigateurs étrangers* (384 pp., Amsterdam, 1867; new ed. Amsterdam, 1960) gives full descriptions of 322 editions, with extensive collation and discussion of points of issue between works; all the Dutch titles are translated into French.

The most complete general bibliography for the sixteenth and seventeenth centuries, covering both parts of the Low Countries, is the *Bibliotheca Belgica: bibliographie générale des Pays-Bas* (founded by F. van der Haeghen, 6 vols, Brussels, 1879 ff; reprinted 1964 ff), totalling about 6,000 well-packed quarto pages; the new edition has been rearranged in straight-through alphabetical order, and has an index that was lacking before. Also extremely valuable is the British Museum's *Short-title catalogue of books printed in The Netherlands and Belgium, and of Dutch and Flemish books printed in other countries, from 1470–1600* (London, 1965). The more specialised bibliographies with a focus other than on history per se are of course also useful, such as the *Bibliotheca Catholica Neerlandica Impressa 1500–1727* (The Hague, 1954). The body of particularly active archivists and editors that Belgium produced in the nineteenth and early twentieth centuries fashioned a good number of specialised tools such as J. Proost, *Inventaire ou table alphabetique et analytique des noms des personnes contenus dans les registres aux gages et pensions des Chambres des Comptes* (Brussels, 1890), often extremely useful for details on individuals.

France

For France the old one-volume standards such as Gabriel Monod, *Bibliographie de l'histoire de France: catalogue méthodique et chronologique des sources et des ouvrages relatifs à l'histoire de France depuis les origines jusqu'en 1789* (Paris, 1888) and Charles Victor Langlois, *Manuel de bibliographie historique* (in two parts, Paris, 1901–4) are still useful but cannot compare with the more comprehensive 'Manuels de bibliographie historique' compilations under the uniform title *Les sources de l'histoire de France*; for this period the subtitles are: *des origines aux guerres de l'Italie, 1494* (ed. Auguste Molinier, 6 vols, Paris, 1901–6); *le XVIᵉ siècle, 1494–1610* (ed. Henri Hauser, 4 vols, Paris, 1906–15); and *le XVIIᵉ siècle, 1610–1715* (ed. Emile Bourgeois and Louis André, 5 vols, Paris, 1913–26).

The old American Historical Association *Guide*'s description of Alfred Franklin, *Les sources de l'histoire de France: notices bibliographiques et analytiques des inventaires et des recueils de documents relatifs à l'histoire de France* (Paris, 1877) as a 'somewhat mechanical compilation; inadequate and antiquated' is not much to the point. It is indeed 'somewhat mechanical', but this is hardly a vice in a work of classified listing that in this case includes an excellent 77-page subject index: though readability and profound analyses are not vices either, bibliography is not a branch of poetry. Its 701 pages cannot, of course, compete with the fifteen Molinier–Hauser–Bourgeois–André volumes in number of citations or fullness of annotation, but it is more 'adequate' in some special regards, such as collections of printed documents (it, for example, describes the contents of the 177 volumes of the *Collection de documents inédits* that had appeared to that date). And certainly with regard to diplomatic (and some aspects of political) history it is not 'antiquated': post-war historians, suddenly repelled by the state and all its works, may have solved the problem for themselves by merely declaring the villain irrelevant and relegating it to the play room, a fit subject only for non-serious historians, but by now more seem inclined not only to lament what states do to each other (and to people) but to look the problem in the face and try to find out how and why—and, not the least likely place to start, what. The much-deplored nineteenth-century romance with that villain may have had a rather different philosophical base but the documents of the subject remain largely the same, many of them published, or continuing series started, fairly early in the century. The main difference between Franklin and a hypothetical analogue published today is that the latter, with a century more of publication to account for, would necessarily be far inferior in coverage of the incomplete but important materials already available by the 1870s. The researcher who expects one source or guide or inventory to be adequate for all his needs is obviously in serious intellectual trouble.

As the bulk of the non-manuscript material that an historian must use is to be found (whether exclusively or not) in national libraries, extensive catalogues provide a priceless listing not only of that library's holdings but of the materials that exist in general for a given field of research—contemporary works, published documents, etc.—some of which one might not otherwise learn of. Next to that of the British Museum, the best and most important of these is *Bibliothèque Nationale. Catalogue général des livres imprimés* (Paris, 1897 ff), though it has shortcomings. It is arranged alphabetically by authors only (not also by subject), and does not include anonymous works, official publications, or periodicals. As each volume includes titles acquired by the Bibliothèque up to the date of publication, and as publication from A to T (Tendil) was stretched out over nearly six decades (1897-1955, in 189 volumes), the later volumes are obviously much fuller; this has relatively little effect, however, on the sources for (as distinct from modern secondary works on) diplomatic history, since much of the more important publication of documents was either done or begun by the beginning of this period, and most of a library's collection of contemporary works would already have been acquired by then.

The standard specifically French bibliography is the *Catalogue générale de la librarie française, 1840-1925* (ed. Otto Lorenz and others, Vols 1-34, Paris, 1867-1945), often cited simply as *Lorenz*, which provides separate author and subject volumes for each period of publication covered (which might be anything from three to twenty-five years).

England

The basic historical listings for the period are Conyers Read, *Bibliography of British history: Tudor period, 1485–1603* (Oxford, 1933; 2nd ed. 1959) and Godfrey Davies, *Bibliography of British history: Stuart period, 1603–1714* (Oxford, 1928; 2nd ed. 1970), whose extensive coverage (e.g., Read, 2nd ed., covers 6,543 titles in 544 pages) gives substantial emphasis to the contemporary. (For later works see American Historical Association *Guide*, VA9–11.)

Contemporary publications are covered in various specialised lists, such as A. F. Allison and D. M. Rogers, *A catalogue of Catholic books in English printed abroad or secretly in England* (Bognor Regis, 1956) and John Parker, *Books to build an empire: a bibliographical history of English overseas interests to 1620* (Amsterdam, 1965), and comprehensively in Alfred W. Pollard and Gilbert R. Redgrave, *A short-title catalogue of books printed in England, Scotland and Ireland, and of English books printed abroad, 1475–1640* (London, 1926; reprinted 1956: 627 pages), and Donald G. Wing, *Short-title catalogue of books printed in England, Scotland, Ireland, Wales, and British America, and of English books printed in other countries, 1641–1700* (3 vols, New York, 1945–51). Welcome indexes to these are provided by Paul G. Morrison, *Index of printers, publishers and booksellers in A. W. Pollard and G. R. Redgrave, 'A short-title catalogue'* and . . . *in Donald Wing's 'short-title catalogue'* (Charlottesville, 1950, 1955). Pollard and Redgrave give a few locations, mostly in British libraries, but can be supplemented by William W. Bishop, *A checklist of American copies of 'Short-title catalogue' books* (2nd ed., Ann Arbor, 1950); Wing does a fuller job of locating copies in both United States and British libraries. D. G. Ramage, *A finding-list of English books to 1640 in libraries in the British Isles* (Durham, 1958) gives 37,500 locations in 144 British libraries (excluding national libraries and

the Bodleian and Cambridge), with a list of the titles included that
are not in Pollard and Redgrave. This list excludes national
libraries and the Bodleian and Cambridge—sensibly so, since
such materials are already well catalogued for them: e.g., *Cambridge University Library. Early English printed books in the University Library, 1475–1640* (4 vols, Cambridge, 1900).

Researchers have been doubly blessed regarding the holdings
of the British Museum, one of the world's largest and finest
libraries. First came the *Catalogue of printed books* in 95 volumes
(London, 1881–1900) plus a 15-volume supplement (1900–5),
later reprinted in 68 volumes (Ann Arbor, 1946–50). A pro-
jected new edition, under the title *General catalogue of printed
books*, managed to cover only 'A-Dez' in twenty-five years
(London, 1931–56), and was dropped in favour of a photolitho-
graphic edition (bearing the latter title) of the museum's official
catalogue itself, in 263 folio volumes (London 1960–6) totalling
some 6,000,000 entries on material published between about 1450
and the end of 1955: quite appropriately called 'one of the great
bibliographical dreams of our time'. (A 50-volume decennial
supplement, 1955–65, was published in 1968.) It is alphabetically
arranged by authors, but includes anonymous works, official publications, and periodicals. The museum's published subject indexes,
in progress since 1901, are only for modern works added since 1881.

(Only about fifteen years after publication, a used copy of
Wing was selling at an *inexpensive*—as those things go—American
bookseller's for $200, while the going bookseller's price for the
British Museum *General Catalogue* as it emerged was $18.50 per
folio volume of about 1,000 columns: a strong argument in
favour of sensibly priced reprints or, better, more adequate initial
printings of publications so obviously widely needed, especially,
as in the Wing case, when it involves a major university press.)

Other routes to published sources

When the historian is faced with the task of discovering what
printed sources exist for his subject the obvious first place to go
is bibliographical aids of the sort discussed above, especially those

that have subject indexes or some applicable classification of materials. A second is to survey in exploratory fashion the contents of miscellaneous collections and series of the sort mentioned earlier in this chapter: though not all are indexed, either adequately or at all, they tend to be placed on open shelves in library reference rooms and reading rooms where the researcher can get at them physically and quickly run through an entire series by volume titles or tables of contents—not a sophisticated application of 'library science', but effective, and in fact rather 'closer to the sources' than a bibliographical list or a card catalogue is (in most European libraries the latter is a pretty hit-or-miss affair anyway).

A third way has the double virtue of leading one into random places where much priceless fugitive material can happily be stumbled on to, and of being immune to the problem of identifying materials by subject in bibliographies indexed or classified only by 'author' and card catalogues that are mainly so. That is to explore indiscriminately, through 'author' listings and wherever else encountered, the total output of those editors one finds most prolific in publishing documents in the general field of one's subject, seeking the widest possible view of their whole production. The nineteenth and early twentieth centuries were rich in notable editors—Louis-Prosper Gachard, Antonio Rodríguez-Villa, Alfred Morel-Fatio, A. L. P. de Robaulx de Soumoy, Edmond Poullet, Guillaume-Joseph-Charles Piot, Joseph M.-B.-C. Kervyn de Lettenhove, Philippe-A.-Ch. Kervyn de Volkaersbeke: every researcher will encounter at least a dozen such before he has been on his subject long.

Since all but two of this somewhat-randomly chosen list are Belgian (Belgium produced a remarkable number of first-rate editors, and a remarkable amount of published material), Sánchez Alonso, specifically directed towards *Spanish* history, provides a fair test of this editor-oriented 'route to the published sources'. In the index one finds four entries for Poullet, three of which (6394/235, 6433/238, 6439/239)[1] are to documents, totalling only

[1] References are to the Sánchez Alonso article number/page in Vol. II of the 3rd edition (1952).

130-odd pages, printed in the *Compte-rendu des séances de la Commission Royale d'Histoire* (CrCRH), the other (5940/182) the *Correspondance du Cardinal de Granvelle, 1565-1586* (12 vols, Brussels, 1877-96) he published separately (with Charles Piot) but on which he published a prior memoir in CrCRH (4ᵉ ser. III, 1876), so that all four could have been encountered or learned of in scanning that series; all that would have been gained would be the citation of various reviews of the Granvelle correspondence as it appeared.

Similarly, all four publications listed for Robaulx de Soumoy would have been encountered in the *Collection de Mémoires relatifs à l'histoire de Belgique* (CMHB)[1] though one would find citations of longish *Historische Zeitschrift* reviews of the latter two. (Conversely, of course, finding these scattered references while exploring relevant sections of Sánchez Alonso might send one scurrying to the CrCRH or CMHB in search of further sources edited by anyone—or in either case to Belgian bibliographies in search of further Poullet and Robaulx de Soumoy items.)

Consulting the three listings for Kervyn de Lettenhove would be somewhat more productive. Supposing that one had been alerted to his name as editor of one of the most widely-known and easily-encountered specialised collections of documents, *Relations politiques des Pays-Bas et de l'Angleterre sous le règne de Philippe II*, published in the *Collection de chroniques belges* (1882 ff), one would learn here (6392/235) that it was continued by L. Gillodts van Severen, that it runs to at least eleven volumes, and that Volume XI, published in 1901, reaches 1589 inclusive. At

---

[1] 6421/237: Pierre Joseph Le Boucq, *Histoire des troubles advenues à Valenciennes à cause des hérésies, 1562-1579,* CMHB XIX (xiii, 178 pp.). 6536/247: Jean Bruslé de Montpleinchamp, *Histoire de l'Archiduc Albert, Prince souv. de la Belgique,* CMHB XXXIV; this was originally published anonymously (Cologne, 1693; 381 pp. duodecimo). 6560/252: *Les mémoires non encore venus du sieur de Féry de Guyon,* CMHB I (1858); the Sánchez Alonso citation 'CMC-Belgique' is a printer's error; Sánchez Alonso also notes the edition reproduced, 'publié par P. de Cambry.—Tournay, 1664, 150 p., duodecimo'. 6562/252: *Mémoires de Frédéric Perrenot, sieur de Champagney, 1573-1590,* CMHB VI (xcix, 426 pp.); Sánchez Alonso adds, 'El autor, servidor de Felipe II, era hermano de Granvela.'

6376/233 one would find him the author of a large and important but widely ignored work on one of the most crucial bilateral relationships in the entire farflung complex of cooperative international Calvinist resistance, *Les Huguenots et les Gueux. Etude historique sur 25 années du XVIe siècle* (6 vols, Bruges, 1883–5). At 4806/44 one would find not only his edition of Charles V's *Commentaires* (Brussels, 1862; translated from the Portuguese) and citation of various other editions, but notation of the period covered (1515–50) and a concise history of that long-lost document.[1]

For one in the early stages of exploring the field, the seven entries for Kervyn de Volkaersbeke would be even more fruitful. One, a contemporary memoir, he might have encountered while assaying so conspicuous a series as CMHB.[2] Four others are all in a similar series, but one sufficiently obscure that it is a far less likely candidate for series-canvassing: the Ghent-based *Messager des sciences historiques de Belgique* (MSHB) (a continuation of the equally obscure *Messager des sciences et des Arts de Belgique*):[3] one might very well have discovered a promising series to check out whether these four items proved relevant to one's subject or not. The same is true of 6402/236: merely fourteen pages of 'Lettres inédites de Philippe II et de Marguerite de Parme' in the 1849 *Annales de l'Académie Royale d'Archéologie de Belgique* (Antwerp). But 6448/240 would lead one around another type of bend. The entry is for Léopold Devilliers, 'Une députation des états de

---

[1] Discussed above, under 'Memoirs'.

[2] 6489/243: François de Halewyn, *Mémoires sur les troubles de Gana [sic; Gand], 1577–1579*, CMHB XXII (xxx, 273 pages).

[3] 5635/152: 'Une pièce inédite relative á la révolte des gantois sous Charles-Quint', MSHB, 1878 (27 pages); the citation 'BSHBel' is a printer's error. 5638/152: 'La dernière lettre [de Charles-Quint] aux États de Flandre', MSHB, 1853. 5702/158: 'La victoire de Muhlberg décrite par Charles-Quint et célébrée à Gand en 1547', MSHB, 1874 (26 pages). 6371/232: a review of Théodore Juste, *Histoire de la révolution des Pays-Bas sous Philippe II, 1555–1571* (2 vols, Brussels, 1855), MSHB, 1858; Sánchez Alonso also cites the work's *Deuxième partie, 1572–1576* (2 vols, Brussels, 1863–7) and three other reviews of one part or the other, and notes that there have been various later editions, including one, under a different title, that goes to 1579.

Hainaut en Espagne (février-novembre 1572)', CrCRH, 5*ᵉ sér.*, 1896, VI, pp. 21–80. This is an excellent article of which one will be glad to learn the existence if it is at all relevant to one's subject but it will have been done quite by accident, for SA 6448 has nothing to do with Kervyn de Volkaersbeke. One's first assumption of a printer's error and one's initial guess of transposed digits both prove right, and the search for the correct article short: 6484/243. This concerns two volumes, crucial to their subject, of *Documents historiques inédits concernant les troubles des Pays-Bas, 1577–1586* (2 vols, Ghent, 1847–9). Thus one has, through a proofreader's oversight, been led with little extra effort to two useful items instead of one, both dealing with the principal focus of international affairs during several decades.

Charles Piot has twenty-two index entries, ten of which refer to published works of his own. Of these ten, six are in CrCRH (two long articles, the rest published documents).[1] The other four are the Granvelle correspondence he published with Poullet (5940/182), his edition (6338/227) of a substantial contemporary work, Renon de France, *Histoire des troubles des Pays-Bas* (3 vols, Brussels, 1886–91)—an important editorial contribution but, being in the *Collection de Chroniques belges*, hardly fugitive—and two important articles: 5785/165, his 'Sur les relations diplomatiques de Charles-Quint avec la Perse et la Turquie' (*Messager des Sciences historiques de Belgique* [where Kervyn de Volkaersbeke

---

[1] 5783/1615: 'Correspondence politique entre Charles-Quint et le Portugal de 1521 à 1522 . . . ,' CrCRH, 4th ser., VII (1879), pp. 11–110. 6521/245: 'Une mission diplomatique des Pays-Bas espagnols dans le nord de l'Europe en 1594', CrCRH, 4th ser., XI (1883-4), pp. 437–520. 6766/273: 'Don Emmanuel, prétendant à la couronne de Portugal et la famille de ce prince. Documents et particularités', CrCRH, 4th ser., V (1877-8), pp. 275–340; Sánchez Alonso notes that he was the bastard son of the Prior of Ocrato, and that he *maquinó* with the Netherlands and other *pueblos enemigos de España* to get control of the crown of Portugal. 7815/378: [?Francisco de Castillo Taxardo?], 'Le siège de Charleroi en 1693', CrCRH, 5th ser., IV (1894), pp. 198–235. 7828/378: 'Un document relatif aux négotiations diplomatiques en Espagne pendant l'année 1668', CrCRH, 4th ser., IV (1876-7), pp. 141–52. 7829/378: 'Les guerres en Belgique pendant le dernier quart du XVIIᵉ siècle', CrCRH, 4th ser., VIII (1880), pp. 31–126.

also published], 1843; 31 pages) and 6514/245, 'Une tentative de réconciliation en 1585 entre Philippe II et les provinces insurgées' (*Bulletins de la classe des Lettres . . . de l'Académie Royale de Belgique*, 1895, No. 6).

The other twelve Sánchez Alonso entries are all for reviews, all published in CrCRH which, their only common denominator being the single reviewer and his period and scope of interest and expertise, point to a wide variety of source and secondary materials. They include the by now well-known J. K. Laughton edition of *State Papers relating to the defeat of the Spanish Armada* (2 vols, London, 1894–5), 6805/277, and Morel-Fatio's *L'Espagne au XVIe et XVIIe siècles. Documents historiques et littéraires* (Bonn, 1878), 4581/12, but also the rather out-of-the-way 'Zwei Schreiben des Herzogs Alba und der Statthalterin der Niederlande Margaretha von Parma, an den Herzog Wilhelm von Cleve vom 22. bezw. 25. September 1567' (*Zeitschrift des Bergischen Geschichtsvereins*, 1893, XXIV, pp. 266 ff), 6434/239. The others include Alessandro Bardi, 'Carlo V e l'assedio di Firenze (da documenti dell'archivio di stato di Bruxelles)' (*Archivio Storico Italiano*, ser. 5ª, 1893, XI, pp. 1–85), 5510/141; Virgilius van Zwichem, *Tagebuch des Schmalkaldischen Donaukriegs* (Munich, 1877); Paul Kannengiesser, *Karl V. und Maximilian Egmont, Graf von Büren. Ein Beitrag zur Geschichte des schmalkaldischen Krieges* (Freiburg-im-Breisgau, 1895); Martin Philippson, *Ein Ministerium unter Philipp II. Kardinal Granvella am spanischen Hofe, 1579–1586* (Berlin, 1895); Carel H. Th. Bussemaker, *De afscheiding der Waalsche gewesten van de Generale Unie* (2 vols, Haarlem, 1895); Albert Waddington, *La république des Provinces-Unies, la France, et les Pays-Bas espagnols, de 1630 à 1650* (2 vols, Paris, 1895–7); Arsène Legrelle, *La diplomatie Française et la succession d'Espagne, 1700–1725* (4 vols, Paris, 1888–92).

From these few examples it will be seen how much useful material one might encounter—published documents one did not know existed, or existed in print; modern editions of hard-to-find contemporary works; corrective bibliographical information (one may have thought that a work consulted, published in 1680 on a 1580 event, was not contemporary—rather an important consideration in early works—and then discover that there was a 1581 edition); secondary works, knowledge of which prevents repeating reliable research already done; and even non-critical details to fulfil the conventional requirements for complete citation—by pursuing Gachard's 48 index entries, Rodríguez-Villa's 54, or Morel-Fatio's 58 in even so ostensibly specialised a bibliography as Sánchez Alonso.[1] (As an incidental benefit, the inevitable resort to the list of abbreviations used in citations leads to what is also a comprehensive international list of well over 800 bibliographical works, collections of published documents, society and government-sponsored series, journals, and so forth, some of which the researcher may be glad to know of.)

Papal Nuncios: a Neglected Source

There has been more diplomatic documentation published for some states than others (and in general more for some periods than others), and these sources have naturally received more attention from historians than those that remain unpublished. But one diplomatic source that has long been available in print has been very conspicuously under-used: the correspondence of papal nuncios, and related documentation. This is printed in substantial quantities in the 'Analecta Vaticana-Belgica', a random example being *Correspondance des Nonces Gesualdo, Morra et Sanseverino avec la Secrétairerie d'État pontificale* [1615-21] (ed. Lucienne Meerbeeck, Brussels, 1937; Analecta Vaticana-Belgica 2nd ser., Vol. IV); under other formal auspices such as *Recueil des Instructions générales aux Nonces de Flandre, 1596-1635* (ed. Alfred Cauchie and René Maere, Brussels, 1904; published by the *Commission Royale d'Histoire*), and separately, both in individual volumes and in journals; as well as such background items as *Documents relatifs à la jurisdiction des nonces et internonces des Pays-Bas pendant le régime espagnol, 1596-1706* (Brussels, 1943; 588

[1] It says something for Sánchez Alonso's thoroughness that *all* of these articles are in the number series used for his first two editions (1919, 1927); many have subsequently been added to.

pages). This material has been used somewhat in treatments of the relations of a given state with Rome and for work on the nunciature as an institution, but with rare exceptions such as the widely-published Bentivoglio correspondence it has been little used for other aspects of diplomatic history or for other types of history. It is a source historians could profitably avail themselves of.

CHAPTER 5

Contemporary Publications

Although chronicles, annals, histories, 'relations', memoirs and other such forms can be spoken of properly as distinct genres, there is considerable overlap among them with regard to method, scope, purpose and nearness in time to their subject matter. There is also a tendency for a 'defective' form to acquire virtues—take on attributes—that make it useful and usable as a source for the historian, though they may not necessarily qualify it for the label 'history' under a given specific modern definition.

The obvious place to start a discussion of them is with the chronicle, descended from that medieval form devoted mainly to the brave *gestae* and tragic fates of kings, nobles, warrior chiefs and such. Principally concerned with military matters and the rise and fall of the great, the chronicle literature of Spain, deriving largely from the action and context of the Reconquista, is not surprisingly particularly full and lively; the form flourished there (far more than elsewhere) well into what we would now consider post-medieval times. By the fifteenth century, when places like 'Aragon' and 'Castilla' had existed as political entities long enough for scholars to want to put together a coherent history for them, great efforts were made to form comprehensive collections of the old chronicles, partly as an accumulation of written history for its own sake, but also to form the basis for new synthetic works: it is, in fact, an effort that still goes on, for, whatever their shortcomings, they are still the principal source of knowledge of Spain's medieval past. And, new chronicles of contemporary or recent times continued to be written, substantially improved in historiographical quality.

While the traditional chronicles were often too narrowly focused on a single person and either drew mainly on limited observation and hearsay when recording recent events or largely folk tradition for more distant ones, they were now subjected to the more stringent critical standards and documentary practices one associates with the Renaissance, thus they became rather more 'modern' in coverage, focus and purpose.

For many aspects of the reign of Ferdinand and Isabel the contemporary chronicles are indispensable, a circumstance reflected in the fact that practically all have had at least one modern edition—those of Diego de Valera (1412–87?), Alonso de Palencia (1423–92), Lucio Sículo Marineo (1444?–1536) and others, as well as many anonymous or partial ones, and several for a work as highly regarded as that of Fernando Pulgar (d. 1492). Many had early printed editions, but this was often only after they had been around a good while, and some not at all. Pulgar's various early editions include an abridgment ('compendiums' and 'epitomes' were very popular) by Pedro Valles in the sixteenth century (Zaragoza, 1567, reprinted 1576) and a 384-page folio edition in the eighteenth (Valencia, 1780) but the earliest seems not to have been produced until seventy-three years after his death (Valladolid, 1565; 313 folios, folio); Andrés Bernáldez' fifteenth-century *Historia de los Reyes Católicos D. Fernando y D*^{a} *Isabel* did not see print until the mid-nineteenth (2 vols, Granada, 1856), and then, with typical bandwagon redundancy in such matters, was given two further editions in the next few years; and Pulgar's continuator, Alonso de Santa Cruz, not until the twentieth: *Cronica de los Reyes Católicos* (ed. Juan de M. Carriazo, 2 vols, Sevilla, 1951) and *Cronica del Emperador Carlos V* (5 vols, Madrid, 1920–5).[1]

This does not mean that they were not in effect published, as they circulated widely in manuscript copies, many of which still exist in the Biblioteca Nacional and elsewhere,[2] but the fact can raise certain problems. As the *Aellii Antonii Nebrissensis rerum a Fernando & Elisabe . . .* (Granada, 1545) supposedly by Antonio

---

[1] On this important continuation see Benito Sánchez Alonso, 'La "Cronica de los Reyes Católicos" de Alonso de Santa Cruz', *Revista de Filología Española*, XVI (1929), pp. 35–50.

[2] As Sánchez Alonso notes (*Fuentes*, I, 327, No. 2393), Gayangos lists the British Museum copy as by Alonso de 'Estanques', a misreading of 'Santa Cruz', later corrected by Fernández Duro.

de Nebrija was published two decades earlier than the first known edition of Pulgar's *Cronica*, one would not normally be on guard against the 'former's' being a mere plagiaristic Latin translation of the 'latter'—there are only the insignificant variations usual in such cases—especially when it has at least twice been given modern publication as an original work.

As the reign of Charles V was of still broader import and impact than that of Ferdinand and Isabel, it found contemporary chroniclers not only among the Spanish such as Pedro Girón, Francisco López de Gomara, Pedro Mexia and others, but among foreigners such as Paolo Giovio, who saw his subject as a 'General History' (Latin ed. 2 vols, Paris, 1553-4; Spanish translation 2 vols, Salamanca, 1562-3; etc.).[1] But while the chronicles continued to have great popularity, creative historians were shifting from a contemporary to a past focus, and to other forms—most conspicuously annals—for contemporary events, and this more often with historians in mind than general readers. The chronicle form continued, but as *past* chronicle and eventually simply died from repeating itself. Prudencio de Sandoval's *Vida y hechos del Emperador Carlos V* (2 vols, Valladolid, 1604-6) was an impressive two-folio volumes that had a new edition in a decade (Pamplona, 1614-18) and subsequently still others (e.g., 2 vols, Antwerp, 1681), and parts of it were published abroad in Latin, English (1662, 1703) and other languages; but much of it was simply copied from Mexia, sometimes word for word. The *Epítome de la vida y hechos del invicto Emperador Carlos V* of Juan Antonio

[1] The baker's dozen Alfred Morel-Fatio chose to deal with in his *Historiographie de Charles-Quint* (Paris, 1913) are Guevara, Mexia, Ginés de Sepúlveda, Ocampo, Busto, Páez de Castro, Padilla, Alonso de Santa Cruz, Giovio, Ulloa, Ruscelli, Dolce, and Sansovino. The critical literature on individuals is substantial; see, e.g., Georges Cirot, 'Florian de Ocampo, chroniste de Charles-Quint', *Bulletin Hispanique*, XVI (1914), pp. 307-36; Peter Rassow, *Die Chronik des Pedro Giron und andere Quellen zur Geschichte Kaiser Karls V. in Madrider Archiven und Bibliotheken* (Breslau, 1929; 35 pages); José de la Peña y Cámara, 'Un cronista desconocido de Carlos V. El humanista siciliano Fray Bernardo Gentile', *Hispania*, IV (1944), pp. 536-68; Angel Losada, 'Un cronista olvidado de la España imperial: Juan Ginés de Sepúlveda', *Hispania*, VIII (1948), pp. 234-307.

de Vera Zúñiga y Figueroa, conde de la Roca, had numerous Spanish editions published at home and abroad (1613, 1624, 1627, 1645, 1654, etc.) and was translated as well—into French in 1663—and has also had modern publication (Madrid, 1941), but for all that it is still just an abridgment of Sandoval's cadging from Mexia.

There continued to be glorifications of every type, such as Marc Antonio Ciappi's *Compendio delle heroiche et gloriose attioni et santa vita di Papa Gregorio XIII* (Rome, 1596), an illustrated 'life' that would do honour to any coffee table, and the chronicles of the old *claros barones* style continued to be popular; they were (and are) too attractive a type of literature not to be. Perhaps the most famous of all post-medieval ones, that on *le Chevalier sans peur et sans reproche* by *le loyal serviteur* (generally agreed to be Jacques de Mailles)—the *Histoire du Chevalier Bayard . . . et de plusieurs choses mémorables advenues en France, Italie, Espagne & és Pays bas . . . l'an 1489 iusques à 1524*—in fact neatly brackets the century of decline of the chronicle form, having been first printed in 1527 and receiving a second edition (Paris) in 1619, edited by Theodore Godefroy (1580–1649), a serious French historiographer; by then it was clearly an anachronism as a type.

One important shift in the approach to contemporary history was from a narration of whatever happened during a given period to a focus upon specific subject matter for its own sake, as in the concentration of Angel González Palencia, Giovanni Godoy, Luis de Avila y Zúñiga, Pedro de Salazar, Lambertus Hortensius, and many others on the Schmalkaldic War. Some were mere propaganda (for or against the Emperor), and some were military history written by soldier participants, so that the limitation of scope was imposed by the occasion and the writer's expertise or purpose, but they all shared a focus upon the event—or rather the crisis—as distinct from either one upon the personal (and glorious) *gestae* of the Emperor or this or that grand chevalier as supra-human hero of a tale to be told, or upon a period as one of glorious deeds to be admired or emulated.

This shift in focus was made easier by—or simply made by—

the evil times that followed in the second half of the sixteenth century and the first half of the seventeenth, with the grand drama of the Great Italian Wars replaced by the hatreds, horror and tragedies of wars of belief, where international struggles were fought out not between mobilised nations but within nations in internal disarray, and where the great crescendos rang more of apocalypse than of glory. It did not, however, necessarily bring with it any profound sociological and psychological analysis of the causes of these troubles. The sizable *Histoire Générale de la Rebellion de Bohème* (Paris, 1623) of Claude Malingre (d. 1653), for example, is valuable for its emphasis on the Austrian role in that struggle, when both the dramatic impulse and the likeliest instincts of a French narrator would make the Bohemian side the more tempting focus, but it still deals mainly with military history—the important but 'surface' matters of military persons (especially Bucquoy), event (the invasion of Bohemia) and drama (the rout of Mansfeld and the capitulation of Prague).

Malingre is a fairly typical example of a combination of two demands: that for a quick treatment of important events, and that for a fuller and more considered treatment than could be had from the oceans of fly-sheets, brief 'true relations' and so forth that gave immediate but comparatively insubstantial proto-newspaper coverage to great events. That a workable compromise between extensiveness and up-to-the-minute coverage could be managed is well illustrated by François de Rabutin's *Commentaires des dernières guerres en la Gaule Belgique entre Henri II, Roy de France et Charles V et Philippes son fils, 1551–1558*, whose first full edition (4 vols, Paris, 1574) is reproduced in Petitot (Vols 31–2, Paris, 1823): the first two volumes, covering 1551–4, first appeared in 1555, and the second two, covering 1555–8, in 1559—a performance that would satisfy even our own recent taste for instant history.

Much of the contemporary work on the *troubles de France* (as well as those of the Pays-Bas), however, reflects a different sort of compromise, that between relevance in terms of present concern and history in the sense of *past* events. Much of this literature in fact is better described not as 'contemporary history' but as the *recent* history of contemporary concerns. That other characteristic that one might require for labelling an account 'history' instead of mere reporting, the concentrated—and at least theoretically critical—use of documentary evidence as the source of one's facts, was often conspicuously present in dealing with either contemporary or distinctly 'past' events. This is true not only of the more famous works such as de Thou's, written earlier but not published until 1620,[1] or Dávila's, both written and published later,[2] but of Jean de Serres' *Histoire générale de France* (Paris, 1597), which was given an expanded English edition by Edward

[1] The *Historiarum sui temporis ab anno . . . 1543 usque ad . . . 1607* of Jacques Auguste de Thou (1555–1617) was not printed until 1620, but the initial preface was published before the period covered by the complete work had passed: J. A. de Thou, *Préface de Monsieur le président de Thou, sur la première partie de son histoire. Mise en français par V. H.* (Paris, 1604). Though the work had various subsequent editions—a pirated Latin edition printed by Peter Kopff in Frankfurt in 1625, a French translation as *Histoire Universelle depuis 1543 jusqu'en 1607* (Basle, 1742), etc., it is appropriately the 1620 edition printed under the title *Mémoires* in Petitot (Paris, 1823) and Michaud (Paris, 1839). See also the continuation of de Thou by Gabriel Bartolemé Gramond, *Historiarum Gallae ab excessu Henrici IV . . . (1610–1629). Quibus rerum per Gallos tota Europa gestarum accurata narratio continetur* (Amsterdam: Elzevier, 1653; Maintz, 1673). The cause of modern historians' difficulty in categorising de Thou is not far to seek: he called his work a 'history of his own times' with an ostensible broad focus reflected in the French title 'Histoire Universelle', and began with the Schmalkaldic War, but it soon becomes essentially a history of the *troubles en France.* Gramond reverses this by using the narrower 'History of France' title but bringing in 'all of Europe' in the subtitle. In view of the exaggerated claims of modernity that are sometimes heaped upon de Thou, compromising the truly admirable qualities of an excellent historian with needless excessive praise, it is significant that Gramond limits his own claim to that of accurate narrative.

For a full account of the many editions of de Thou see Samuel Kinser, *The Works of Jacques-Auguste de Thou* (The Hague, 1966: International Archives of the History of Ideas, No. 18). For the subsequent period of French historiography see, for example, W. H. Evans, *L'historien Mézeray et la conception de l'histoire en France au 17ᵉ siècle* (Paris, 1930).

[2] Henrico Caterino Dávila, *Historia delle guerre civili di Francia* (1st ed. Venice, 1630), covering the period 1559–98, has had some 200 editions (Venice 1642, 1,056 quarto pages; Venice, 1692, 834 pages, etc.), including numerous translations: e.g., *The History of the Civil Wars in France* (2nd ed. [London] 1678;

Grimestone, *A generall historie of France, written by Iohn de Serres unto the yeare 1598. Much augmented and continued unto this present out of the most approouved authors that have written of that subiect* ([London], 1611; 1419 pages); Gabriel Chappuys ('Secretaire Interprète de sa Majesté'), *Histoire de nostre temps. Soubs les regnes des Roys Tres-Chrestiens Henry III Roy de France et de Pologne, & Henry IIII Roy de France et de Navarre: Contenant tout ce qui s'est passé, tant en France qu'és autres païs circonvoisins, iusques à la Paix faite entre les Roys de France et d'Espagne. Dédiée à Monseigneur de Rosny* (336 pages, and the simultaneously published 63-page extract *Histoire véritable des guerres entre les deux maisons de France et d'Espagne. Durant le regne des Tres-Chretiens Roys François I, Henry II, François II, Charles IX, Henry III & Henry IIII. Roy de France et de Navarre à present regnant. Iusques à la Paix de Vervins, et mort de Philippes second Roy des Espagnes 1598. Avec la Genealogie de la Royalle Maison de Bourbon* (both Paris, [1600]);[1] Pierre Matthieu's *Histoire mémorable des guerres entre les deux maisons de France et de l'Autriche* (n.p., 1599), covering 1515–98 in 157 octavo pages, and his more extensive *Histoire des derniers troubles en France soubs les regnes des Rois . . . Henry III . . . Henry IIII . . . seconde édition . . . de l'histoire des guerres . . .* (Paris, 1600; n.p., 1606; 4 vol duodecimo ed., n.p., 1742); and other similar works, all specifically notable for their extended chronological coverage of essentially 'contemporary' matter.

Modern historians' acceptance of the work of early predecessors as respectable in quality and perhaps even usable in practice has tended to run to fad, and usually to be limited to a quota of only a few at a time. Until Ranke discredited him, Francesco Guicciardini was very big; recently his nephew Ludovico has been well

734 pages folio). Dávila was an Italian (born in Padua in 1576) of Spanish extraction who spent most of his life in France—a multi-hyphenated mixture of 'nationality' that has caused his modern readers a certain amount of under-standable disorientation.

---

[1] The British Museum catalogue gives both as 1606, but the M.VI^c of both title pages would mean 1600: one M plus VI centuries, with no odd years noted.

regarded, both for his description of the Low Countries and his *Commentarium de rebus memorabilibus, quae in Europa, maxime vero in Belgio* (Antwerp, 1566, covering 1529–60). It is encouraging that de Thou has seemingly been added to the canon, though it is not so certain that he has or will be used, or that increased attention to him means that the canon is actually broadening.

In any case, the tendency to grant de Thou the accolade of 'historian', which seems to be partly based on the deliberate quest for and serious use of documents (which was neither unique nor particularly new) and mainly on the peculiar notion that authentic historical work can be defined simply by universality of subject, is clearly a case of a right decision insufficiently founded. One need not argue that de Thou's universality was more a matter of intention than of practice, nor the obvious fact that worthless pseudo-history can be written on a wide scale at least as easily as on a narrow one, nor the inverse-proportion difficulty that exists between breadth and depth. It is enough to note that three other characteristics that are also important are conspicuously present in many works of the period of less than universal scope: the quest for the past of a nation, place, institution, or whatever, not for the purpose of glorifying it but of knowing it; the attempt to use the past to explain the present (the current one or some previous one); and the attempt to deal with events over a span of time sufficiently long that they may make some interrelated developmental and explanatory sense.

An accurate assessment of either the breadth of historical activity (and thus the availability of contemporary histories) or its level of sophistication (and thus the degree and nature of its usefulness) is not helped by the 'star system' that commonly prevails in discussing not only historical works per se but writings on historical method, the nature of history, etc. One does not, of course, argue with the quantitative limitations of space but with the impression, usually fairly explicit, that the few named are not prominent ones but isolated ones: there is a considerable difference between an eminence in a plain and the peak of an iceberg.

Barnes, for example, in his *History of historical writing* describes

Jean Bodin's *Methodus ad facilem historiarum cognitionem* (Paris, 1566) as 'the first extensive treatise on historical method'. He correctly notes that Bodin places 'the emphasis on interpretation rather than upon criticism of sources', but strangely (or disingenuously), in a chapter whose title 'Humanism and historical writing' accurately describes the specialised terms of his treatment, does not note that this is a rather serious departure from the Humanist preoccupation with textual criticism (though he does undercut Bodin a bit by introducing him as 'Scaliger's publicist contemporary').

Barnes adds: 'Especially significant was the stress which Bodin placed upon the influence of geographical factors in historical development, thus opening the way for Montesquieu and Ritter. His book was therefore more a forerunner of the first chapter of Buckle's *History of Civilisation in England* than of Berheim's *Lehrbuch.*' This is relevant to one side of the 'history of historical writing', the development of it to the present (1st ed. 1937), but is hardly so to the history of historical writing in that period or for that matter the next two centuries, all of which it completely ignores. It was perhaps easier for Barnes than for the present writer to see a seminal 1566 book on historical method, influential in its own time, uniquely as a forerunner of a chapter to be published in 1857.[1]

As a result (however one defines '*extensive* treatise') one would never imagine the existence of such earlier treatises as the *Consilium Historiae Universitatis Scribendae* (Florence, 1548) by the Swiss scholar Christophorus Mylaeus, in which he discusses the collecting of historical documents, the comparing of texts, the study and evaluation of sources, the proper scope and organisation of written history, and much else, with extensive reference to earlier historians and chroniclers as well as contemporary

---

[1] Harry Elmer Barnes, *A History of Historical Writing* (2nd rev. ed., New York, 1962), p. 117; Barnes misleadingly gives it an English title in connection with its 1566 first publication. One notices that it is the only 'Interpretation of History' title earlier than Marx in the old American Historical Association *Guide*, and even it has been dropped in the new edition.

authorities; or François Balduin's *De Institutione Historiae Universae* (Paris, 1561), which analyses the work of recent historians by comparing their treatments of the reigns of Charles V, Francis I, etc.; or that as early as 1579 a Basel publisher (Perna) could issue a two-volume collection of ten important works by seven writers on the subject (bound together in two volumes): Antonio Riccobonus, *De Historia Liber* (the first item, which gives the set its title), two by Mylaeus, two by Uberto Folieta, two by Theodor Zwinger, etc., only one of which—Zwinger's second piece—is based to any considerable degree on Bodin. This concerted enquiry into the subject continued to flourish and to produce a substantial literature, such as Ioannus-Iacobus Beverus, *Synopsis Historiarum et Methodys Nova* (Hanau, 1599), which discusses the use of history as a guide for the future, the problem of periodisation, etc., and adds a useful series of national bibliographical lists—Greek, Roman, German, French, English, Slavic, etc.

There was, in fact, a substantial and rapidly-burgeoning historical literature to record: Cornelius van Beughem in his *Bibliographia historica, chronologica & geographica* (Amsterdam, 1685; 812 pages) manages to list some 5,000 historical works published just since 1650 (he also includes portraits of some 6,000 eminent persons). Long before that, quantity justified even one-nation bibliographies, and demand justified re-editions of those, such as André Duchesne's *Bibliotheque des autheurs qui ont escrit l'histoire et topographie de la France* (2nd ed., Paris, 1627). Publication of these and other types of historical reference works went on apace, and the extensive author and subject indexes of Gotthelf Struve Burckhard's *Selecta biblioteca historica* (Jena, 1705; 815 pages) reflect a level of editorial sophistication that was in fact reached quite early. The widespread interest in history and historical study is reflected in the publication of numerous other types of tool as well, such as O. Brianville, *Abrégé méthodique de l'histoire de France: par la chronologie, la généalogie, les faits mémorables et le charactère moral et politique de tous nos rois* (Paris, 1664).

While the literature involved usually lacked some of the characteristics of the modern doctoral dissertation, much of it possessed qualities that justify calling it history. In contrast to annalistic compilations of current events (sometimes no more than a superficial outline narrative) or literary rehashes of recent ones (usually adding nothing new), many of these works delved far into the past. If in doing so the writers did not always deal with progression in terms of cause and effect, they did seek, in the whole work, to trace the evolution—especially political and constitutional—of their society through the past to the present. Fairly typical are Pierre de Sainct-Julien, *De l'Origine des Bourgongnons, et Antiquité des Estats de Bourgongne . . . Plus, Des Antiquitez d'Autun, de Chalon, de Mascon, de l'Abbaye & ville de Tournus* (Paris, 1581), a work of 674 pages based on extensive research in old archives, abbeys, etc., and Jean-Jacques Chifflet's more narrowly focused *Vesontio* (Lyon, 1618), which traces the development of the city of Besançon from Roman times to Chifflet's own.

The Netherlandish historians, determined to give their 'country' a present identity by providing it with a historical past, were especially concerned with reaching back; and when they came to writing of the Netherlands revolt they tried to treat it as a complex historical phenomenon and to explain what had brought it about—sometimes even military chroniclers, such as Pedro Cornejo in his *Sumario de las Guerras civiles, y causas de la Rebellion de Flandres* (Lyon, 1577). Even when they did not pretend to deal comprehensively with more than the present or the recent past they still felt a need to give their subject a necessary historical background.

Though there had been a certain amount of historical work there as elsewhere before that time, the watershed in Netherlands historical writing and publication seems to occur with the very beginning of the *troubles des Pays-Bas*. Or at least one may say that the relationship is rather precisely symbolised (even though the editor was French—Henri II's official historiographer) by Denis Sauvage's publication (Lyon, 1561-2) of three volumes of earlier chronicles, beginning with the venerable *Cronique de Flandres*, progressing through an anthology of other anonymous ones, and capped by *Les Mémoires* of Olivier de la Marche, published here for the first time, covering 1435-88. Continuing interest, both in the Netherlands and abroad, is reflected in publication of new editions of Hadrianus Barlandus (Adrian Baarland), *Rerum gestarum a Brabantiae Ducibus Historia, conscripta usque in annum 1526*, a chronicle of the dukes of Brabant covering more than 1,200 years, first published in 1526, published here with a third part bringing the account up to 1532 (Louvain, 1566) and his *Hollandiae comitum historia et icones* (Leyden, 1584) and of *Annales sive Historiae Rerum Belgicarum* (2 vols, Frankfurt, 1580), a collection of works on the subject by Baarland (d. 1539), Gerard Geldenhauer (d. 1542), Jacob Meyer (d. 1552), Lodovico Guicciardini (d. 1589) and Jacques Marchant (d. 1609). And even during 'the troubles', when that crisis itself made obvious demands on historians' attention, there continued to be new, serious, extensive work done on the past, such as Guillaume Paradin, *Annales de Bourgongne* (Lyon, 1566), 995 folio pages tracing Burgundian history from the early Middle Ages to 1482. The above few titles serve also to illustrate two distinct lines of treatment: the one finding the origins of this recently created state in its Burgundian past, essentially a dynastic approach (though sometimes institutional as well), the other a more purely national approach, sometimes almost of the history-of-a-people type.

Many of these long-span treatments were of course no more than summaries (true also of the many compendiums of longer works), and so of little use to modern historians except as evidence of what people wrote, read, believed, etc., but many others have a sheer physical bulk that allows them to be quite comprehensive, such as the 1,600-plus folio-size pages of Louis de Mayerne Turquet's *Histoire générale d'Espagne jusques à la conqueste . . . de Portugal faicte par Philippes II* (2nd ed., Paris, 1608).[1] Some historians went back to what might be called historio-

---

[1] The 1st edition, of 1587, was recalled and is today very rare. On the author and his influence see Benito Sánchez Alonso, 'Mayerne Turquet y los historiadores españoles del siglo XVI', *Estudios Menéndez Pidal*, I (1950), pp. 589-99.

graphically viable beginning points, often well chosen, beginning this same subject, for example, with the end of the Gothic period,[1] or its beginning.[2] Others, less wisely, went back to the deluge,[3] or all the way back to Adam (as the starting point of Spanish history),[4] or to the creation itself.[5]

These, certainly, often fell down—a not unusual failing of briefly sketched backgrounds. Some, in fact, did not get beyond the background period itself. Manuel Correa de Montenegro's *Historia general de España* (BNMS 2088; Salamanca, 1606), for example, claims in its grandiose full title to begin with the deluge and come up to 'our times', but in fact begins with the creation, does not even get up to Adam until folio 21, and in the full 183 folios never makes it past 1 b.c. But it is too easy to be snide and condescending about this sort of thing and thus miss the more significant point: the need to fill—albeit with fantasy—historical gaps, to provide historical antecedents, for which knowledge was lacking (and so the historically foolish results) but which an admirably historical attitude assumed nevertheless had to be filled.

[1] E.g., José Antonio de la Serna, *Historia brebe de los 48 Reyes de Asturias, Leon, Castilla y Reynos unidos*, which begins with Pelayo and ends with Philip II. The Biblioteca Nacional has a two-volume manuscript copy totalling 1,660 folios (MSS 1217–18, incorrectly cited in Sánchez Alonso, *Fuentes* I/p. 23/103, as 1817–18), plus a three-volume copy (MSS 7043–45).

[2] E.g., Julián del Castillo, *Historia de los Reyes Godos que vinieron de la Scitia de Europa, contra el Imperio Romano y a España: y la succession dellos hasta el Catholico . . . Philipe segundo* (Burgos, 1582; folio, 158 folios). An edition of 1624 has a continuation up to Philip IV by Jerónimo de Castro y Castillo.

[3] E.g., Francisco de Cepeda, *Resumpta historial de España desde el diluvio hasta . . . 1642* ([Madrid?], 1643). The 2nd edition (Madrid, 1654) has a continuation up to 1652 by Luis de Cepeda y Carvajal, the whole encompassed in 173 quarto-size folios.

[4] E.g., Diego de Soto y Aguilar, *Historia general de España desde Adan hasta . . . 1621*, the original 692-folio manuscript of which is at BNMS 8366.

[5] José Pellicer de Ossau y Tovar, *Anales de España . . . desde la creacion del mundo hasta la perdida de España por Ruderico ultimo Rey de los godos*, a 1638 manuscript copy of which is at BNMS 2472 (266 folios). Marginal notations carry both the years of the world and of Christ. An epitome of 137 folios is at BNMS 2474.

It is also fair to note that treatment of these earlier periods naturally drew heavily upon Biblical history and early Christian tradition which, in the nature of things, personal piety and social pressure would often not allow one either to criticise or to ignore; that traditions and myths (secular ones were also drawn heavily upon) are often more historically relevant to later beliefs, attitudes, etc.—certainly to constitutional development—than the 'true' (i.e., correct) facts of the matter; and that the *use* of tradition seems neither better nor worse here than, for example, in the hagiological treatment given to the rise of Parliament by many of England's leading historians (to the benefit, one might add, of later parliamentary development).

Most important of all, however, if researchers are to make fruitful use of this vast but largely unexploited literature, is the need to distinguish between the historically useful and the ahistorically useless, not to judge one by the other and throw the baby out with the bath: only the immature or the improvident would judge the whole of, say, Mariana's history of Spain by his starting with the deluge or his unhistorical treatment of those early times.[1] Unfortunately, modern historiographers have usually taken the position that his treatment of the early period, or indeed his treating it at all, compromises the historian and thus the whole work, though it would make rather better sense to judge on its own merits that later and principal part of it that is truly measurable by modern secular standards of historical writing and either forget the rest or relax and enjoy it. When viewed in context and a little less glibly, it is perhaps more appropriate to say that Mariana's standing (he is clearly the

---

[1] Juan de Mariana (1535–1624), *Historiae de rebus Hispaniae* initially reached 1516 in 25 books (Toledo, 1592–5, 1168 pages, folio), later extended to 30 books (1st full ed. Mainz, 1605), reaching 1621 in rather summary fashion; further extensions are by other hands; the Spanish translation (Toledo, 1601) is by Mariana himself. See Georges Cirot, *Mariana Historien* (Bordeaux, 1905, 480 pages). For his activity in other fields see John Laures, *The Political Economy of Juan de Mariana* (New York, 1928); Gunther Lewy, *Constitutionalism and Statecraft during the Golden Age of Spain: A Study of the Political Philosophy of Juan de Mariana, S.J.* (Geneva, 1960).

Spanish historian in the period most widely respected outside of Spain, though others such as Jerónimo de Zurita [1512–80], chronicler of Aragon, are technically better) should, on the contrary, make the *practice* less compromising.

Most of these histories, whether dealing with the distant or more recent past, suffered from the bias of patriotism and other religious and philosophical predispositions, the narrowness of view of restricted geographical scope, and the distortions derived from the peculiar focus, the artificial egocentricity with regard to the world at large, of national history. But the best of them were the products of extensive and careful research and of serious consideration not only of the purpose of the work (which might be quite subjectively didactic) but of objective standards of truth, accuracy and historical relevance in pursuing that end. Certainly, then as now, historians did not always follow those standards and often accepted tradition and evidence too readily, but they could also refuse to be uncritical about precisely the subjects about which conformity was most expected and critically-based 'new views' least wanted. Mariana is a good example of that as well. He came under attack from Pedro Mantuano in his *Advertencias a la Historia del P . . . Mariana* (Milan, 1611, quarto, 216 pages; but especially the 2nd ed., Madrid, 1613, quarto, 322 pages), an attack which turned into a public debate with the publication of Tomás Tamayo de Vargas' *Historia general de España . . . de Mariana defendida . . . contra las advertencias de Pedro Mantuano* (Toledo, 1616, quarto, 341 pages); the controversy was still going on generations later in Gaspar Ibáñez de Segovia, marqués de Mondéjar, *Advertencias a la 'Historia' del P . . . Mariana* (Valencia, 1746, folio, 131 pages) and Gregorio Mayans y Siscar, *Prefación a las advertencias del Marqués de Mondéjar* (Madrid, 1795). The principal bone of contention was that Mariana—hardly an anti-traditionalist—had attempted to demonstrate in his history that Santiago had never come to Spain: not the most popular thesis to put forward in his time and place.

In any event there was a good deal of bad history and a fair amount of good history written in the sixteenth and seventeenth centuries, which is also true of the nineteenth and twentieth. From a practical point of view, which period has the better balance of good and bad is rather beside the point, especially since the careful historian can make good use of both.

In a period in which individuals dominated events as much as in any, and with humanist scholars' great interest in movers-and-shakers, biography was naturally an important historical genre. The great variety of quality, coverage and subject is only faintly suggested by the following few examples, which span a century of active publication: Aubert Miraeus, S.J., *De Vita Alberti Pii* . . . *Belgarum Principis Commentarius* (Antwerp, 1622), in which the quality of the writer (as well as the substance of the subject) rises above the standard eulogistic occasion;[1] the *Histoire du connestable de Lesdiguières. Contenant toute sa vie, avec plusieurs choses mémorables, servant à l'histoire générale* (Grenoble, 1638; 2nd ed. 1649; 3rd ed., revised and augmented, 1650) by his secretary Louis Videl; Tomasso Tomassi's anonymous life of Cesare Borgia, *Vita del Duca Valentino, detto Il Tiranno di Roma* (2 vols, duodecimo, Monte Chiaro, 1670), which rather panders to the (our) natural taste for the history of evil men; and the Abbé Jacques Marsollier, *Histoire de Henri de la Tour d'Auvergne, duc de Bouillon* (3 vols, Paris, 1719), or his *Histoire du Ministère du Cardinal Ximenès* (Toulouse, 1693), which had various new editions corrected and augmented by the author, a translation (in German, Hamburg, 1719), and an anonymous refutation: *Marsollier découvert et confondu dans ses contradictions écrivant l'Histoire* . . .' *Avec un abregé de la vie du même Cardinal qu'on a tiré du sieur Marsollier por mieux faire remarquer ses contradictions* (n.p., 1708). Though one should probably count as a debit the fad for 'parallel' lives—Ximénes de Cisneros and Richelieu, Richelieu and Buckingham, etc.—the body of contemporary biography is a rich and vastly under-exploited source.

Sixtus IV set B. Platina Cremonensis to work writing a history

[1] See also A. Miraeus, *Diplomatum Belgicorum libri II* (Brussels, 1628); F. Foppens, *Auberti Miraei opera diplomatica* (4 vols folio, Louvain and Brussels, 1723–48); B. C. De Ridder, *Aubert Le Mire, sa vie, ses écrits* (Brussels, 1863).

of the papacy, *De Vita et Moribus Summorum Pontificum Historia* (its various editions include Venice, 1518; Cologne, 1529), which Fueter calls 'an important step in the secularisation of history. He is the first who combined church history with secular history'; but even that is essentially a 'history of the popes', with little attention to the papacy as an institution in the analytical manner one has come to expect from 'secular history'. But this literature could be analytical (though seldom self-consciously so), especially in examining what went wrong in bringing about a given crisis. As the range of works already mentioned indicates, however, they were not limited to biography, nor for that matter to national histories or 'universal' ones or the distant past or accounts of what happened to have happened in a given segment of time, nor even to internal problems within a given state (which tended to be civil war) or within Europe itself (whose conflicts historians increasingly tend to think of as civil wars within the European civilisation). None of these categories is fitted, for example, by a wide variety of works such as Achille Tarducci da Corinaldo, *Il Turco Vincibile in Ungaria* (Ferrara, 1600), which deals with a 'European' problem but an external one, and not only deals with Turkish penetration into eastern Europe at least partly from the Turkish end but delves also into the origin and growth of Turkish power itself: if it is never in doubt which side the author is on, it is also never in doubt that what he is after is knowledge of the facts and that what he seeks to present is a reality-based description of a serious problem, including its enemy element, and not a mere literary study in black and white.

Of the part of this vast literature that deals with the period itself, much is usable as a source regarding persons, events, etc.— sometimes in considerable detail—and of a great many kinds of specific data. Most of it, regardless of period covered, is extremely valuable in recovering the context of the times: what opinion-makers were writing, what knowledge of the past and the present was available to them and to the public at large (much more than we often suppose), in sum the factual and ideological view of the world of those who were acting out (or living through) the history that one is attempting to write; if one is writing social or intellectual history, that is in fact part of the 'history' itself, and even for the proper sort of drum-and-trumpet it is an inseparable part of the fabric. It naturally must be used with care, but that is true of any historical literature: the alternative is to use it blindly. If it poses more difficulties in use than that of more recent periods, the problem is more one of cultural distance than of difference in historical or historiographical relevance, and bridging that distance, far from being a mere nuisance necessity for the technical handling of sources, is in fact the basic part of the historian's task. Even the most 'unreliable' of such works will help with that task, and the better ones will help get at the 'facts' themselves.

As evidence of what was being said—as distinct from what the facts of a matter might have been—nothing is more relevant in the area of domestic and international political history than polemic and propaganda: what was said in either of these manners was itself often an historical event of some importance.

One type of polemic, the religious one, is rather specifically characteristic of this period of Reformation and Counter-Reformation. Some of these are no more than anti-papist and anti-heretic diatribes, often more pertinent to keeping one's own co-religionists in a properly feverish lather of hate or panic of fear than to convincing anyone else. Others are full-blown theological disputes across the hostile gulf between Catholic and Protestant worlds. These were apt to be serious formal scholarly efforts, sometimes running to several volumes; to lapse into scurrilous invective; and to have a political application, as in the case of tyrannicide in which one debated the propriety of murdering a king who opened his eggs at the wrong end.[1] A comprehensive

[1] The public exchange on tyrannicide with the greatest relevance to international affairs was that between James I of England and Francisco Suárez, but it was debated by others as well, many going back to ancient Rome for their authorities, not just to scripture, the church fathers, etc. Treatment of the general area shades off into both abstract 'political science', such as Juan de Mariana's defence of the subjects' right to depose (and assassinate if necessary) the monarch (a seemingly radical position, but actually conservative in Spain at

intellectual history of the period itself (as distinct from merely the roots of later trends of thought) would very largely be taken up with international theological controversy.

Others are less unique to the period. Pamphlets questioning Elizabeth's virginity, Lerma's honesty, or the statesmanship of the Duke of Buckingham are typical writings of enemies, rivals and malcontents. William the Silent's slanders of Philip II were a mixture of self-defence and policy, and Antonio Pérez's similar libels, while more dramatic than most, are not otherwise much different from the standard exposés of wickedness behind the scenes still being written by disgruntled ex-government employees.

Some of these, such as James I's various debates with both Catholic and Protestant opponents, affected international affairs, and others—such as resistance theory, obviously—the internal affairs of the state. But nothing perhaps is so relevant to the history of the workings of the European state system as the sort of literature that is best labelled propaganda, defending one's actions, dynastic claims, etc., or attacking those of others. The line between this and purely polemical literature is in many ways inevitably imprecise, and in a sense arbitrary. Both often had the dual purpose of convincing others of the rightness of one's position while simultaneously preserving or increasing the support of the adherents one already had; both combined positive arguments in justification of one's own actions, claims, etc., with a negative attack on those of one's opponent; both could involve a co-ordinated barrage of numerous publications as well as isolated occasional ones; both could involve books of substantial size as well as pamphlets and fly-sheets; both could involve extensive scholarly research as well as spur-of-the-moment products dashed

the time, reflecting the tradition of circumscribed powers and limited status of the crown at a time when royal absolutism was becoming the *dernier cri* in Europe) in *De Rege et Regis Institutione* (Toledo, 1599), and works on resistance theory written for the needs of the moment by both religious camps—and sharing the same arguments: on the latter aspect see Robert M. Kingdon, 'William Allen's use of Protestant political argument', in *From the Renaissance to the Counter-Reformation* (ed. C. H. Carter, New York, 1965, pp. 164–78).

off in haste and sometimes carelessly. With regard to each of these qualities the balance in what I would call specifically 'propaganda' is towards the former, in that of merely 'polemical' literature towards the latter. But the distinction is more than one of degree with regard to one essential characteristic. Polemics may be fired by or at rulers and may be sponsored by governments, but they may have almost anything as source and almost anything as target. The literature in question here is *government* propaganda, directed by one state against the actions, claims, etc., of another state (and justifying its own); as insurgent causes, including independence movements, are often at the centre of international as well as domestic affairs in this period, it also includes the exchange of pro- and anti-government propaganda.

Good propaganda usually requires at least a certain basis in fact, its distortions achieved not so much by outright lies as by inflation of truths, in which case the historian can learn a good many actual facts simply by discounting exaggerations, ignoring pejorative adjectives and adverbs, and otherwise restoring proportion with a large grain of salt. Sometimes an intentionally one-sided account is achieved by merely telling one side: the account may be quite reliable so far as it goes, giving the researcher a very useful source for that part of the story; he must go elsewhere of course for the rest, but that is usually true of the best of sources. And sometimes the claims, complaints or cause may be good enough to preclude any need for distortion in presenting one's case to the public: being imbued with a healthy distrust of propaganda per se and a sensible scepticism about any purportedly rational argument whose logical conclusions unerringly come out on the side of the arguer, we are often inclined to forget that some propaganda is true.

Even when propaganda is not a reliable source of the facts of the matter, even when it is too distorted for the truth to be sorted out, it is still, obviously, precise and exact evidence of what was being claimed (often at least a second-degree manifestation of government policy decisions or of the real nature of insurgents' complaints or aspirations, and of course a first-degree one, an integral part, of their attempted implementation), and of what some people *may* already have believed to be true and some others, the potential audience, *may* have been successfully persuaded was so. These things, whatever their relation to the actual facts in the usual sense, are themselves essential historical facts that the historian simply cannot ignore: United States participation in World War II would at the very least have been much different, Pearl Harbor notwithstanding, had we not known that all Japanese (i.e., Japs) had buck teeth and murdered their prisoners, and historians of that participation will not understand their subject if they ignore that fact.

Throughout this period, and especially from the latter half of the sixteenth century and increasing thereafter, literature of this sort was ground out in great quantities and in all shapes and sizes in all parts of Europe. In the nature of things, however, the bulk of these contests found Spain on one side (when conducted on a scale of any importance these were normally of course two-sided affairs, merely the propaganda aspects of extended real confrontations), even more so than her French successor as preponderant power, and quite apart from religious alignments, simply because her extensive and far-flung European domains involved her in a greater number of local disputes than any other power, were conspicuous targets for the territorial aggrandisement of others, and gave her a variety of non-Spanish and non-Castilian subject populations some of whom raised serious (in two major cases successful) rebellion against 'foreign' domination. Just as the actual power struggles were more serious, so the propaganda barrages were more extensive when the context involved Spain in all or most of these things: an attempted takeover of Spanish domains, local disputes, her perennial rivalry with France (the next greatest land power), local rebellion of subject populations, and foreign intervention in that rebellion.

Propaganda by one state against another was of course nothing new, either between equals or against the preponderant power: Charles V was attacked on an almost profligate scale. But some of the potential components listed above were still missing. Most of them were present in the Netherlands revolt; given the high degree to which government propaganda machines (and the technical requirements for non-government ones) were soon to be developed, the first decades of the Netherlands war, from the 1560s on, might almost be called a developmental period. In any case, the development was quite full by the 1640s, when they had the risings in Catalonia and Portugal to focus upon.

The pro-Catalan side got off to an early start, with a great variety of publications including such as Josep Zarroca, *Politica del Comte de Olivares. Contrapolitica de Cathaluña* (Barcelona, 1641, 41 folios),[1] covering events from the beginning of 1640 to 18 May 1641; Gaspar Sala y Berart, *Secrets Publichs. Pedra de Toch de les intencions del enemich y illum de la veritat* (n.p., n.d. [1641], 47 pages) published anonymously, by order of the *Diputació*, the local government body that had taken the lead in the rebellion, soon published in Portuguese (Lisbon, 1641) and French (Rouen, 1642) translation as well; and (among many anonymous pieces) *Apoyos de la verdad catalana contra las objeciones de una justificación que se hizo en nombre del Rey Catholico contra esta provincia* (Lisbon, 1642, 28 folios), a pertinent double example, both of the insurgents' support in another rebelling province, it being published in Portugal, and of the audience apparently aimed at, it being written in Castilian.

France's position was at least as well represented, being supported by both Catalan and French propaganda production: Francisco Martí y Viladamor's *Cataluña en Francia, Castilla sin Cataluña y Francia contra Castilla. Panegyrico glorioso al . . . Monarca Luis XIII* (Barcelona, 1641, 497 pages) and *Praesidium inexpugnabile Principatus Cataloniae pro jure eligendi Christianisimum Monarcham* (Barcelona, 1644, 184 pages folio) bracket such works as

[1] As the scale of such works is obviously relevant I have generally indicated their length, either in pages or folios, according to which system of numeration is used. As the size of the work indicated by a given number of pages obviously depends upon page size, I have usually indicated the format when other than quarto (the most common format for this particular literature). The use of the term 'folio' with regard to format (the largest one) and with regard to foliation (regardless of format) should of course not be confused.

[Charles Sorel], *La Deffense des Catalans. Ou l'on void le juste suiet où ils ont eu de se retirer de la domination du roy d'Espagne. Avec les droits du Roy sur la Catalogne et le Roussillon* (Paris, 1642, 349 pages, 12°), Francisco Fornes, *La catalana verdad contra la emulación. Cataluñia, electora según derecho y justicia. Luis XIII verdaderamente electo en conde de Barçelona* (Paris, 1643, 36 pages), [Pierre de Caseneuve], *La Catalogne françoise. Ou il est traité des droits que le Roy a sur les Comtez de Barcelonne, & de Roussillon; & sur les autres Terres* . . . *de Catalogne* (Toulouse, 1644, 202 pages), and Joannes Nicolai, *Galliae dignitas adversus praeposterum Cathaloniae assertorem vindicata* (Paris, 1644, 168 pages).

Spain, for her part, not only laced the field with the usual steady fire of propaganda grapeshot but brought up her heavier artillery, especially in the person of José Pellicer, the royal historiographer, who (a veteran of this sort of war from the previous decade) apparently oversaw a good deal of the operation and himself produced such contributions as *Idea del Principado de Cataluña* (Antwerp, 1642, 598 pp., duodecimo), an attack on the notion of Catalan separatism.

The propaganda surrounding the Portuguese rising was much the same, except that France, though sympathetic to the rebels, did not make any territorial claims for herself and so had no real position of her own to maintain. On the Spanish side Pellicer did yeoman service, as one might expect, among other things providing a medieval historical basis for the Spanish crown's claims in his brief but thoroughly argued *Sucession de los Reynos de Portugal y el Algarve, feudos antiguos de* . . . *Castilla* (Logroño, 1640, 39 pages). At the heart of the propaganda battle in the early years was a *Manifesto do Reyno de Portugal presẽtado á Santidade de Urbano VIII* . . . *pelas tres Nações Portugueza, Franceza, Catalana, em que se mostra o direito com que* . . . *João IV* . . . *possue* . . . *Portugal* . . . (Lisbon, 1643, 60 pages; first written in Italian, it is apparently to that earlier edition that the first response was made), published anonymously by Pantaleão Rodrigues Pacheco, and the *Respuesta al Manifiesto del Reyno de Portugal* . . . *en la que se demuestra el derecho de Felipe IV a la Corona Portuguesa* (Antwerp, 1642, 198 pages; Latin translation Louvain, 1642) published anonymously by Juan Caramuel Lobkowitz—a likely challenger since before open rebellion had begun he had published *Philippus prudens Caroli V Imp. filius, Lusitaniae legitimus Rex demonstratus* (Antwerp, 1639) to prove the Spanish claim to the Portuguese crown at a length of 430 folio pages. This set off a rash of 'anti-Caramuel' publications. The same year as Caramuel's *Respuesta al Manifiesto* appeared, Antonio de Sousa de Macedo attacked both this and his earlier book in *Juan Caramuel Lobkowitz . . . convencido en su libro* (London, 1642, 140 pages), followed quickly by Manuel Fernández de Villareal, *Anticaramuel o defença del Manifiesto . . .* (Paris, 1643, 252 pages), [Pedro García], *Caramuel ridiculus Caramueli convicto* (n.p., 1643, 91 pages duodecimo), and so forth, the Spanish side in turn defended by Antonio Fuertes y Biota, *Anti-Manifiesto o verdadera declaración de los derechos de los Reyes de Castilla a Portugal* (Bruges, 1643, 280 pages) and other such. And this of course involves only one particular exchange. So far as I know, no one has attempted to ascertain the actual scope of this type of publication (oddly it has received very little attention), but some notion of its prominence may be conveniently had from the listings in Sánchez Alonso: his entire 'Separación de Portugal' section, covering twenty-odd years, contains only some 112 items, including about two dozen modern ones; of the limited remaining quota—a bit under ninety articles—about five dozen are propaganda pieces by one side or the other just for the 1640s alone. The mind boggles at what the total number might be.

Over a decade before these two internal crises erupted, Carlos García had written a disquisition on *La oposición y conjunción de los dos grandes luminares de la tierra, en la qual se trata de la dichosa aliança de Francia y España, con la antipatía de españoles y franceses...*, had it translated into French (*Antipathie des François et des Espagnols . . .*) and, antipathy notwithstanding, published the two texts on facing pages (Rouen, 1630, 401 pages duodecimo). This is neither polemic nor propaganda but a description of a situation that is manifest in much of the diplomatic documentation at the time: the French hated and despised the Spanish and the Spanish hated and despised the French, a fact which informs much of Spain's and France's relations with each other, radically extending the limits of aggressiveness for which one could count on having the support of one's own subjects. One could hardly ask for a more appropriate contemporary work in the present context, for these were the two essential home audiences in what was naturally the main arena of propaganda exchange, that between the two major military powers. It is also impeccably timed, appearing precisely at the moment of France's entry into the Thirty Years' War by Swedish proxy, after which time it was generally considered that relations between the two were irreparable and both sides began preparing the public relations ground to place the blame on the other when war did break out, which finally did occur in 1635: a five-year period during which the Franco-Spanish contest, fought only indirectly in the German wars, was fought directly with printing presses, followed by twenty-four years (1635–59) during which propaganda was an important adjunct of open war. The 1630s were the beginning of what might be called a Golden Age of Propaganda.

The anonymous *Justificación de las acciones de España. Manifestación de las violencias de Francia* (n.p., n.d., 51 pages; there is a manuscript copy at BNMS 5708) and [Bezian Arroy], *Questions decidées sur la justice des armes des rois de France, sur les alliances avec les herétiques ou infidelles et sur la conduite des gens de guerre* (Paris, 1634, octavo) are fairly typical of the run-of-the-mill production. As war approached and then arrived, both sides increased production and made heavier use of established scholars. The *Mars gallicus, seu de justicia et foederum regis Galliae libri duo* of Cornelis Jansen, a response to Arroy's *Questions decidées* written under the pseudonym Alexandri Patricii Armacani, had numerous editions —1635, 1636, 1637 (442 pages octavo), 1639—and was translated into both French and Spanish in 1637. On the Spanish side Gonzalo de Céspedes y Meneses contributed *Francia engañada, Francia respondida* (?p. 1635, 154 pages) under the patriotic pseudonym Gerardo Hispano, and José Pellicer a *Defensa de España contra las calumnias de Francia* (Venice, 1635, 199 pages octavo, anon.; see also BNMSS 10438, 10785); from Belgium Jean Jacques Chifflet, whose *Visontio* was mentioned earlier, weighed in with an anonymous *Vindiciae hispanicae* (1st ed. apparently 1645; 'altered edition' Antwerp, 1645, 250 pages; it had at least one other edition, in 1647), answered anonymously by Marc-Antoine Dominicy in *Assertor gallicus contra Vindicias Hispanicas Joannis Jacobi Chiflettii* (Paris, 1646, 230 pages). And of course there were formally historical works used to the same purpose. Examples of either type could be listed more or less endlessly. Oddly enough, there seems to have been only one serious study made of even part of this vast and historically important literature: José Maria Jover's *1635. Historia de una polemica y semblanza de una generación* (Madrid, 1949, 565 pages).

CONTEMPORARY REFERENCE WORKS

The type of contemporary publication most inexplicably neglected as a source by modern historians is the general category of reference works. Most conspicuous of these were the wide-ranging encyclopaedias, the taste for which was shown early by the demand for the ancient one of Pliny the Elder: 'The *Natural History* was enormously popular in the fifteenth and sixteenth centuries. By 1544 more than forty printed editions had been published.'[1] The demand was met by an impressive array: Gregor Reisch, *Margarita philosophica* (1503); Raffaele Maffei Volaterranus, *Commentarii rerum urbanorum* (1506); Joachim Fortius Ringelberg, *Lucubrationes vel potius absolutissima* (1541); Paul Skalich, *Encyclopaedia seu orbis disciplinarum epistemon* (1559); Theodor Zwinger, *Theatrum humanae vitae* (1565); and others. These usually appeared in numerous successive editions, including translations, growing in size and in coverage in the process. The crowning example is Sebastian Münster's *Cosmography*, which between 1544 and 1628 had thirty-five full editions in German, Latin, French, Italian, and even one in Czech, plus several

[1] Gerald Strauss, 'A Sixteenth-Century Encyclopedia: Sebastian Münster's *Cosmography* and its editions', in *From the Renaissance to the Counter-Reformation* (ed. C. H. Carter, New York, 1965, pp. 145–63; 148).

epitomes and extracts in English.[1] They could also be adapted to particular national audiences. Christóbal Suárez de Figueroa, *Plaza Universal de todas Ciencias y Artes* (1615, 1630, 1733, etc.), for example, is a translation of Tomasso Garzoni's *Piazza Universale* reoriented towards Spain, with pertinent subjects added or expanded and references to Spanish works added for various subjects.

Some of these had an intentionally circumscribed topical coverage which may not coincide with a given researcher's needs; others, more truly encyclopaedic, cover such a wide range topically, geographically and chronologically—they naturally reflect the great contemporary interest in the New World and in ancient times—as to be most useful to historians as evidence of what information was available to the general reader at the time, as a measure of the knowledge of the world they brought to their affairs (the historian's subject), as well as reflecting both their interests and the reading that may have helped shape their thinking.

Many works, however, were quite sharply focused in topic, and concerned with describing the present world (usually a very manageable part of it) and compiling data about its past. When the latter involves a concentration on the preceding century or two, and when they were compiled late enough in the period in question here (the two centuries or so up to about 1700), they can in fact comprise comprehensive reference works for most of the period itself. Some of the more valuable early ones gave detailed descriptions of the major cities of Europe, including a good deal of specific data important to modern historians. Perhaps the most useful of all, however, are those that focus on a particular country or region.

Among the best of the earlier examples of this genre are Paolo Giovio's *Descriptio Britanniae, Scotiae, Hyberniae, et Orchadum* (Venice, 1548) and Ludovico Guicciardini's famous description of the Netherlands, first published in 1560 and in various

[1] These are discussed briefly in *ibid.*, and Münster's work of course in considerable detail.

editions thereafter. But this was essentially a synthetic genre that could not really get off the ground until a sufficient number of basic works had been produced to provide raw material for synthesis, a point which presumably had not been reached until the early seventeenth century. It was at any rate not until then that large-scale publication of this sort was launched by the pioneer in the field, the Dutch publishing firm of Elzevier, in a superb series of small volumes that are so useful and so convenient to carry that one wonders how any of them could have survived to the present: with pages about $2\frac{1}{8}$ by $4\frac{1}{4}$ inches and about an inch thick—they average about 500 pages of fine print— they are a sort of early Pocket Books, and enormously popular in their own time. Based upon the works of Giovanni Botero and other respected compilers plus supplementary data specially compiled, they include (to cite a few representative volumes only) *Hispania, sive de Regis Hispaniae Regnis et opibus Commentarius* (Leyden, 1629), *Suecia* (Leyden, 1633), *Portugallia* (Leyden, 1641), and *Respublica sive Status Regni Poloniae, Lithuaniae, Prussiae, Livoniae, etc.* (Leyden, 1642), some of which were published under a particular compiler's name, such as Joh. Bapt. Veri, *Rerum Venetarum libri Quatuor* (Amsterdam, 1644), which, as the title suggests, is a bit different from the usual series layout.

The Portugal volume is fairly typical, its fourteen chapters including a 'Geographica & Hydrographica descriptio generalis' of the kingdom, a description of its people, customs, etc., lists of kings, noble families, chapters on its laws, its African and Atlantic domains, and so forth, often presenting the conflicting data of various earlier authorities rather than choosing arbitrarily among them; to this (pp. 1–369) are added 13 appendices (pp. 370–460) on topics ranging from the Castle of St George that dominates Lisbon to Malacca and other Portuguese holdings in the Far East; the volume also has a brief introduction, a table of contents, and an index containing nearly 250 page references.

Other publishers fairly quickly started bringing out their own series modelled on the 'Elzevirian Republics'. Like the Elzevier series their individual volumes collectively blanketed almost every corner of Europe and branched out beyond as well. The focus ranged from the prosaically local to the exotically distant: in the Jansson (Amsterdam) series, for example, from Johannes Bertelius, *Respublica Namurcensis, Hannoniae et Lutzenburgensis* (1634) to Gabriel Sionita and Johannes Hedronita, *Arabia . . . seu Arabum Vicinarumque Gentium Orientalium Leges, Ritus, etc.* (1633). The Johannes Mair (Leyden) series included quite Elzevier-like volumes such as *Republicae Moscoviae et Urbes* (1630), but also *Respublicae Hollandiae et Urbes. De Antiquitate Reipublicae Batavicae*, made up of writings of Grotius, Ludovico Guicciardini and Peter Scriver, plus a section of elegant verse by Caspar Baerle praising princes, cities, etc.

The individual volume perhaps best known to English readers is *Angliae notitia, sive praesens Angliae status succincte enucleatus . . . Accedit Historiae Angliae . . .* (Leyden, 1686), but literally dozens of volumes deserve to be equally well known, such as J. B. Montalbano, *Turcici Imperii Status* (Leyden, 1634). Some were later translated into vernacular languages: M. Van Goch, *Hedendagsche Historie of Tegenwoordige Staat van alle Volkeren*, for example, whose Volume V, *Het Turksche Ryk in Asia en Afrika*, and Volume VI, *Van het Europisch Turkyen . . . de Griekschekerk . . . Polen . . . Litthauwen* (Amsterdam, 1733–4), dealing with areas occupied by the Turkish Empire, are a Dutch translation of the work of Thomas Salmon.

Both the geographical coverage and topical focus varied as well. Johannes Angelius Werdenhagen's *Universalis Introductio in omnes Respublicas sive Politica Generalis* (Amsterdam, Jansson, 1632) is, as the title indicates, a broad survey that could either stand on its own at that generalised level or serve as an introduction to the large body of available specialised volumes. The thinning effect of broadening the geographical area covered was sometimes counteracted by limiting the kinds of subject matter included, as in Alphonsi de Vargas, *Relatio ad Reges et Principes Christianos* (n.p., 1642).

Some gained still greater detail by restricting both physical and topical areas of coverage, some by the simple expedient of producing a bigger book, some by a combination of both, as for example the Zyllius (Utrecht: later Zyllius and Ackerdyck) series of specialised geographical compendia, published in a considerably larger format (about three by five inches) than the Elzevier one: an *Italiae Brevis et Accurata Descriptio* (1650; 432 pages text plus 15 pages of detailed itineraries, with distances between places and page references to the text for many); *Hispaniae, Cum Insulis eo spectantibus & in Europa Sitis compendiosa descriptio* ([1658: the title page's 1568 is a printer's error]; 81 pages plus 15 pages itin.); *Galliae accurata descriptio* (220 pages) together with *Galliae Descriptioni adjunximus paucas vicinae Provincias Belgicas, et Leodiensem Dioecesin* (1659; pp. 1–220, 221–367, plus 41 pages itin.). These and a brief world-wide *Geographiae Compendium* (1658; 42 pages) were all reissued together as *Compendium Geographiae Item Hispaniae, Galliae et Italiae* (Utrecht, 1659), making a priceless reference volume of some 993 pages.

The great contemporary success of works on the model of the Elzevier Republics is perhaps best illustrated by the *Respublica Achaeorum et Veientium iuxta sua fata in usum praesentis saeculi delineatae* (Utrecht, Zyllius, 1664) of the Dutch scholar Martin Schoockius (1614–69), historiographer to the Elector of Brandenburg, which applies the same method to the ancient world 'for the use of the present century', his subject matter ranging from ancient historical works to Latin treatises on truffles. Whatever value this may have for the study of ancient history, it seems quite obvious that the vast body of similar works these people compiled on the contemporary world would, on the history of that period, well serve the *present* present century. There have been recent editions of Robert Peterson's 1606 translation of Giovanni Botero's *Of the Greatness of Cities* (ed. P. G. and D. P. Waley, London, 1950) and G. Braun and F. Hogenberg, *Civitates Orbis Terrarum* (Cologne, 1572–1618; facsimile ed., Cologne, 1965), and both have been used as sources by H. G. Koenigsberger and George Mosse in their excellent examination of *Europe in the Sixteenth Century* (New York, 1968), where they accurately describe the latter as 'a kind of sixteenth-seventeenth century super-guidebook with magnificent engravings of townscapes' (p. 55 n), but the use of such works as sources and re-publication of them to make this more feasible for historians are both very rare. In an age of 'publication explosion' in which publishers fill their lists with umpteenth editions of all manner of old chestnuts, it seems curious that they have not got around to publishing dozens of these far more vital sources, either in the original Latin or in translation into one of the major modern languages—including, surely, the basic Elzevier series *in toto*. Beyond that lies a remarkable literature ranging from the Roman guidebooks of Marliani, de Rossi, and Albert Reimar to such specialised works as Kirchmair von Reichwitz's *Von den Königlichen Französischen Finanzen/ Renten/Gefällen und Einkommen und deren Ober-Aufsehern und Verwaltern* (Nürnberg, 1665). Copies of much of it are quite hard to come by, even in the big European libraries, for they were so informative they were apt to be read to tatters and quite out of existence, but they are no less informative now and no less useful. Conscientious publishers should republish more of this literature, and conscientious historians should consult more of it when they can.

RELAZIONI

Fairly early in the Italian development of permanent diplomacy the custom was adopted of having an ambassador returning home from a tour of duty present a formal written 'relation' of his embassy, in effect a comprehensive 'debriefing' (they naturally varied in length; twenty-five or thirty folios was fairly typical). This was in part a summary account of his mission itself, a sort of précis of what he had reported in his despatches during that time, and in part a 'relation' of the country he had been posted to, including both a general description—physical, institutional, etc. —and a more particular account of present conditions, prominent persons in government, and so forth.

Those of the Venetians are well known, and the two basic groups published have been widely used: *Relazioni degli ambasciatori veneti al Senato* for the sixteenth century (ed. Eugenio Alberi,

15 vols, Florence, 1839–63: ser. 1, European states outside Italy, 6 vols; ser. 2, Italy, 5 vols; ser. 3, 'Ottoman states', 3 vols; appendices to all three series, 1 vol.) and *Relazioni degli stati europei lette al senato dagli Ambasciatori Veneti nel secolo decimosettimo* (ed. Nicolò Barozzi and Guglielmo Berchet, 10 vols, Venice, 1856–78: ser. 1, Spain, 2 vols; ser. 2, France, 3 vols; ser. 3, Italy, 3 vols; ser. 4, England, 1 vol; ser. 5, Turkey, 1 vol. in 2 parts). But this is only a part of those available.

There are others more fugitive, such as those published by Arnaldo Segarizzi as 'Volume 19' (3 vols in 4: 1912–13, 1916) of the *Scrittori d'Italia* collection. Some have been published by the countries they pertain to, such as *Relazioni Veneziane: Venetiaansche berechten over de Vereenigde Nederlanden van 1600–1795* (ed. P. J. Blok, The Hague, 1900) or *Relations des Ambassadeurs Venetiens sur Charles-Quint* (Brussels, 1856), *Relations des ambassadeurs vénetiens sur Charles-Quint et Philippe II* (ed. L. P. Gachard, Brussels, 1855; Spanish translation by Ciriaco Pérez Bustamente, Madrid, 1944), and *Relations inédites d'ambassadeurs vénetiens dans les Pays-Bas sous Philippe II et Albert et Isabel* (ed. G. Hagemans, Brussels, 1864), a body of sources discussed by Gachard in 'Les monuments de la diplomatie Vénetienne, considerée sous le point de vue . . . de l'histoire de la Belgique en particulier' in *Nouveaux Mémoires de l'Académie des sciences et belles-lettres de Bruxelles* (Vol. 27, 1853).

There are still others unpublished, not only in the Archivio di Stato at Venice; substantial numbers of transcripts are to be found in foreign repositories as well, not all of them regarding only the country the archive pertains to. A random example from the Biblioteca Nacional (MS 8509), a 384-folio group of thirteen seventeenth-century transcripts of 'Relationi diversi', mainly of the 1550s and 1560s, contains one on a mission to Charles V, one on another to him and to Francis I, and another on Spain in 1561, but the bulk are on Rome, Florence, Savoy, France (2), Turkey (2), Persia and Armenia, and—a Savoyard relation—Poland.

The last item, on Poland, illustrates another sometimes overlooked fact, that there is a substantial body of Italian *Relazioni* besides the Venetian ones; these too are often found in non-Italian repositories; and some have been published, as for example: *Relazioni inediti di ambasciatori lucchese alla Corte di Madrid, secoli XVI–XVII* (ed. Amadeo Pellegrini, Lucca, 1903, 96 pages), and Raffaele Ciasca's in-progress *Instruzioni e relazioni degli ambasciatori genovesi* (Rome, 1951 ff), beginning with five volumes on Spain, 1494–1721.

Attempts outside Italy to follow this custom were rare, but one does encounter them, even in print: Charles Cornwallis's *A discourse on the State of Spain, written in . . . 1607* was printed separately in 1751 and included in the Somers *Tracts* (in Vol. 2 of the 1752 edition, Vol. 3 of the 1810 edition), and George Carew's *A relation of the State of France with the character of Henry IV and the principal persons of that court* (1609) is included in Thomas Birch's *Historical view of the negotiations between . . . England, France, and Brussels . . . 1592 to 1617* (London, 1749).

As is the case with diplomatic correspondence, contemporary publication of this genre is mainly in the second half of the period 1500–1700; these include non-Italian ones such as the *Legatio Rhaetica* (Paris, 1620) which Charles Paschal addressed to Louis XIII concerning Switzerland. Others were not regular ambassadorial relations but modelled after them, such as Andrea de Mendoza, *Relatione compitissime di quanto e successo nella Real Corte de Catholico Re Nostro Signore* (Milan, 1623) and the *Raggvaglio della solenne comparsa, fatta in Rome . . . dell . . . Signor Conte di Castelmaine Ambasciadore . . . di Giacomo Secondo . . . all 'Udienza della Santitá . . . Papa Innocenzio Unidecimo* (Rome, 1687) by Michael Wright, a member of Castlemaine's suite.

This is perhaps the place to note one other different sort of published diplomatic source, the summaries of incoming Venetian ambassadorial reports in M. Sanuto, *I Diarii* (ed. G. Berchet and N. Barozzi, 58 vols, Venice, 1879–1903), covering 1496–1533.

NEWSLETTERS, PROTO-NEWSPAPERS, TRUE RELATIONS

In the function that accounts for the greater part of their contents —reporting on a wide spectrum of events, conditions, etc., that are judged to be of interest to the intended readership—ambassadors' reports are essentially newsletters, a fact that is basic to understanding the practical nature both of those reports and of the separate genre that traditionally bears that label. The latter, newsletters properly so called, were sometimes privately sent from one individual to just one other, were sometimes intended for wider circulation or even distribution, and in the course of becoming more public would normally become commercial ventures. They might entail sending 'home' news abroad, such as John Chamberlain's already-mentioned letters to English ambassadors (some 470 over nearly three decades, 1597–1626, mostly to Dudley Carleton), or sending foreign news home, such as the contemporaneous Salvetti Newsletters.

The commercialisation of such enterprises and the public demand for their product led to a rather impressive development of what was intended as a serious and continuing periodical press, a development examined for various countries and from various points of view in M. A. Shaaber, *Some forerunners of the newspaper in England* (New York, 1966), Henry F. Schulte, *The Spanish press, 1470–1966: print, power and politics* (Chicago, 1968), C. Leber, *De l'état réel de la presse et des pamphlets, depuis François Ier jusqu'à Louis XIV* (Paris, 1834), Fanny P. Folke Dahl and Marguerite Boulet, *Les débuts de la presse française: nouveaux aperçus* (Paris, 1951), and similar works.[1] These early periodicals (a term which should not require precise periodicity) naturally flourished best under official sponsorship, but even then their performance is often impressive, as for example the Paris-based *Gazette de France*, for which the royal physician Théophraste Renaudot (1584–1653) was granted the necessary 'privilege' by Richelieu in 1631, usually considered the official government organ of his ministry and later Mazarin's. *La Gazette* appeared in fairly frequent regular editions of from eight to sixteen quarto pages, plus numerous extras (*extraordinaires*) devoted to particular

[1] There are also reference works, such as E. Hartzenbusch, *Apuntes para un catálogo de periódicos madrileños desde el año 1661 al 1870* (Madrid, 1894), which runs to 415 quarto pages.

topics, usually newsworthy major events, crises, theatres of action, etc., ranging from Scotland to Turkey to the New World (e.g., several extra issues of the 1640s deal with the English Civil War), plus round-up issues on the *Estat General des Affaires*. When Renaudot's withdrawal to St Germain with Mazarin and the court during the Fronde troubles of 1649 interrupted publication, his sons filled the gap with twelve issues of an emergency newssheet, *Le Courier François*.[1]

There were numerous publications of the sort, either under government aegis or independent commercial ventures. One encounters the same popular titles—Gazette, Courier, Mercury, etc.—in many diverse parts of Europe. Some lasted a considerable time, some failed fairly quickly, and some lasted only so long as the conditions that gave them birth did, as in the case of the rival royalist and parliamentarian papers of the English Civil War.

Other publications serving the same market were far more substantial, gave far more detailed treatment than one can label even 'journalism in depth' or 'background journalism', relied more on documentary sources than on the usual ones of journalism, and often extended their coverage of 'recent' events quite far into the past, giving them a scale, purpose and function that makes them not popular journalism but 'pop' history, an effect also created by later re-publication of works originally fairly contemporary. Various of these qualities can be seen, for example, in a random sample of the publications of Vittorio Siri: *Il Mercurio overo historia de' correnti tempi* (3 vols, Casale, 1647; also Geneva, 1647); *Mémoires secrets tirés des archives des souverains de l'Europe, depuis le règne de Henri IV* and the same . . . *contenant le règne de Louis XIII* (the French editions of both are n.p., n.d.); or *Mercure, contenant l'histoire générale de l'Europe depuis 1640 jusqu'en 1655* (translated by M. Requier, 18 vols duodecimo, Paris, 1756–9).

---

[1] The above description is based upon the newspapers themselves. For the various sides of this early editor-publisher's career see G. Gilles de la Tourette, *Théophraste Renaudot d'après des documents inédits. La Gazette, les monts-de-piété, les consultations charitables, etc.* (Paris, 1884).

A quite distinct genre is the small-scale one-shot account of a single subject, comparable not to book-length treatments-in-depth nor to continuing newspapers but to the occasional special issues of the latter. They usually bore a long descriptive title, most frequently beginning 'True Relation of', 'Second Relation of' (when there was opportunity for a sequel), etc., or, second most frequent, 'Letter written by soandso describing suchandsuch', and in size ranged from mere fly-sheets to pamphlets of quite substantial length, in quarto or folio format as often as not. As, far more than individual issues of a continuing periodical, they had to stand or fall by themselves, they reflect far better the tastes and interests of the public they were intended for. Much of that interest was not in 'hard' news but in pageantry and the doings of celebrities, and in events of a striking nature: the formal *entrée* of a ruler or other notable into any town of importance was sure to be described in pamphlets hot off the press, while striking occasions were given coverage in such as *Maniere de la deffiance faicte par les heraulx des roys de France et Dengleterre a Lempereur, etc.* (Antwerp, 1528), an early example now almost extinct. Many travel accounts were also published.

In varying degrees according to the persons, purpose and setting involved, diplomatic missions also received quite frequent coverage (though naturally more limited to a home audience), including one referred to in Chapters 2 and 6: *Relacion muy verdadera del recibimiento y fiestas que se hicieron en Inglaterra á don Juan Tassis, conde de Villamediana* (Sevilla, 1603), *La segunda parte de la embajada de don Juan de Tassis, conde de Villamediana y embajador de Felipe III, para el Rey Jacobo de Inglaterra* (Sevilla, 1602 [sic]), *Relacion de la jornada del Excmo Condestable de Castilla á las paces entre España é Inglaterra, que se concluyeron en Londres en el mes de Agosto* (Valladolid, 1604), etc.

The taste for spectacle, for high drama (or melodrama) and for international affairs could be all simultaneously gratified when the subject was war. As with any other subject these varied in quality, but perhaps no other had so many contributions by eminent authors, making it questionable whether one should classify as journalism or 'instant history' such works as Jean Boyvin's *Le Siege de la Ville de Dole, Capitale de la Franche Comte,* widely considered the most reliable account of the event, and *Relation de Tout Ce Qui S'Est Passe au Siege . . . de Breme* in March 1638 (published together in a single quarto volume, Antwerp, 1638). In spite of the title the *Relatione dell' Assedio di Parigi* (Bologna, 1597) of the papal historian Filippo Pigafetta must surely be classed as an historical work (and hardly an 'instant' one, with a seven-year lag), but it is worth emphasising that the intended audience seems to be essentially the same as that of the right-after-the-event relations.

Events of a given type naturally resembled one another, and relations of them usually followed the same basic structure, varying mainly in details (and sometimes having to strain to do that). Royal (and analogous) *entrées* were much alike: the entourage should be quite large (state how large) and include numerous persons of rank (state how many and name at least those of special importance); at least the more important part of the company should be splendidly outfitted, the city officials will be decked out in ceremonial garb and the people will be out in numbers in their Sunday best (describe); there will be welcoming oratory and probably commemorative verses by local Latin scholars (reproduce as quality indicates) and whatever pageantry the locals can provide (describe the living tableaux, etc.); only with luck will there be some untoward incident to mar the occasion and enliven the account. Even sieges run to formula, the besiegers outside the walls going through standard military procedures, the besieged inside suffering standard miseries, almost ritual matters that vary mainly in detail: for the 1590 siege of Paris, for example, Pigafetta reports 13,000 deaths from starvation and 30,000 from disease. (The besiegers might be attacked by a relieving column, the siege might be raised, etc., but these are standard variations with their own variations of detail.)

It is precisely these details of quite conventional events that give this pamphlet literature its greatest value for the historian (though relations of unique events—natural disasters, local

miracles, etc.—can be of both interest and value). Since battles
were far briefer than sieges they provided less narrative grist for
the writer's mill, requiring him to strain harder for basic details
to fill out his pages, the full title of a relation of the Battle of
the White Mountain provides a somewhat fuller example of
what this detail might amount to: *The famous victory that the
Emperor of Germany, Ferdinand of Austria, brother of the Queen Our
Lady doña Margarita, who is in glory, has had against the Count
Palatine, and rebels and malcontents of those states, near the town of
Prague, Monday 9 November 1620. [Recounted] as well are the
famous captures and deaths of Princes, knights, captains, infantry,
cavalry, wagons, baggage and artillery that [our side] made of the
enemy. And the quantity of infantry, cavalry, pontoons, catapults and
vessels of war that His Holiness sent in aid, and the King Our Lord in
the charge of the Marquis Spinola, and the King of France, dukes and
lords of Italy, and Catholic cantons, and Catholic electors and other
potentates and supporters of the most illustrious and Catholic house of
Austria* (Málaga, 1620, folio; the title is of course in Spanish). In
addition to the list of data included, one notices two things in
particular here. It is a relation of an event in east-central Europe
printed in a smallish port in Andalucía; that Spanish readers
should be interested in that particular battle is not surprising, but
it is less obvious that that interest would be sufficiently widespread
to support publication by provincial presses. And, given the date
of the battle, it would necessarily have come off the press within
a few weeks of the event if the publication date has not been
falsified (which is a constant possibility).

How reliable is this detail for the historian's use? Although one
should not push the analogy too far, it is in important ways
comparable to that of modern newspapers. Relations of spectacles,
oddities and such are, alas, often no better than today's Sunday
supplements, glib feature stories, etc.—then and now, descriptions of predictable ceremonies might be written in advance, and
are not unknown to have come off the press before the event
had actually occurred (especially embarrassing when the event
has been delayed: when the above-mentioned Count Palatine

married an English princess and took her back to Heidelberg, accounts of their reception there were in circulation before they had even left England)—yet many which can be checked against other types of sources prove to be quite accurate and honest descriptions. News of battles, the taking of besieged towns, etc., can suffer similarly from the rush to get into print (as do first accounts of casualty figures and similar details now), and even later versions can differ substantially from one another. But this also is as now: shortly before this was written the Irish Finance Minister was unable to deliver his (Spring 1970) budget speech to the Dail because he was 'in hospital with concussion after hitting his head on a beam' (*Irish Times*), 'after being thrown from a horse' (*Financial Times*), and after being 'knocked unconscious by a piece of guttering which fell from the roof of his house' (*Daily Telegraph*). One of course does not argue that the above-mentioned Málaga publication of 350 years ago is more dependable than the *Financial Times*, that contemporary True Relations are more (or as) accurate on detail than present day newspapers, but quite the reverse side of the coin: both can be wrong as well as right—certainly these three highly regarded papers are doubtful sources on what happened to poor Mr Haughey (while the Málaga relation got the date of the battle wrong: it was 8 November). It is in this fact that the pertinent comparability lies, not in the question of which has the greater *degree* of accuracy or inaccuracy (especially since it does not involve a choice between sources for the historian, the *Telegraph* not having covered the White Mountain anyway). Neither can be used blindly by the historian (nor can *any* source, for that matter), but with the requisite (and should-be-routine) caution and judgment and in conjunction with alternative sources by which they can be tested for accuracy both can be used to good effect.

[As Sanchez Alonso says:] This literature fed not only on oral narrations of travellers and on private letters but also on official documents. Reports made by ambassadors, captains general, etc., were immediately printed and sold profusely among the people, *vulgarizándose* the most important matters of international character.

The Relations are initiated at the end of the sixteenth century, reach their apogee in the middle of the seventeenth century, and sustain themselves, with little life by then, until the beginnings of the nineteenth century, when the development of the periodical press makes them unnecessary.[1]

As one might expect, the standard product was usually quite brief, most typically amounting to two or four quarto-size folios. But many were larger, and so varied in size even on a given type of subject that it is difficult to draw the line at some reasonable limit for 'pamphlet' literature as one escalates gradually from, say, the *Libre harangue faicte par Mathault en la presence de monsieur le prince en son chasteau d'Amboise, le 16. jour de juin 1614* (n.p., 1614), a small-octavo volume, to F. Rapine's *Recueil très-exact et curieux de tout ce qui s'est fait et passé de singulier et mémorable en l'Assemblée générale des Etats tenus à Paris en l'année 1614 et particulièrement en chacune séance du tiers Ordre. Avec le cahier dudit Ordre, et autres pièces concernans le mesme sujet* (Paris, 1651) in 720 quarto pages—an extreme example that is also clearly beyond any reasonable definition of contemporaneous, another matter so varied as to make definition necessarily arbitrary.

Nor is it clear what precise designation is most appropriate for such partisan publications as *Les ouvertures des parlements, faictes par les Roys de France, tenant leur lict de justice. Ausquelles sont adioustées cinq remonstrances, autrefois faictes en icelles au Parlement de Paris. Reveuës et augm. . . .* (Paris, 1612) by L. Dorléans (1542–1629), a lawyer correctly described in Michaud as 'un des plus fougueux partisans de la ligue', or such official ones as the *Edict du roy sur la pacification des troubles de ce royaume leu et publié . . . 14 May 1576* (Paris, 1576). But precise labels and exact frontiers seem less important than the existence of this vast body of one-shot publica-

[1] B. Sánchez Alonso, *Fuentes*, II, 5, where he also agrees with Gayangos' inclination to classify them as *gacetas periódicas*, not only because of a technical role as progenitor but because in their own time they performed a function later performed by the periodical press; he is somewhat ambiguous about the latter, however, speaking of it here as though it did not exist before the eighteenth century but treating earlier *gacetas* here and in his listings as quite distinct from one-shot relations.

tions on current events produced for public consumption and surviving now in large quantities for judicious use by historians. In addition to individual survivals, and occasional individual modern reprints, they may be found in such general published collections as the *Somers Tracts* and the *Harleian Miscellany*, and in smaller ones focusing on specific events, such as *De moord van 1584. Oorspronkelijke verhalen en berichten van de moord op Prins Willem van Oranje* (The Hague, 1884) on the assassination of William the Silent, or *Die Explosion des Mechelner Sandtores (1546) in Flugschriften der damaligen Zeit* (ed. R. Foncke, 1932), a smallish (120 pages, octavo) collection of contemporary fly-sheets about the explosion of 800 barrels of gunpowder in Maline in 1546, reported to have destroyed over 800 houses—two collections which at the very least reflect the variety of the literature.

CHAPTER 6

Code, Cypher and Security

Webster's Collegiate Dictionary, pertinent here because it is so widely used, defines *code* as 'a system of words or other symbols arbitrarily used to represent words'; but just as that dictionary is an abridgment, so is the definition. It, and the underlying common usage of the word as a generic term, are quite inadequate for application to diplomatic documents.

In reality, 'code' in this generic sense is of three broad types, the essential differences between them being the magnitude of the linguistic unit the symbol replaces, the nature of its normal use, and the degree of secrecy involved. One type is public, of which 'Morse code' is perhaps the best known, but naval flag signals, pictographic highway signs, and the death's head on a bottle of poison are also examples. Its meaning is intentionally made as widely known as possible—by purpose and function the very opposite of secretive. It is free of linguistic requirements—coded radio messages may be conceived in one language, transmitted in this neutral lingua franca, and understood at the receiving end in a totally different language; pictographs and other warning symbols can be understood without language and even without literacy. And it is the most efficient of the three in substituting single symbols for whole meanings rather than just for single words or letters—'I am in trouble, please send help'; 'Pavement slippery when wet' (graphically conveyed by a silhouette of a skidding car); 'Danger—poison—keep out of the reach of children'. This type of 'code', intended to be widely understood, is similar in some of its characteristics to 'code' in general, but in others is different from or contrary to the two types that are pertinent to diplomatic documents: code properly so called, and cypher.

The distinction between these two can be simply put. Cypher is the use of symbols in substitution for letters of the alphabet (or for diphthongs, syllables, common combinations of consonants, and other linguistic components below the level of full words) in the writing of a *message*; *words* are normally not substituted for, they being merely the middle-magnitude linguistic units in which language structure requires that the whole message be expressed: one might say that words are the basic units of language, but that the basic units of cypher are individual letters or combinations thereof. Code, in contrast, is the substitution of a symbol for a word, normally one of special importance such as the name of a person or place; it does not ordinarily convey any meaning in the sense of message.

The distinction between the two may be illustrated in two ways. The code indicator in the system used by a given state might be a number or other non-linguistic symbol, or it might be another word—classical or mythological names assigned to living persons, for example; in the latter case, *code* names can be put into *cypher*: 2468 means 'Ajax', which in turn means 'the king of France', or to reverse the example, 'Ajax' could be spelled out in 'clear' in an otherwise cyphered letter with its uncyphered meaning still concealed by the use of code. Secondly, though for efficiency's sake modern cypher has adopted the code-like custom of using a single indicator for frequently used common words such as 'the', the strength of the distinction in the early modern period is reflected in the fact that even the commonest words were usually spelled out, and that if such special words as 'soldiers', 'money', etc., were given individual indicators they were often listed in the code key, not the cypher. Contemporaries in fact had little of that particular 'code' feeling that values expression in arbitrary symbols as a vehicle for the succinct, as well as secretive, transmission of meaning. They would simply write what they would ordinarily write, and encypher or encode whatever part of it security seemed to require, sometimes encyphering all or practically all of a many-page letter with no attempt at compressing the text or even eliminating verbosity: from the point of view of compression one almost never has the slightest notion, viewing a copy of a letter, whether it was ever in cypher or not.

All cryptic systems are subject to the human inclination to make them easier to use. In the case of cypher this is compounded by the fact that the system of commonly used symbols one is substituting for has a conventional order of sequence, making it tempting to substitute for it by ordered analogy, which (usually) is to say by numbers in parallel sequence. The whole principle behind cypher assumes the unintelligible transmission of intelligible meanings by the substitution of random symbols for ordered ones. Symbols that have neither linguistic meaning nor any very significant rational order—dots, circles, triangles, etc.—are the truly cryptographic ones, as they are not susceptible to any sustained analogy (though even they are to a degree: one might progress through the vowels with an increasing number of dots, or of bars, sides to a figure, etc.). Ironically, perhaps the best substitute for letters is letters, as the only available 'analogy' is the same alphabetical one; since that would hardly do—it has been tried, but being limited to a sliding scale approach it is far too transparent to last very long—the identity of order makes random substitution imperative in a way that separate analogy does not. Number substitution can be, and often has been, properly random, but it often has not.

Contrivers of cyphers perhaps fancied that they were applying parallel orders in a sufficiently random way to be properly cryptic, but such compromises themselves were based on rational principles and so are fairly easy to figure out. The English in the early seventeenth century, for example, used several individual cyphers (as did others)—one for correspondence between ambassadors and the king, another between ambassadors and the official handling their dispatches, another for correspondence among ambassadors, etc.—but the variations among them were slight, and easily deducible. In parallel alphabetical and numerical order one cypher might assign the quota of numeral indicators (two apiece, say) through the consonants, then through the vowels (where the quota would usually be higher, and varied), then a

few for 'nulls' (meaningless indicators to be scattered about to
cause confusion should anyone attempt to break the cypher), then
the bigger numbers as code indicators for names, places, etc.;
another would 'vary' this merely by running through the vowels
first and then the consonants; others by doing one or the other
but starting with number ten instead of one. It seldom occurred
to them even to use the abandoned first digits as nulls: the lack of
any single-digit numbers in a cyphered English text is a dead
giveaway that the whole system has simply been slid forward a
few notches. As will be seen later, breaking such an overly
rational cypher is essentially child's play (though an interesting
game—more entertaining than crossword puzzles).

This simplicity, however, is pertinent in an opposite way as
well, crucial to an understanding of the nature (real, not fancied)
of cyphered documents and coded references, and of the context
in which they were used. Cryptic writing had two rather distinct
purposes: to bury its contents in secrecy if the document should be
stolen (essentially a matter of security of the mails), and to bury
them in unintelligibility in the event of their being seen by unauthorised persons in a more routine situation, even within one's
own government—or especially so. For the latter purpose, a
simple cypher would be quite sufficient. For the former, the
situation arose with surprising infrequency, and when it did any
cypher would usually be ultimately insufficient.

The fact is that relatively little diplomatic correspondence was
ever stolen in the mails, largely because such activity was limited
almost entirely to third parties. The Huguenots, in their period,
sometimes waylaid couriers going to or from Spain during times
of unrest, and the Dutch and others made similar raids, but this
accounts for very little and could usually be got around by sending
duplicates by other routes since such conditions would rapidly
become known. From the researcher's point of view it involves
very few documents that are not otherwise available in one form
or another. It is perhaps more important in the effect it can have
on the historical significance of the document itself: a surviving
draft will reveal the policy position arrived at for its writing, but

if it were ultimately undelivered it naturally forms no part of the basis of the addressee's subsequent actions.

The mails were relatively secure simply because the party with the strongest interest in seeing most diplomatic correspondence, the government of the 'other' country to or from which it was being sent, had even stronger reasons for not tampering. The English naturally wanted to see everything the Spanish ambassador in London wrote home and everything he received in reply from Madrid, and the converse was true of the Spanish, or of any other pair of states, but there were several sound reasons why they seldom violated the other's mail and usually found it unrewarding and even counter-productive when they did.

First of all, they knew perfectly well (what historians have often failed to recognise) that an occasional theft that would net only a few documents now and again would usually provide only fragmentary evidence of what the other government was up to, an incomplete and therefore inaccurate picture that was not particularly useful at best and at worst could be dangerously misleading. But if they attempted it on a sufficiently substantial scale the victim would necessarily shift to more secure channels, normally by sending every dispatch by special courier; as the victim would have struck back in kind, the initial offender would have to do the same, and, as the alternative means were far more expensive than the more vulnerable ordinary ones, would have succeeded only in escalating the cost of regular communication for both sides. At worst this could disrupt communication to the point of destroying the liaison on which diplomatic exchange depends. The pragmatic fact is that violating mails was not the best way to get one's hands on another state's diplomatic documents anyway.

It was quite routine for every major state to have sympathisers or spies or both within every important government with which they had regular diplomatic relations (and in other states as well), and so had access to more documents than went through the mails—not only correspondence to and from a particular ambassador (all that was apt to be found in any given mail raided) but any and all ambassadors in various countries (like raiding *all* the mail couriers), and important council documents as well—and better access at that. If one was to be able to go on getting one's hands on documents out of government files, it was necessary to keep one's success a secret, and the advantage of seeing the contents of documents was often mainly in knowing in advance what was going to be sent and received; that advantage would be lost, and one would again be in the dark, if the purloined document were actually kept and presumably another, perhaps far different one, written and sent in its place. Both these considerations made it far preferable to copy the document, have it returned quietly to its proper files, and allow the machinery of government to continue to turn undisturbed and unknowing.[1] It was seldom possible for an agent to remove something stealthily from the mails, copy it, and return it in time to avoid detection of its loss, so in such cases despatches were usually simply made off with even when it did not involve a physical attack on the courier. An agent within the government, however, could make his own copy as opportunity served or slip the document out for a few hours and take it to the embassy for copying before slipping it back into the files: one had time to make a full copy and to return the stolen document. One also had time and the necessary trained personnel to make accurate copies of cyphered documents, a far trickier copying task than clear text, should that be necessary, but the fact that it infrequently was touches upon another advantage of acquiring one's stolen documents from a government's files instead of from the mails: if one waits until a letter has been delivered, one's agent can steal an already-decyphered copy, relieving one of that task.

It not only relieved the embassy of transcribing the cyphered text into clear, but of breaking the cypher to begin with; but even that was a matter of convenience only. Though an enormous

[1] Walsingham, whose role as a spy-master occupies a rather large part of his historical image, sometimes hired handwriting experts such as Peter Bales to forge alterations in the contents of intercepted correspondence before returning it to its normal channels in order to mislead the recipient, but whatever success such flummery may have had—in uncovering the Babington Plot, for example —it was, for the reasons stated, impractical as a permanent practice.

amount of material was put into cypher, it was of course taken back out of cypher for reading by the addressee, with two countervailing forces at work: the more important its contents the more closely the decyphered copies would be guarded, but the more important its contents the more people were apt to be consulted about it and the more copies made for consultation and thus potentially for stealing; thus the bulk of the documents that were stolen were not in cypher even if they once had been. If they were, an agent who could steal a secret document could usually also steal a cypher key; if he could not, the embassy, after copying, had plenty of time and usually the expertise to break the cypher; failing that, the still-cyphered document could be sent to the home government where someone would be available capable of breaking almost any cypher. Thus while cypher guarded secrecy in a limited and temporary sort of way, encyphering a document did not conceal the contents of earlier drafts or later decyphered copies, nor for very long that of the cyphered original itself if stolen.

For all these reasons together, though ambassadors and governments employed cypher extensively, their greatest problem was security at home, the greatest danger circuitous espionage—not the direct action of those directly involved, which was often in fact the one flank on which one could be reasonably sure of being safe. Even during the period when the English ambassador in Madrid was mailing home copies of the very stolen documents already mentioned on several occasions, if other means were not departing soon enough he often sent his despatches by the Spanish courier with no more than moderate qualms, and the Spanish government, even after they knew what he was up to, did not hesitate to use Digby's courier; and the same was true in reverse and between other combinations of states. It was simply a matter of playing the game and being able to count on others to do so, to everyone's benefit; outside the baselines, of course, such as in each other's own secretariats, the rules did not apply, but where they did for long periods of time between given states they were kept surprisingly well. (This was not, of course, universal: I do not recall in the period anyone's sending their despatches by a French courier, for example, though I expect the Dutch would have been more willing to do so than the Spanish or English.)

Code indicators being one-shot affairs, not strung together to form linguistic constructs, and being substitutes for a wide variety of people, places and miscellaneous things, not for an ordered alphabet, one would suppose that a code would be harder to crack than a cypher, but this is not necessarily so. Both of these considerations in fact touch upon routes of access to the meanings of individual indicators and into the heart of the code itself.

A coded meaning is indeed contained in a single symbol and so is not vulnerable to analysis of its structure, but it is not an *isolated* symbol and therefore not an isolated meaning. As it appears in an intelligible context (either originally in clear or now decyphered: if still in cypher, the coded parts would hardly matter anyway) its possible meanings will be limited, sometimes quite narrowly. As appearances of the same designator multiply, the contexts vary and the nature of the narrowing with it, cutting across each other in a manner that often reduces the possibilities quite rapidly. If, for example, the passage refers to a letter '134' wrote to someone, this at very least makes 134 a person or a group, not a place or a thing; a reference to 134's wife or son narrows that down to a person; mention of his ambassador makes him a ruler; if it is his ambassador to Madrid he is not ruler of Spain; etc. Often before one has encountered 134 even that many times one will learn that he lives in the Louvre or some other detail that could apply to only one person: even the most innocuous references that make clear quite ordinary things he must be or could not be—young or old, married or single— eliminate possible contenders from among those otherwise quali- fied (if 134 has received a papal blessing it is not Queen Elizabeth). A consideration like the latter would in fact decide a typical case, where the possibilities have been reduced, say, to the only two available rulers recently widowed, but one Protestant and one Catholic.

Knowing that 134 is the king of France puts an opening wedge into the code. One soon collects indicators for his wife, chief minister and others in France, and others elsewhere by the context of his relationship with them: if, on a given day, 134 is reported to have signed a peace treaty with or declared war upon 109, the available treaty signings or war declarations by the king of France on that day will make rather clear who 109 is.

But a soon-acquired familiarity with the codes in question will often open another route into a given code that is even quicker, once one has the initial wedge of a few designators for which the meaning is known (preferably several, but a relative few will give a very good start). There is in fact a potential rational organisation of the meanings of code designators at least partly analogous to numerical order, which allows one to give code lists a logical coherence that some states could not resist. This is a combination of classification into logical groupings and of logical ordering within and, to the degree possible, among groups. That is, to group together all persons or institutions in each given country and assign them consecutive designators, these also being assigned according to a rational and consistently applied order within the group, and with the groups themselves ranged in a logical sequence, normally one's own state first, followed by the others in a descending order of importance, then these followed by the usual miscellaneous groups of places, commonly used words, etc. (there is seldom a rational order applicable either within or among these latter groups, but they normally come last, and in the usual groups of sequential numbers).

The nature of such codes, the degree to which the code can be further unravelled by inference, and—more importantly—the degree to which further knowledge can be gained by inferences drawn from limited data in hand, can be illustrated fairly succinctly. A corner may be cut for this by choosing a case where one does not have to start so nearly from scratch. For example, in a typical letter to James I, his ambassador in Madrid uses forty-one different code designators (employing those attached to the 'king's cypher', of course).[1] All of these are decoded on the manuscript

[1] John Digby to James I, Madrid, 13 September 1613, SP94/20/73–6.

itself and so pose no problem for the historian, but forty of these (they being numbers) are spread from 71 to 179, a span of 109 numbers, all or almost all of which are apparently being used as designators, but of which (from this letter alone) we know the meanings of only forty.

This raises the question of whether one can, from these forty, deduce the meanings of at least some of the other sixty-nine for future use in reading similar despatches that may not have the decode so conveniently written on them. The answer in such a case is generally 'yes', and in this particular case one can by a little reasoned inference be fairly sure of about two dozen (or at least narrow the possibilities down to two or three in each case) and make fairly good guesses of at least the sort of things the rest have to be (sometimes one is able to establish a series of three or four almost-certain meanings in an almost-certain sequence that can be placed almost certainly within a one-slot range of its proper place). The list on the opposite page will illustrate the subsequent comments.

The weakness of the system, of course, is that the indicators are assigned in rational groups—a given country, its ruler, the royal family (if any), followed by the leading ministers and (where applicable) a key institution; then another country in the same fashion, the lists even following a declining order of precedence as consistently as was probably possible. It is only slightly less orderly (and transparent) than the custom sometimes followed of neatly reserving all the 70s for one state, all the 80s for another, and so forth: once one knows that that system prevails and knows even a few random meanings, even unknown indicators reveal a good part of their meaning. For example, since anything so systematic can also be trusted to be in order of precedence as well (80 being the state itself, 81 the monarch, etc.), though one may not know what state the 80s apply to, 81 is clearly the ruler; if it turns out that 81 is a minor, or has just been married, or has just fired his chief minister or has only been on the throne a year, his identity and the necessary meaning of at least 80 and 82, and the state all the 80s pertain to, have all been revealed. But the latter

71 ENGLAND
72 King of England
73 Queen of England
74 Prince Charles
[75: blank]
76 Princess Elizabeth
77 The Count Palatine
[78: blank]
79 English Privy Council
[80–85: 6 slots]
86 Viscount Rochester
87 French ambassador to England
[88–103: 16 slots]
104 IRELAND
[105: blank]
106 Earl of Tyrone
[107: blank]
108 SPAIN
109 King of Spain
[110–114: 5 slots]
115 Duke of Lerma
[116: blank]
117 Constable of Castile
118 Marquis Spinola
119 Juan de Idiáquez
[120: blank]
121 Juan de Ciriza
122 Pedro de Zúñiga
[123: blank]
124 English ambassador to Spain
[125: blank]

126 Papal nuncio to Spain
[127–131: 5 slots]
132 The Pope
133 FRANCE
134 King of France
135 Queen Regent
[136: blank]
137 'the 2nd daughter of France'
[138–141: 4 slots]
142 Villeroy
143 HOLLAND
144 The States General
[145–146: 2 slots]
147 FLANDERS
148 The Archduke Albert
[149: blank]
150 Duke of Savoy
151 Prince of Piedmont
[152–153: 2 slots]
154 money
155 shipping
[156–158: 3 slots]
159 soldiers
[160–165: 6 slots]
166 The English seminary in Madrid
167 Virginia
[168–169: 2 slots]
170 Paris
171 Rome
[172–178: 7 slots]
179 Milan

is only a convenient extreme of orderliness; what is crucial is that a consecutive segment of numbers is involved, and in an at least partially predictable order. As may be seen in the present case:

75: Should be a member of the royal family, as one would not put anyone else ahead of Princess Elizabeth. As none are available, it seems probable that 74 is a generic 'Prince of Wales' designator, which would have indicated Prince Henry until his death some ten months before (6 November 1612), but would now indicate Charles, then 75, merely leaving his previous designator (75) unused.

78: Probably a person, as one would not likely list another group or institution (e.g., the East India Company) ahead of the Privy Council; if the assumption made regarding 75, that the list had been in use for a while, is valid, then this could be Salisbury (who died 12 May 1612, only six months before Henry) and so would also be vacant. Alternatively, the inclusion of Frederick V, who had recently married the Princess Elizabeth, in (or at least next to) the royal family, opens the door of possibilities to the King of Denmark (the Queen's brother) or perhaps even the duc de Bouillon, Frederick's uncle, who had been much involved lately in arranging that marriage; in any event, as Frederick would have been added fairly recently, this lower part of Royalty Row obviously then had room for an addition, and that may be true of 78 now.

80–85 (six slots): Almost surely privy councillors, probably in the order Abbott–Ellesmere–Nottingham–Northampton–Suffolk, plus Sir Thomas Lake, currently the closest thing to a secretary of state (most likely following them, especially since it would follow the pattern used for the Spanish Council of State).

The decoder's rendering of 86 as Viscount Rochester would, had it been necessary here, fix the time of the decoding, and thus the approximate date of the document, at some time between Robert Carr's elevation to that title (25 March 1611) and his later promotion to Earl of Somerset (26 December 1613), but his last-place position at 86 strongly suggests that this code list itself antedates his elevation to the viscountcy.

88–103 (16 slots): The first few of these should be other ambassadors resident in England. As the Spanish ambassador is oddly *hors de serie* (60, the only number used that is not within the limits 71–179), the next, in the probably-used order of precedence, would be the Venetian, then the Archdukes' ambassador, with the order of the others—Savoy, the United Provinces—being less easily guessed; this probably starts with 89, however, as the Spanish ambassador had previously been 88 (though not necessarily in this particular code), as one knows from earlier correspondence, and his being randomly out of place now suggests that the designator may have been changed for security reasons (the meaning presumably having been either discovered or simply figured out: the joke of labelling the Spanish ambassador '88' is rather thin), in which case 88 would now be either vacant or filled by a recent addition to the list (though a mere clerical slip is a possibility never to be ruled out in such surmises). These presumed ambassadors *could* be followed by some non-ambassadorial foreigners resident in England and/or some Englishmen prominent enough to list but not otherwise classified (e.g., the Catholic archpriest), but some of the later slots (before Ireland) are perhaps given to one or more members of the government of Scotland and perhaps Wales, with designators also perhaps for governing councils there.

105, 107: Both are surely Irish or concern Ireland (105 would definitely be); regarding 107, it is improbable that a single slot for some other category would intervene before Spain, and it is unlikely to be simply unused, as three specific designators are hardly too many for Ireland, one of these almost certainly for the Lord Lieutenant, the other probably for the Irish Parliament, probably in that order.

110–114 (five slots): At least the first few will be members of the royal family (probably all, since Lerma would likely be the first to be listed after them); the queen is recently deceased, but if the assumption of slight obsolescence made regarding 74–75 is correct, 110 would be her indicator, now vacant (the pattern of state-king-queen is obvious, though this is not the place to speculate on Louis XIII's being paired with his mother [134–135]); next would come the heir, the future Philip IV, with the king's other offspring probably coming in the usual order of precedence, in order of their nearness to the throne (males, then females, in descending order of age), but James's long-time interest in a Spanish marriage for the Prince of Wales *could* place the Infanta Ana higher on the list (and conceivably the younger Infanta María, though she had entered the picture only since it had become clear that Ana was destined for Louis XIII, so that the likelihood of her having been placed high would depend on how long ago this particular set of designators was drawn up; the indications are that she would not be).

116, 120: Both should be high-ranking councillors, unless one supposes that the secretary of state who does *not* handle the papers of English affairs is included, in which case he would presumably be bracketed (as 120) with the one who *does* (121). It is hard to guess who would be listed ahead of the Constable of Castile, but an English list would not be bound by Spanish court protocol (and perhaps not that familiar with it), and James might have been inclined to list the Count of Villamediana, who, with the Constable, had headed the extraordinary embassy that had negotiated the Treaty of London in 1604, and since the latter was mainly a titular head and Villamediana the very active working head, the pragmatic James might well list Villiamediana first in spite of the Constable's far higher rank. (One notes that Pedro de Zúñiga, who was the first Spanish resident in England after the peace, and had also since gone as extraordinary ambassador there, for which occasion he was created Marquis of Floresdavila, is listed *below* secretary Ciriza, and therefore presumably a later addition, probably in connection with his recent mission (during his residency he would have been covered by the generic designator 'Spanish ambassador to England'). It is also interesting to note that Spinola, a Genoan whose service to the Spanish crown had been almost entirely in the Netherlands, is in the 'Spain' list, not that of 'Flanders' as one might expect.)

123: Another councillor, added since Zúñiga, or an available slot still vacant, as (unless there was a later shortage of numbers) 124 surely begins an *English* list of ambassadors to Spain.

125: An ambassador to Spain, since it is between two others; if the above assumption about 123 is correct, precedence (which, by the ample evidence of the forty decoded items, this list follows quite consistently) would make this the Emperor's envoy if he is listed, and otherwise the French ambassador.

127-131 (five slots): At least the first few, and probably all, would be other ambassadors resident in Spain. Aside from the Imperial and French ambassadors, the likeliest order would be Venice, Flanders, Savoy, Florence (or Florence, Savoy), Genoa, in protocol order. (In actuality, as will be seen later, the English code list apparently lacked a designator for 'the Emperor's ambassador here', and even one for the Emperor himself.)

136: Presumably the first daughter, for whom James had been dickering (for the Prince of Wales) before shifting to 137: one might expect that in other letters 136 would pop up as the prospective bride of 111.

138-141 (four slots): Except for Villeroy, ministers and other prominent political figures are conspicuously missing from this list (Concini and his wife, Foreign Secretary Puissieux, Condé, and the duc de Bouillon would be leading candidates), but so are ambassadors to France; at the very least the *English* ambassador, and surely the Spanish, would be included, and perhaps others (the anomaly of their coming before Villeroy might be explained by his being a recent addition to the list); the 'third daughter of France', who eventually became Queen of England, would join the English code lists sometime, but it may be too early for her to be 138 here.

145, 146: two prominent persons in the United Provinces, one certainly Maurice of Nassau, the other perhaps Frederick Henry but more likely the English ambassador there.

149: In conformity with the ruler-consort pattern of sequence this should be the Archduchess Isabel, with that of the state-ruler pattern it should be Savoy, and with general practice in this and similar lists it should be the English ambassador: a case where possible inferences cancel each other out until further evidence is encountered (e.g., reference to something that happened in 149 would make it Savoy, reference to a letter written by 149 would limit it to persons, reference to 149's sovereignty would necessarily make it the Archduchess, etc.).

152–153: Preceding 154–155, one or both *could* be similar words, but they seem more probably other miscellaneous princes: among Italian ones the Grand Duke of Tuscany is conspicuously missing from this list, as are the kings of Sweden and Denmark, the Holy Roman Emperor, etc.

156–158 (three slots): Certainly other frequently-used key words such as those before and after.

160–165 (six slots): Somewhere here (not necessarily at the round number) should be a switch from key words to the names of places-other-than-cities, probably with no other type in between, probably at or near the beginning since one clearly needs designators somewhere (and having them here would follow the list's logical organisation) for the Indies (perhaps East and West separately). A few groups such as the Hanseatic League, the Evangelical Union and the Catholic League of Germany, the Huguenots, etc., should also appear somewhere in this list.

168, 169: Probably further miscellaneous names of places neither states nor cities; could be names of cities, but since ten slots (170–179) seem plenty the only argument for it is that London seems likely to come first (i.e., before 170) in an English list of cities.

172–178 (seven slots): Seem certain to be cities.

Post-179: Though the 'limit' of the list here is merely the highest designator that happens to have been used in a particular letter, it seems unlikely that it extends much further. An English list that makes room for only two persons (including the English ambassador) in the United Provinces, and perhaps only one in the Spanish Netherlands, is not apt to have a much longer list of cities than this, and there are practically no other customary code-list categories not already accounted for.

A random example may illustrate the relative ease of cracking a simple and non-random cypher, especially one used lazily. At SP 94/19/221 is a letter (apparently of 1612) in the same handwriting as John Digby's despatches from Madrid, mostly in cyphers. A covering label reads as follows:

A 4.50.21.46.42.60.50.8.70.
109.54.16.42.30.44.26.61.
30.50.70.12.46.27.60.40.17.
2.41.27.39.5.50.51.26.66.
32.46.30.11.61.30.12.44.54.
44.18.22.42.26.50.53.25./.

Even without a key or the help of some other decyphered letter, one can work out a good deal of the cypher used just from this, drawing upon common sense, the need for meaning (the Achilles' heel of any cypher, and made still more vulnerable here by combining cypher and code), some familiarity with commonly used cypher conventions and the general nature of the English cyphers (which the historian quickly picks up), and a sufficient familiarity with contemporary linguistic and orthographic usages (necessary for research in documents in any case).

First of all, since one knows what this is a label for, and the encypherer has tipped off the construction by foolishly leaving the initial article in clear,[1] the label almost certainly begins 'A copie [Digby's normal spelling] of a letter' or 'A letter [from or to]' someone, or a close variation using one or the other of those beginnings. Secondly, as it is plain from the document—from their isolated occurrence in clear passages—that the three-digit numbers are code indicators for persons or places, this beginning passage must be completed in the first line, before 109: to say 'A letter to/from 109' or 'A copy of 109's letter to . . .', or some

---

[1] Which, except for a possible slip in grammar, precludes the possibility of plurals (it could not say 'A copies' or 'A letters', though it could say 'A copie of several letters'), and of all following words beginning with a vowel—here, words such as 'extracts', not important to meaning but important to making a first crack in the code; in other cases, if the choice were, say, between 'king' and 'ambassador', the slip would reveal essential meaning as well.

such. Thus isolated, there are nine indicators available for spelling it out, one too few for 'letter from', eliminating that possibility, one more than needed for 'letter to', two more than needed for 'copie of'.

Any unused indicators are presumably nulls. The basic reason for using these meaningless indicators is to suppress letter frequency and in general to cause confusion, but since the English commonly gave them the double-duty function of separating words—a wholly idiotic procedure that makes word length obvious and cracking that much easier—that is the best trial assumption. As two would be needed to separate even cyphered words only, the eight-indicator alternative is incompatible with the assumption, leaving 'copie of' as the only candidate (if it does not work out, one can try 'letter' abbreviated 'lr', and other less likely alternatives); it is the best candidate, anyway, as there is a double letter in the following line, making it a likely candidate for 'letter' (a bar, dot or some such over an indicator was commonly used to indicate a double letter). If the second word is indeed 'of' (or any other two-letter word) the nulls used, before and after it, would be 60 and 70, which also fits the usual pattern of having one's nulls *hors de serie* (most of the numbers here are below 60, plenty to provide at least two indicators for each letter of the alphabet), and thus makes likelihood seem greater: this would leave precisely the five indicators needed for 'copie'. If one thus tentatively fills in the appropriate letters, one has:

C O P I E O F

A 4 . 50 . 21 . 46 . 42 . 60 . 50 . 8 . 70 .

The first thing that strikes the eye is that at least one number, 50, seems confirmed, as it comes out O both times, which also suggests that one is on the right track. (Use of the same indicator when there are more than one for a given letter is lazy encyphering, but the implication would have been the same with adjoining letters.) Secondly, all the vowels are high numbers, and all the consonants lower numbers. Thirdly, the numerical order of both consonants and vowels parallels their alphabetical order. Thus one has a good start on one's own code key:

```
              C           F
 1   2   3   4   5   6   7   8   9  10  11  12  13  14  15
              P
16  17  18  19  20  21  22  23  24  25  26  27  28  29  30
                                          E
31  32  33  34  35  36  37  38  39  40  41  42  43  44  45
 I           O
46  47  48  49  50  51  52  53  54  55  56  57  58  59  60
```

Assuming this parallel order to prevail throughout, with all the consonants first and then all the vowels, the series should start off with B, with D coming between C and F, G to N coming in sequence between F and P, and Q to Z thereafter, as there is obviously more than one indicator per letter but not enough room between F and P for three each, the number clearly must be two for the consonants (though likely more for the vowels). Assuming this number to be consistent throughout (fairly typical of consonants, though not of vowels), this turns out to fit perfectly up to P (there is almost never a separate indicator for J, the I doubling for it—as it commonly did in spelling as well). By continuing on the same basis one can construct a tentative key through T, after which point one faces the uncertainty of whether there is an indicator for V or if the U indicator is used (either would be likely) and for double-U, and the possibility of single indicators for the little-used tail-end letters X and Z (a problem which would have been helped by having an A indicator). It would look as follows.[1]

[1] The six letters deduced from the first line of the label are given in CAPS; the twelve further inferences confirmed in lines 2–6 are *italicised*. The further inferences yielded by applying the tentative key to these latter five lines have also been added here in parentheses (the four confirmed by the obvious spelling of words they occur in, plus the less immediately obvious 51 and 53) or in square brackets [the three assigned on the principle of consecutive indicators, plus 52, added later].

b *b* *c* C *d* d f F g g *h* h k k l
1 2 3 4 5 6 7 8 9 10 11 12 13 14 15
l *m* *m* n n P *p* q q *r* r s s t *t*
16 17 18 19 20 21 22 23 24 25 26 27 28 29 30
[w] (w)   (a) [a] (a) E [e] (e)
31 32 33 34 35 36 37 38 39 40 41 42 43 44 45
I   O (u) [u] (u)
46 47 48 49 50 51 52 53 54 55 56 57 58 59 60

Applying known letters and inferred consonants gives this reading:

```
    c   o   p   i   e       o   f   [?'s]    l   e  tt       r
A 4.50.21.46.42.60.50.8.70.109.54.16.42.30.44.26.61.
    t   o       h   i   s           m b     ss     d   o       r
30.50.70.12.46.27.60.40.17.2.41.27.39.5.50.51.26.66.
    i   t h       t h•           m   p   e   r   o       r
32.46.30.11.61.30.12.44.54.44.18.22.42.26.50.53.25./.
```

This directly confirms three of the indicators in the initial first-line reading (42, 46, 50) plus twelve of those that were added inferentially to the tentative B–T key, some of them two or three times. Four post-T slots may also be considered confirmed by the obvious words they occur in, three others (31, 40, 43) by the assumption (consistently true elsewhere) of consecutive indicators: 44 (three times) can only be E, 41 and 39 A, 32 W (also, since V would not likely be given only one indicator, it can be safely inferred that it has none—that the U indicators are used—and that 31 is thus another W indicator); in contemporary spelling 40 could be either A or E, but must be A here because it falls between two confirmed A indicators (by the same principle, 43 must be E); 51 and 53 remain momentarily problems.

The most important consideration is that along with 61 (used twice) and 66, 54, also used twice, is an obvious null, and (assuming the consistency that is maintained throughout elsewhere) those following as well, making all vowels come before 54. The pattern of ordered sequence would require U to come at the end;

as in this cypher it could not conceivably have fewer than two indicators (certainly not fewer than the consonants), 52 and 53 should be U; if one assumes consistent spelling, 51 and 53 should be the same, and in fact U is the likeliest spelling available here ('-our', not '-oor', though the unavailable '-or' would be somewhat more common); thus 51 also can be assigned to U with some confidence. This leaves six indicators between 44 and 51, two of them (46 and 50) already confirmed for I and O, which could be either of two ways. I and O might have as many indicators as E (which would be bad practice, as E's higher frequency needs to be suppressed), or E might have four, leaving five to be divided between I and O—in which case I (with the greater frequency, and doubling for J as well) would necessarily have priority. The former would give E 42-43-44, I 45-46-47, O 48-49-50, the latter E 42-43-44-45, I 46-47-48, O 49-50, with the duplications leaving only 45 (E or I) and 48 (I or O) in doubt; actual use of the key would readily clear this up.

This leaves only the six spaces 33-38, which just fit the two-per-letter consonant pattern for X Y Z (Y commonly being found among the consonants, if at all); it is possible but unlikely that A might have four indicators if E has, but definitely not if E has only three, so that the possibility that 38 might be A needs to be kept open only as a matter of routine prudence.

The question of who 109 is (whose letter to his ambassador to the Emperor it is) is hardly in doubt: this copy was stolen in Madrid by the English ambassador there, which indicates the likeliest answer; the fact that most of the purloined letters Digby sent were to or from Philip III increases the probability, as does the fact that few others *had* ambassadors to the Emperor. Internal evidence should confirm this.

And the contents of the letter are in fact at one's fingertips, since one has muddled out virtually the entire key to its cypher from the nine cyphered words on the label. Viz.:[1]

[1] SP94/19/221. Decyphered from Spanish cypher, translated into English and put mostly into an English cypher; there is no indication whether the combination of cyphered and clear passages bears any relationship to the original.

By the inclosed lett^r wch I have sent to 17.36.64.40.17.1.41.27.39.
6.50.51.26 in 171. you shall see the Answeare that I make concerning
the business of 27.51.$\overline{4}$.50.52.26. Demaunded by 30.11.44.60.3.50.20.
6.42.54.26.4.17.2.41.16.6.49.58.6.42.62.4.50.16.40.15.30.50 the 42.17.
22.44.26.50.52.25.28.67.54.41.17.2.40.$\overline{28}$.39.6.50.52.26. of 132. signi-
fying that in case 132 should not bee pleased to 40.$\overline{27}$.46.28.30.69.12.
46.17. that the 44.17.22.42.26.50.52.25 should bee forced to helpe
12.46.17.27.42.18.7.44 of a 64.4.44.26.30.40.46.20.43.54.8.44.51.6 of
the 42.17.21.46.26.43.63.4.40.$\overline{16}$.42.5.$\overline{61}$.4.50.18.40.$\overline{4}$.46.48. W^{ch} the
4.11.51.26.3.12.44 now 22.50.$\overline{27}$.42.$\overline{28}$.44.30.12. wth out 60.46.20.51.
42.27.30.52.26.43. I require 40.20.6.61.4.50.$\overline{17}$.40.51.20.6.66.36.50.52.
that according to the 4.50.20.30.42.20.29.28. of the 46.20.4.16.50.27.
44.6.60.16.42.$\overline{30}$.44.25 that 36.48.51. doe all possible good 50.7.46.4.
42.27. wth the 42.17.22.44.26.50.52.25. for the 42.33.4.51.28.46.20.9.
and preventing of all distastes that may arise betwixt 132 and 12.46.
17.27.44.16.8.47. And 35.50.52. shall bee carefull to advise 64.17.$\overline{42}$.
from tyme to tyme of all that passeth heerein.

Applying the tentative key to the text confirms 51–52–53 for
U, and the unequal division for I (47–48–49) and O (49–50); the
only vowel indicator it does not confirm is 45, but since I would
not have four and E only three, it has to be the latter (this also
illustrates encypherers' typical lazy failure to use all the indicators
available: this obvious fourth for E is unused throughout). It
also confirms 33 as X and 35 and 36 as Y, and by inference 34
as X and 37 and 38 as Z. It also confirms that encypherers are
human, here having three times taken an indicator one place
away from the correct one (twice in 'himselfe', once in 'you').
As the Emperor's ambassador has attempted to force aid from
132 by threatening seizure of a feudality that the Church possesses,
132 is obviously the Pope; as the Pope is the only person in
Rome apt to be on an English code list (i.e., no Queen, Prince,
etc.) it is less unusual that their indicators (132, 171) should be
numerically unrelated. The fact that there is apparently no code
indicator for the Emperor casts an interesting reflection on his
place (or lack of one) in English foreign policy thinking as of
1612, as distinct from six or eight years later.

One might add that the method used here for establishing an entry into the cypher was chosen because it was the most direct one, an apt illustration of the accessibility of the simpler cyphers to the researcher (when necessary) and of the obviously limited role cypher played in practice—mainly that of masking contents from the 'enemy', protecting them more against sight reading than against decyphering when copies were actually in another's possession. For an expert cryptologist (a category that does not include the present writer) there would be equally obvious routes: one sequence of indicators in the label and two in the text are so similar as to catch an expert's eye as essentially identical—i.e., variations of contiguous indicators spelling out the same word; another set appears once in the label and four times in the text. Both are obviously important words and would be worth some trial guesses; the fact that both are long (assuming a right guess that it is indeed one word) has two advantages: the number of possibilities is vastly reduced, and if correctly guessed would yield enough indicators to enable one to unravel the rest of the cypher more quickly (by assigning assumed meanings to further cyphers to see if they yielded sense). The cryptologist might not guess 'emperor' too readily for the latter set, but 'ambassador' is a likely word to be used in this context, it would be an extremely likely recipient as clearly is meant in the beginning of the text, and all three examples of the former set have a double letter (a bar over the indicator, a dead giveaway) at just the place it comes in 'ambassador'. Had a still simpler route not been available, an expert cryptologist (then or now) would have seen this probability, tried it, and cracked the cypher in a couple of minutes; the rest of the task, filling in the remaining blanks in the reconstructed key, would be essentially scribe's work.

Chosen for its particular advantages as a working example (not least its convenient length), this document serves also to illustrate a generalisation made earlier about the frequency of the researcher's need in practice ever actually to decypher documents: two folios away (223) there is the customary decypher copy with 132 and 171 also decoded.

The more sophisticated cyphers, such as those used by the Spanish, are more difficult to crack for a number of reasons. They often shifted the relationship between indicators and meanings by shifting the setting of the wheel or other mechanical device used for deciphering, sometimes as often as every line; since the patterns for the various settings were randomly chosen and thus unrelated to each other, one had to start over with every shift. Even without this the cypher was far more extensive, using far more symbols and thus making more to figure out, and far more complex and (especially) random, making the figuring out more difficult.

Perhaps the most confusing characteristic was the avoidance of symbols capable of rational order that might parallel alphabetical order and thus be rationally deducible, as number indicators are. They used numbers, but they were interspersed with a good many symbols that had the virtue of being totally meaningless linguistically and incapable of rational ordering: diamonds, triangles (right side up and upside down), various types of crosses, apparent adaptations of medical and chemical symbols, and a variety of little things that look like child-drawn Christmas trees and other such fantasies. They even met the problem of avoiding analogies of order and meaning head-on by using letters for letters. Though a systematic element crept in, it was at least not a simplistic one, letter symbols often being used in combination (pq means b, pr means c, etc.), obliquely (given first letters mean that the meaning of the second letter is a specific number of places later or earlier in the alphabet), and even boldly (a specific first letter indicates that the second means exactly what it says). And any of these types of symbol were used in a manner designed to suppress letter frequency and linguistic patterns. Vowel frequency was suppressed by assigning indicators for the various combinations with them (ba, ca, da . . .); as q is almost invariably followed by u and the recurring combination eventually becomes a dead giveaway, qu or que was given its own indicators, as were such frequent consonant combinations as cl, tr, etc. But the most important factor is that this complexity and variety were usually made use of, in contrast to the lazy use of the far simpler English cypher discussed above, where suppression of frequency by assigning several numeral indicators (generally two, three or four in sequence) to each letter was frustrated by encypherers' habit of generally using the one easiest to remember, sticking with the first one, or one that happened to be a round number.

A Spanish cypher of the same period uses letters as symbols for letters, then employs them in pairs representing two-letter combinations in which the first letter is cypher but the second is in clear. When J is D, L is M, and N is L, '*ja la*' means '*dama*', '*la na*' means '*mala*', etc.

This sort of cypher very effectively combines three excellent characteristics. Its indicators and meanings are randomly, not rationally paired: the above designators J, L, N (in alphabetical order, as they would be listed in a decyphering key) correspond in properly muddled fashion to the letters D, M, L; when these latter are ordered alphabetically D, L, M (as in an encyphering key) their corresponding indicators are J, N, L. Using two-letter units of meaning vastly increases the numbers of items whose frequency of appearance would have to be calculated and evaluated in order to break the cypher by that standard route. (In the 26-letter English alphabet the possible combinations would soar from 26 to 776, all of which are available if one chooses to ignore syllables and simply march through words two letters at a time; here the first entries, both indicator and meaning, are consonants, the second vowels.) And combining clear with cypher, though it is a bit too systematically done here, adds considerable confusion (the last best guess for the meaning of A would ordinarily be A).

The latter two considerations make it far harder to gain initial access to the cypher than to the one-letter one discussed above. But once entry has been gained, a few meanings learned, only the randomness will protect the rest of the cypher. Once an ordered analogy is introduced the jig is up, but even the Spanish, with their generally more sophisticated cyphers and codes (using unorderable classical names instead of numbers) sometimes fell into this tempting trap. As, for example, in another Spanish cypher of the period, in which two-letter meanings are used but numbers are used as indicators, and for which one happens to have discovered ten scattered meanings for numeral indicators ranging from the 30s to the 60s:

32		37 SA	42	47		52 GA	57
33 RE		38	43	48		53 GE	58
34 RI		39	44 TI	49		54	59
35 RO		40	45 TO	50		55	60 FO
36		41 SU	46	51		56	61

The lowest of the known indicators happen to be in sequence, 33–34–35, meaning RE–RI–RO; after an unknown slot, 37 is SA, and after three gaps 41 is SU; then three gaps, 44 TI, 45 TO, six gaps, 52 GA, 53 GE, six more gaps, 60 FO, and ten more gaps before 71 is known to be the single letter N. Besides the obvious fact that these are all combinations of consonants with vowels, one notices two things: that the consonants R–S–T are in immediate alphabetical sequence, and that the three consecutive R vowels are as well. At second glance one notices that G–F is reverse alphabetical order. More importantly, the two consecutive G vowels are in normal sequence. Less obviously, so are the S vowels—and with exactly the number of slots between them needed for E–I–O. A quick count from SU to TI, TO, thence all the way (starting over again at 47) to GA, GE, and thence on to FO finds all of the known vowels falling in their proper places. The pattern turns out to be childishly simple, the vowels simply being repeated *seriatim* over and over in conjunction with one consonant after another:

32 *RA*		37 SA	42 *TA*	47 *?A*		52 GA	57 *FA*
33 RE		38 *SE*	43 *TE*	48 *?E*		53 GE	58 *FE*
34 RI		39 *SI*	44 TI	49 *?I*		54 *GI*	59 *FI*
35 RO		40 *SO*	45 TO	50 *?O*		55 *GO*	60 FO
36 *RU*		41 SU	46 *TU*	51 *?U*		56 *GU*	61 *FU*

Thus for these thirty indicators, of which one initially knew only ten, one now knows the full meaning of twenty-five, and lacks only the first letter for the other five (47–51). The only violation of straight numerical/alphabetical order is the switch in initial letters from R–S–T to ?–G–F, but even this indicates with fair certainty the structure of this consonant-plus-vowel part of the cypher.

First, several such vowel sequences are grouped together in alphabetical order (either forward or backward) by the initial letter. Secondly, since 71 happens to be known to stand for the single letter N (and 72 for L, 77 for D), there is not room to continue the G–F–D–C–B pattern beyond D, there being only nine open slots and five per initial letter being necessary, so the vowel sequences for B and C will necessarily be elsewhere, and perhaps D as well.

Thirdly, even if D is here (62–66) there will be room for only six other consonants in the span 1–31, making, with the six in 32–61, a total of only thirteen. Unless some are scattered elsewhere in the number system (possible but not probable), some consonants will necessarily have been left out, most likely the less used X and Z and the more vowel-like H and Y (for V the B indicator was customarily used), leaving room for the likeliest thirteen, B–C–D–F–G–J–L–M–N–P–R–S–T. As five and presumably six (counting D) of these are known, this leaves only seven to discover. Any one such discovery would of course give its whole vowel sequence, and would also give probabilities as to alphabetically sequential neighbouring consonants. Given the pattern here, it is a fair assumption that in 1–31 there is either one ordered group of six consonants or two of three each. On the above working assumption regarding exclusions (which would make T the last consonant included), and supposing no sequence to be isolated from a small grouping, the best bet for 47–51 would be J, the next consonant available in the backward G–F sequence. As Q combines with only one vowel, the mandatory U, the odd number strongly suggests that it is somewhere in 1–31, the best bet being 31 as that would put it in alphabetical order before R, and otherwise 1 or 16 (between two groups of three vowel sequences). In any case, application of the known indicators to the cyphered text would, by exposing obvious words, reveal still further indicators until they all were known.

Thus even these more sophisticated two-letter codes reveal themselves with surprising readiness once a fairly minor entry has been made. More important, they provide the most literal examples available of how much further knowledge a certain amount of mulling and common sense will extract from even the most cryptic documents of any kind.

CHAPTER 7

Research in the Diplomatic Sources

Some of the problems and other issues involved in research in the diplomatic sources of the period are peculiar to them, or to some particular type of them; some are characteristic of sources in general in this period, or of these kinds of sources in any period, or of historical research in general. Such problems and influencing factors give every sign of being unlimited in number; one naturally cannot pretend to comprehensive coverage of them within the scope of this book's purpose. Yet such documents have no real modern existence apart from their use as historical sources, any more than they had in their own time apart from their active role as historical entities. For the historian history, in the sense of relevant past actuality, is what the sources tell him it is; for others, who do not go to the sources, it is what the historian tells him the sources say it is. But what the sources tell the historian and the historian tells the layman depends not only upon what is written in the sources but upon how they are used, and whether they are. Thus a 'description' of the sources in realistic terms requires giving some attention to at least the more conspicuous influences that bear upon this process.

CANONICAL HISTORY AND CANONICAL SOURCES

The most pervasive single influence upon historical research and writing in the early modern period is the established canon of events, issues, problems and persons that one begins with, and the corresponding canon of sources themselves for these things: a canonical historiography that in the past has served to delimit both subject and sources and whose research-shaping mould remains deeply imprinted upon both.

The problem with canonised sources is not that they are bad (they are no more than normally so), or that they are limited (one has to begin somewhere), or that they are old-fashioned (the continual change in historians' criteria of importance is not one of regular progression but of jumping from type to type; a three-hundred-year-old collection may be as relevant to current historical interests as one fifty or twenty years old—it is an almost random relationship), but that most of them have been used to death.

It is not surprising that this is especially true of published sources, since that form has been strangely elevated to a favoured position over manuscript sources, so that when one speaks of a 'standard' published source for a given subject one is speaking of an individually canonised example of a broadly canonised genre— a double halo of sanctity that generations and centuries of veneration have given a tradition of inviolability. Not that one may not occasionally go to the apocrypha for research in matters of indifference—events, issues, problems, persons not included in the books of the canon. But those extraneous topics, and findings about them, do not affect the central, canonised body of historical truth; and that whole historical truth, dogma already established based upon the evidence of its own assertions, cannot be further proved nor expanded and certainly not corrected by apocryphal, even alien sources.

This is, of course, insane, but it is only a little exaggerated, nor is it a matter solely of nineteenth-century whigs, the problem now dead with them. Only a few years ago, for example, an article I had submitted for publication was rejected by the *American Historical Review* on the judgment of a consultant (termed 'one of our finest specialists') based on the double grounds that it was in conflict with received opinion and that it was 'based upon sources that are rather too Spanish and Catholic'—a reasonable documentary foundation, one would think, since the subject was a Spanish ambassador, and the sources his own despatches, conciliar documents related to them, etc. Even so, I suppose these *are* Spanish documents, since both he and his government were Spanish; but one is left to wonder whether they are 'Catholic' because he was, or because some of them have a little cross at the top. And to wonder also, of course, whether the documents of,

say, Edward the Confessor are Catholic—and therefore unreliable. (It was encouraging to find that this absurd Anglo-
Protestant jingoism—apparently nurtured in an American Heart
of Oak—found no echo in England, where [*amour propre* being
also served] the same manuscript was immediately accepted by the
Historical Journal, the editor, F. H. Hinsley—in some contrast—
commenting, 'I like controversial articles'.)

Of the principal shortcomings of these sanctified sources, four
deserve special mention. Firstly, they breed the spurious notion
that the limited subject matter contained in them is the sum and
substance of relevant history, that all else is trivia, marginalia, or
at best important only as it can be related to the topical, con-
ceptual and other contents of the already-established canon. This
in spite of the fact that the canon took shape under the influence
of specific circumstances, attitudes, interests and such like which
continue to change and expand; to believe not only in the factual
accuracy and so on of the canonical sources and the soundness of
interpretation, etc., of the body of orthodox literature based upon
them, but also in the centrality of the contents of canonical history
itself, the particular subject matter covered, and in the special,
perhaps unique, relevance of the particular facts about individual
topics that have been selected for inclusion, requires one to believe
that the canon was formed in a sort of inspired patristic age, that
an analogue formed under different circumstances would not be
equally authentic, and that this one not only was authoritative
but continues to be so regardless of change in the context or
historical study. If one can.

As all dogmas are, this one, too, is more dependent upon faith
than upon reasoned, critical examination. It requires belief, for
example, that the course of development of political institutions
in northern Europe hung solely on the outcome of military
engagements, with the social forces shaping those institutions to
be somehow automatically turned off by a few thousand mer-
cenary soldiers routing a few thousand others from some stretch
of Flemish sand or German pasture; that Portugal was an authentic
separate nation, its natural and proper condition that of a separate

sovereign state, and Catalonia was not; that it was morally imperative for the English to support the Dutch against Spanish tyranny and papist repression of the true religion (and of course that Protestantism is essential to political freedom), but that it was morally acceptable to make war against them a few years later for commercial reasons; and, most importantly, that these and certain specified other things like them, big and small, are what is important in history; all else is commentary.

It is in fact not necessary to argue that the accepted interpretation of these things may be wrong, or that there may be other things besides this limited canonical agenda that are of equal or even greater importance; so much is obvious. What may be less obvious is that any one of these traditionally prominent issues, events, movements, problems, persons, etc., may not be important at all. Put differently, this central body of historical content may be valid but—parts of it, at least—simply not central at all.

Secondly, the sanctification of a limited number of sources breeds the equally spurious (and equally convenient) notion that not only is the body of important historical content limited but that this limited body of sources is sufficient for establishing certainty about it (logically inevitable since the canonical content is defined by the canonical sources), and, by extension, that sufficient certainty about any historical matter can be achieved by consulting a conveniently small body of sources, that historical knowledge and understanding are easily come by, the vast body of extant historical evidence merely a reference tool to be flipped through to the right place, where truth, in its simplicity, waits to be noted down, and that, sufficient evidence being such a simple matter, almost any convenient handful of applicable evidence will do. In sum, that (excluding, where necessary, foreign and infidel sources) historical evidence is all of pretty much the same value (an odd implication to come from canonical discrimination), and that Historical Truth not only may be easily had but can be fitted comfortably on to a three-by-five-inch note card.

Thirdly, and still equally speciously, the canon exalts printed sources over manuscript ones. There are undeniable advantages to printed sources. They allow access to documents where access to archives is not available, allow what access one does have to archives to be devoted to still other documents, leaving the printed ones to be dealt with at home, assemble scattered documents in one place, and so on: one can hardly imagine historical research on a proper scale without them. But 'indispensable' means neither 'only' nor 'best'. Indispensable they certainly are, but they are neither sufficient by themselves (a point already belaboured somewhat), or at least are not known to be until the full body of documentation has been seen, nor are they any more than a *pis aller*, imposed by practical considerations that have no relation to criteria applicable to sources. They are by themselves in some ways inferior, lacking those benefits of familiarity, nuance, etc., to be had from handling the originals themselves in their natural archival environment. Contrary to common belief, they do not even provide any great advantage in readability: not too far into the sixteenth century secretarial handwriting (which *is* difficult in the fifteenth and before) becomes sufficiently easy for most diplomatic documents to be read about as fast in manuscript as in print. Once one is accustomed to it, of course: reading manuscript documents, like riding a bicycle, is difficult only for those who have not yet got around to learning how; either one is an easy skill to acquire, and exceedingly simple thereafter.

But the worst thing that can be said about printed documents is that they interpose a stranger between the historian and his sources. In a given case the editor may have greater archival expertise than the historian, but this is not necessarily so, need not remain so for long as the historian gains experience, and certainly should not be so when the historian is dealing with a more specialised body of documents than the editor is: his collection or his total archival activity may be very general and thus his expertise spread far more thinly, including that employed in editorial annotation—identification of persons, etc.—an area in which a competent researcher will soon be far more expert than someone more broadly engaged can ever hope to be.

More crucially, in using published documents the historian is limited to the types selected for inclusion by the editor; as interest and criteria of importance vary from individual to individual and change with time (now favouring political content, now economic, etc.) the chances of the editor's selection matching the historian's needs are not great, and they diminish further when the historian's subject happens to be more specialised. If the historian adjusts his treatment to fit these particular sources—cuts his coat to fit the editor's cloth—he is not writing his own historical work but someone else's. If the editor's criteria are outdated and the historian adjusts to them, he is merely writing outdated history.

Regarding the specific documents chosen for publication within a given type, the historian is not only dependent upon the competence, interests and criteria of the editor (totally random factors from the historian's point of view) but is limited to the choices actually available to the editor at the time or under the conditions of editing. If the editor worked before archival organisation was improved and extensive cataloguing done, the range of choice was extremely limited—the reason why some of the older publications drawn from large archival collections are very hit-or-miss. For some, the *pis aller* factor is reduced to the vanishing point: they really are not better than nothing at all.

When this tendency to push the historian further away from the manuscript sources is extended to calendars—removing him from the full text in any form—the effect is, of course, extended with it.

And (fourthly) the worst thing that can be said about canonised sources in general is that they are no longer the source of anything much. If a source is a source of something fresh—new to historical knowledge, not just to a continuing succession of novices—then some of them are not sources at all. Certainly different historians will make different things of the same piece of data and extract different things from the same piece of evidence, and it may take many to thresh out some semblance of historical truth, but there finally comes a time when a piece of evidence has nothing left in it that has not already been found and made use of, exposed to critical examination in numerous secondary works.

To ignore the latter and insist on going back to the former for all of the same old details is simply playing at scholarship, a fitting and useful exercise for schoolchildren but above that level a sham: to march conscientiously back past Trevelyan, Macaulay, *Biographia Britannica*, and Bishop Burnet only to consult the same sources they all used—rerereresearch that is unlikely by now to produce new results—can hardly be called 'going back to the sources' in a very meaningful or creditable sense, and is certainly not a step forward on the path to further historical knowledge. Research implies going to some kind of source, but since the time available for it is finite, one might as well spend it on new ones, not on old, exhausted over-harvested ones ready for inclusion in a kit for children. A better cliché might be 'to go *forward* to the sources'.

How does this process work? The *Dictionary of National Biography*, the best of the national biographies, an indispensable tool for anyone working in English history—and a magnificent accomplishment by any standard—is both shaped by and a shaper of the English canon of sources and so a useful example here. On a broad scale, a small handful of sources figure prominently, repeatedly, as principal bases of its 29,000 articles (7,812 on the sixteenth and seventeenth centuries). On an individual scale, the typical article on a given person—including ambassadors and others relevant here—is further based mainly on a few—one or two or three—particular sources more specifically applicable to him, many of which are shared by, for example, several contemporary ambassadors. For the collectivity of English ambassadors at any one time the result is a network of interlocking sources used repeatedly, creating a mutually reinforcing orthodoxy of sources, and of treatment of English diplomatic history in the period, even when written by several different authors.

To precisely what orthodox sources does one refer here and in all the above? They are far too many to list here, and of course inclusion in the group would necessarily be increasingly arbitrary at its outer edges, but any student of history could make his own list of principal cases from the citations he knows like a litany from having encountered them endlessly in the footnotes of one work after another. For Spain there is most of the sixteenth-century material in the *Colección de documentos inéditos*; for France, Sully's slippery memoirs, a doubtful source even if it were not over-used, and some of Richelieu's more over-cropped papers; for Belgium, the Lonchay-Cuvelier-Lefèvre *Correspondance de la Cour d'Espagne sur les affaires des Pays-Bas au XVIII siècle* (rather poor analyses anyway); for England, Ellis, Oglander (his opinions of the realities of English government may be safely forgotten), many (but not all) of the collections of printed documents, and the *Calendar of State Papers, Venetian*.

Whatever one may once have been able to say in praise of these and others like them, they are by now guilty of the double crime of exhaustion and of diverting conscientious historians from going on to new and fertile fields. There is in fact a case to be made for rigging all published documents to self-destruct after a given number of uses. But this is perhaps a vain hope: someone has just issued—complete with a big advertising campaign—expensive, and durable seeming, new reprint editions of the *Winwood Memorials* and the *Sidney Papers*.

The historiographical canonisation either of particular collections or of particular ambassadors will separately establish a substantial bias in the sources conventionally used for, and the contents conventionally found in diplomatic history, but one even encounters canonised ambassadors whose papers themselves have been blessed by the canonisation of one particular collection of them to the exclusion of others; since it is usually original scripture and not later revisions (whether improved or not) that are considered specially blest, this is usually also the oldest, and often the least satisfactory edition available. To take only one of many possible examples: historians have bled to death the posthumously published *Reliquae Wottonianae, or a Collection of Lives, Letters, Poems . . .* (London, 1651, 1654, 1672, 1685—its successive editions include increasing smatterings of Wotton's correspondence), but seem to have seldom used the purportedly complete correspondence published in Logan Pearsall Smith, *Life and Letters of Sir Henry Wotton* (2 vols, Oxford, 1907), nor even the less complete *Letters and dispatches from Sir Henry Wotton to James I and his ministers . . . 1617–20* (Roxburghe Club, 1850).

If there is a canon of historical personages, significant events and established sources, there is no less an authorised litany of accepted ideas about given specific situations within which actions and events took place, decisions were taken, etc., and which inevitably shape the historian's handling of the discrete facts involved; when the accepted idea is wrong, the handling of the facts, the understanding of them, interpretations placed on them, and so forth must all go equally wrong. If one cannot understand international affairs properly (or learn the details of them accurately) without a proper understanding of the process of making foreign policy decisions, one cannot hope to do the latter without a proper understanding of who is taking a leading hand in doing so (and, usually, in domestic government as well). In the period of my own research there is a useful triple example, a trilogy of comparable, contemporaneously received truths, each of which is treated as axiomatic: that the duc de Luynes was a near-cypher in government who played no role of importance in the shaping of French policy; that the reverse was true of Lerma in Spain, he being in practically sole control of both domestic and foreign affairs; and that in England the ministerial function of administrative decision and execution was exclusively Salisbury's until his death in 1612, and only then did Northampton and Suffolk get their hands in. All three of these notions are wrong. Continued research increasingly shows Luynes to have been a minister of fair competence, force and influence, and to have been the deliberate promoter of policies usually associated with Richelieu (the uniqueness of that greater genius obviously having been successfully imposed upon history with near-Napoleonic cunning). Lerma's role in decision making was (as noted in the discussion of ambassadors' reports) very much less than is usually said. And, unpalatable though it may be to traditional despisers of the Howards (especially the implacable haters of that 'viper' Northampton), for much of the near-decade of James's reign before Salisbury's death, England's affairs were managed (under the king) by a triumvirate made up of Salisbury, Northampton and Suffolk; as this is perfectly clear in even the most heavily used of the old canonical sources it bears impressive witness to the power of conventional truth to blind and desensitise generations of honest and sensible scholars.

Though we unquestionably know more about the past than we once did, the lamentable fact is that we know very little and understand less. Though it is undoubtedly not the only problem involved, what must be done with regard to this one is clear: expand beyond the canonical sources and content; deny the past canon any special status within the broader scope; and not, in the process, establish a new one.[1] The problem is not one of finding the *right* canon or merely widening the old one, but of freeing research from any such pre-ordained focus—not obliterating historical priorities, certainly, either of source or content, but leaving them always subject to re-examination, modification, and above all further expansion.

THE PROBLEM OF BIAS

Anyone who wishes to test whether unnoticed influences have an effect upon the shape of research needs only to turn to the bibliography of the historical work nearest at hand, place his finger between M and N—the middle of the alphabet—and see if he is not far beyond the middle of the list. What has happened is fairly simple. The preliminary bibliography that an historian compiles is usually larger than needed. He will start working his way through his bibliographical cards until he has satisfied his needs, a point often arrived at (there perhaps being no need to

[1] The third point is far harder to achieve than the first, as any historian knows who has ever found legions of lemming-like would-be researchers breathing down his neck on the track of his own footnotes, and thus been faced with the startling fact that the Petits Fonds 2468, just exploited for the first time, is in danger of being as overworked (to the exclusion of other, still-fresh sources) as any of the older chestnuts have been.

read all forty accounts of the same minor battle) before exploratory bibliography is exhausted. Usually this will have been done in alphabetical order. The same is true where redundancy is concerned: if the same ground is covered equally well in two separate works, either one sufficient for the historian's specific needs, if he calls for only one in a library the odds are that (in orderly-minded logic) he will call for the one by Brown, and only if that is unavailable will he shift to the one by Smith. This tendency is both natural and innocent, and perhaps usually harmless, but it does not mean that when one goes beyond the 'imperative' authors the interpretations espoused, new facts added or aspects emphasised by Aaron or Abercrombie will have greater use and acquire greater currency than those of Zimmerman or Zoepfl.

This is perhaps a relatively harmless matter, but others are more serious in varying degrees and various ways. It is bias of this pragmatic sort—not the conspicuous ones of nationality, religion, and so forth—that I wish to touch upon here. Although there is naturally much overlap, the biases mentioned briefly here— only a few of many such—can be described as of three broad types: personal ones the individual researcher may be affected by, those inherent in archival and other working conditions, and those inherent in the sources themselves.

There is the bias of archival facility which in its effect is one of progressive exhaustion of particular sources. The history of archival exploitation by researchers has been very largely the history of developing archival organisation. In the past this has meant that those sources systematically shelved, and subsequently those with published catalogues, especially those catalogued extensively and analytically, were the ones most frequently used, their collective contents shaping the state which historical knowledge of the subject had reached at any given time. This bias, of course, continually declined in effectiveness as the body of well-organised and publicly catalogued materials has broadened, but it was accompanied by an alternative one: the cumulative exhaustion of sources as the period of repeated use has grown longer (since expanding the body of easily-accessible sources entailed *adding to* the old ones, not abandoning them for the new). One is justified in postulating a loose but generally valid rule: the freshness, and in extreme cases the profitable usability, of catalogued sources can be roughly measured by the publication date on the catalogue's title page.

There is the bias of readily available information about particular sources, principally those associated with more famous men, the availability influenced by the figure's importance in more general history rather than the document's importance to diplomatic history. For example, the *Dictionary of National Biography* (long before Conyers Read's monumental work on the man) indicated where one may find the diplomatic papers of Francis Walsingham, but not those of, for example, Philip or Thomas Hoby or Valentine Dale. Yet one would hesitate to say that Walsingham's three years' service in France (1570–3) were more important than Philip Hoby's two decades (1535–56) of varied and numerous missions to the Emperor, Spain, Portugal, France and Flanders, or that French affairs were important to England only in 1570–3 and not in the decades before (Philip Hoby, 1551; Thomas Hoby, 1566) or the further three years immediately after (Valentine Dale, 1573–6).

There is the bias of irrelevant fame. In the strictest sense one could categorise thus the Walsingham example, since it is not his importance as a *diplomat* that causes the location of his diplomatic papers to be specified in his country's most important (and much used) biographical reference work, though this is not really applicable to a statesman involved in both domestic and foreign affairs. Where it does, however, seem applicable, is in the case of persons whose fame derives from activities totally unrelated to any government affairs. Any diplomatic historian could name, off the top of his head, at least twenty unstudied ambassadors whose diplomatic careers demand study for sound historical reasons pertinent to the history of international relations, but in whom no researcher has yet shown any interest. Yet we are blessed with several serious studies of the diplomatic doings of a man, merely passingly involved in such things, whose fame derives from his mastery at painting fat Flemish women. Similarly, much of the earlier publication of English diplomatic correspondence, much of which has provided the 'standard' documentation for standard English history, tended to be not that of prominent ambassadors per se but that of persons prominent or active in literary pursuits, whose essays, poetry, or whatever, apparently gave a sort of publication impetus that dragged in their diplomatic correspondence as well—and some was actually published to exemplify humanistic style, liberal character, and whatnot. Henry Wotton's diplomatic correspondence, for example, would as such have a fairly low priority for publication.

There is the bias of self-publication, self-promotion, and plain literary fad. One need go no further for an example than that of Cardinal Guido Bentivoglio, whose various 'letters', 'relations', etc., saw countless editions, translations, and publication in various countries, which gave them an even more widespread readership. Almost any library a researcher is apt to use will have several— they are still rather a drug on the old-book market—and they are equally apt to end up in his footnotes. (The present writer is no exception, his use of sources here being no doubt biased by the several Bentivoglio works on his own bookshelves—acquired for about the cost of a meal in a good restaurant.) Another, the Maréchal de Bassompierre, whose various memoirs had wide circulation in the seventeenth century, had his posthumously-published journal republished in the nineteenth as well, and even achieved a two-volume biography.[1]

[1] H. Noel Williams, *A gallant of Lorraine: François, Sr. de Bassompierre, Marquis d'Harouel, Maréchal de France, 1579–1646* (2 vols, London, 1921). The *Mémoires de Bassompierre* (Cologne, 1665) were published as *Journal de ma vie: mémoires* (ed. Marie J. A. de La Cropte, marquis de Chantérac, 4 vols, Paris, 1870–7) by the Société de l'Histoire de France, and in Petitot as well (*2e sér.,* Vols 19–21). Again, the present writer has happily exploited the *Ambassade de Bassompierre en Espagne l'an 1621* (Cologne, 1668), which perhaps illustrates a sort of medium-force influence of availability on sources used: I did not focus upon that particular embassy *because* this convenient volume was available; but because it was I used it instead of either seeking out all the originals or employing alternative published sources.

The bias of availability sometimes reaches the point of outright conspicuousness. There is surely no type of document this is more true of than Instructions to ambassadors. Besides (and because of) their undoubted attractions as sources discussed in Chapter 2, they are the easiest source to come by for nearly any given diplomatic topic in the period. Contemporary secretaries often grouped them in separate files, and later archivists have often assembled further special *liasses* of them, which cataloguers almost always list as such: if for a given period the catalogue lists a hundred *liasses* of vaguely identified 'Letters and Papers' and one of 'Instructions to Ambassadors' and the researcher has time to look at only fifty, or ten, the latter will be among them though the choice of the rest might necessarily be random. (Similarly, when a catalogue, as is common, gives partial lists of each volume's contents, any Instructions found will almost always be noted—the only type of diplomatic document, aside from treaties, for which this is so consistently true.)

The same bias occurs in published documents. An editor may print only a small fraction of an ambassador's correspondence, but he will almost never exclude any Instructions found. Many of the nineteenth-century editors who were particularly active in publishing various kinds of collections of documents published a good many collections of Instructions. The *Recueils des instructions données aux ambassadeurs et ministres de France depuis les traités de Westphalie jusqu'à la Révolution Française*, edited by Albert Sorel, Gabriel Hanotaux and other distinguished scholars and published on a massive scale under government auspices over a period of forty-five years (25 vols in 26, Paris, 1884–1929) is surely the ultimate example. When the temptations and the real virtues of the form as source are coupled with so powerful a combination of comprehensiveness and editorial excellence, and the collection is constantly advertised in citations and even quite short bibliographical lists (e.g., in both editions of the American Historical Association's *Guide to Historical Literature*), then one may be assured that the particular kind of evidence that happens to be therein will weigh more heavily in historical literature than whatever particular kind of evidence, and knowledge, and so forth, is to be had in other documentary forms, less attractive, less conveniently available, less conveniently compact, and less well known.

The favourable bias, however, seems to be limited to ambassadors. By contrast, historians seem to have made little use of analogous materials, such as a volume of 'Instructions that the King of Spain have given . . . to their Viceroys and Governors . . . of Naples and Milan' covering 1559–1668 (BNM MS 6938) or two volumes of 'Letters written by the Kings of Spain to the Viceroys of Sicily' covering 1600–59 (BNM MS 910–11) or similar collections scattered around many archives.

There is the bias of the sources' geographical proximity. That researchers, being both human and faced with practical limitations, will use the sources located nearest them more frequently, more extensively, and perhaps exclusively is obvious, but some of the effects of this are worth noting. The most immediate is that most diplomatic historians deal mainly with the foreign affairs of their own country; the very important corollary of this is that most of the history of any country's foreign affairs is written by natives, most of them imbued with the values, traditions, prejudices and presuppositions of that country. While this need not necessarily result in the extreme distortions of nationalistic history, it still results in national history, which is totally anomalous in international affairs; there is a significant and lamentable lack of (for example) English research in French foreign policy and of French research in English foreign policy—if we must have one-state studies at all. A sports reporter who reported, in detail, one side of a football game without the other would be a laughing-stock; the analogy, though unkind, is quite apropros. International relations are, on the working level of diplomatic exchange, mainly bilateral; on a broader scale they are multilateral for the whole of a given diplomatic system or between or among lesser multilateral combinations within the larger group. The notion of unilateral international relations is patently absurd; unilateral diplomacy is a solitary vice that nature has allowed man the ability to conceive of and to practise in his imagination but not actually to perform.[1]

Unfortunately, even when the diplomatic historian's focus is, as it should be, bilateral or multilateral, the distance of foreign sources—almost all of the archival ones, many and perhaps most of the printed ones—will still (unless he has sufficient time and money for extensive research abroad, or is able to solve the problem with microfilm, or—the best solution—a combination of both) impose a bias in the quality and comprehensiveness of sources used (and their nature—the foreign side will necessarily be limited almost entirely to printed sources, with the limit which this places on choice of 'archival' material), and thus an inequality in familiarity, facts encountered, evidence available, etc.

Unless the bias can be overcome in a positive way (with time, money and film) it can be so only by equalising the disadvantages, working in the affairs of countries other than one's own—but at the price of losing the advantage (bias-producing or not) that one was born with regarding at least one subject country. (American diplomatic historians of early modern Europe automatically gain the virtue of a more equalised accessibility to archival sources without the pain of self-abnegation.) A bias of sources still remains, however, as foreign archives are not equally distant or otherwise equally practicable for a given historian, and the printed sources available at home will be comparably imbalanced: an English library will be better equipped for French history than Spanish, a Spanish library better equipped for French or German or (the bias of historic ties) Belgian history than for English (here the bias of foreign language competence is also at work): the source bias in American libraries will favour England and France, but at a given place could fall in any direction.

One must note one further 'distance bias', seemingly trivial

---

[1] The argument here is of course not that there is anything wrong with an historian's interest in the foreign affairs of his own country, but that he will never find out what they were like by the unilateral approach because that is not what they *were*.

but with considerable, and not particularly admirable, impact on the shape of historical research in the past: the local (intra-country) one. In the past, the more productive historians usually either were attached to the central university, located (on the Continent) in the capital, or, literary figures, resided in that national cultural centre where the national library and usually the principal state archive and some lesser archives were also located. Though many did an enormous *amount* of research, few diplomatic historians bothered with research in local or other archives outside the capital. This inevitably had its greatest effect in Spain: the Archivo General, the official repository of state papers and thus of the vast body of basic and indispensable diplomatic sources, being located in an ancient castle in a small village near Valladolid, far out in Old Castile, almost all diplomatic (and political) history was based almost entirely on sources in the Biblioteca Nacional and a few (excellent but limited) private and other government archives scattered around Madrid. Happily, this effect has been lessened by the growth and high-quality staffing of provincial universities—in the Spanish case, a notable improvement in this remarkable under-use of the nation's principal archive is perhaps due as much to the University of Valladolid as to a sudden onset of scholarly virtue among Madrid-based historical writers—but its effects are still more than they should be, and sometimes not on a cross-country basis but a crosstown one. Some cannot bestir themselves even that far out of their customary milieu; some prefer to do all their work in a place that is both archive and library; and some eminent historians (vanity apparently will not be denied) have confined their research, with unsurprising results, to the one where they happen to have a prestige-bearing reserved seat in the *salle de lecture*.

The principal point intended here, of course, is a didactic one: that this sort of influence should be resisted by researchers who are subjected to it. But two further practical results of the bias may be noticed as well: its inevitable effect on what narrative literature exists for the researcher to draw upon and which documents are already available in printed form; and conversely which sources are largely exhausted and which (sometimes entire collections or even whole archives) remain to be tapped by future researchers, and which subjects remain sufficiently or perhaps entirely unexamined by previous historians.

There is the built-in bias of unequal accessibility of languages for historians, both individually and generally. That the historian with excellent German but no Italian and another with the reverse will choose different areas of study, each appropriate to the language tools possessed, is both natural and desirable. But the effect that the difference would have on their treatment of Swiss affairs, say, or on the sources used for Anglo-French relations beyond those in English and French is a more nebulous and sometimes more treacherous matter.

Beyond individual variations, for the Western historical community as a whole sources used and areas covered are governed largely by comparative familiarity with languages, with frequency and extensiveness naturally diminishing as general familiarity with the area's language is less. The effect of this is perhaps not important where the importance of the area itself to broader history is comparatively slight: there are probably as many historians conversant with Montenegrin or Icelandic as the needs of European history require. But Spain, Poland and Sweden, to cite only three, have an importance in the history of part or all of this period far in excess of historians' ability to deal with evidence in those countries' languages.

When the area involved is important and the language truly remote, the problem becomes still more acute, usually one of availability of translations. For example, Persia in the early seventeenth century was a target of attempted political penetration by Spain and of successful commercial penetration by the English; one can get a good deal of information from the Spanish documents on the former and from many sources, most conspicuously the Purchas collections, on the latter, but for the typical historian of European affairs there is little available— linguistically accessible—from the Persian end. (The shape of the present writer's own research has been similarly affected by his ignorance of Czech—a signal lack during the period when the Bohemian revolt is the principal factor in international affairs.)

An unusually useful example of bias in the handling of documentation is Algernon Cecil's *Life of Robert Cecil, First Earl of Salisbury* (London, 1915) since to its patent religious and national prejudices are added the personal, and since his 'handling' of documents on at least one critical matter—his illustrious ancestor's alleged Spanish pension—involves an absolute refusal to accept what some documents say, as well as what can most charitably be described as calculated ignorance of the facts, a perverse refusal to look at, or into, sources that might confirm the unpalatable allegation.

Through some ten pages (357–66) he works very hard at trying to talk it away: it does not fit Salisbury's honest character; he probably accepted the pension as a trick on the Spanish (presumably compatible with an 'honest character'), etc. The author then tries to clinch this charitable speculation by casting doubt on the matter of actual payment (though the evidence shows him not only getting paid but demanding and getting a rise). 'The evidence against him,' this stout defender of the family honour asserts, 'is all of it ultimately derived from Spanish sources: the memorandum of Villa Mediana instigating and outlining the pensions; the despatches of the Spanish Ambassadors in London reporting their disappointment at the insufficiency and untrustworthiness of the information supplied; and the despatches of the English Ambassador at Madrid, himself much puzzled to read the riddle of the revelations [which, however, he successfully did] and whose considered reflections on the subject are buried for us beneath the symbols of a cipher despatch.[1] [Cecil's footnote] 'What certain proof is there,' the pained descendant asks, 'that money sent over from Spain ever passed out of the hands of the Spanish Ambassadors, and that the alleged complaints of Cecil at the amount of the payments made him were not a fraudulent shift to cover the Ambassador's opportunities of lining his own pockets?'

The latter argument is too outlandish to comment upon, but

the matter of the undecypherable evidence is worth looking at more closely. Cecil's footnote reads: 'S.P. For., Spain. 16th Dec. 1615. Digby to the King. I am not aware of the existence of the key to this cipher.' This raises the question of how badly he really wanted to dig up those 'considered reflections'—or anything else about the matter that might be embarrassing. The letter in question was actually originally sent on 14 December; this version (SP 94/21/198–205v), a signed duplicate dated the 16th, was sent with an English merchant going by sea (see the covering letter at SP 94/21/206); as extra insurance of its safe arrival (both in England and in the king's hands), still another duplicate was later sent by the Spanish post. It is quite true that the crucial passages of this version—the only one to be found at its appropriate chronological place in the State Papers—are in cypher, that they have not been decyphered (as is usual) on the face of it, and that no key is provided. Since the original did arrive safely (or at least we know that its bearer did), and as the duplicate sent later by Spanish post probably arrived before this one, and at least one of those would have been decyphered, there was no need to repeat the job on this one (and, given the sensitive nature of its contents, an undecyphered text would be the most appropriate version to put in the regular files, if any was going to be).

The accuser the author is principally concerned to defend Cecil against is clearly S. R. Gardiner, whose reference to the contents of this document make it reasonably certain that he had read it all, which seems not to have occurred to A. Cecil. There is nothing particularly miraculous about this. The documents near by in the same volume are covered with decyphers of the same cypher used here, the decyphered words written conveniently just above the corresponding indicators. From these a person can make his own cypher key in a matter of minutes, merely noting down the indicators used for each letter of the alphabet; since it is a ridiculously simple cypher anyway, a moderately intelligent child could do it—assuming, of course, that he wanted to. The only thing the author required to get at these 'hidden' contents was the will to know.

Except that he also needed the right document. This one is of December 1615. The Earl of Somerset's troubles were just then commencing, and James had asked Digby for whatever information he might have about Somerset's possible involvement with the Spanish, including the question of accepting a pension; Digby's answer on that point was that, while Salisbury had, so far as he knew Somerset had not. That is, there is no more than passing reference to Salisbury here; the document is about some-one else. The Digby letter to James that *is* the clinching evidence (and was at the time when the pensions were exposed), and which is the one Gardiner cites in that regard, is of December 1613, two years before and 130 pages away in Gardiner's text.[1] One ought to be able to demand a minimum standard from would-be historians, no matter how personally biased they may be: if an author is going to mount a specious, know-nothing attack on other people's use of historical evidence, he ought at least to apply his spurious arguments to the right document. (The author's argument that 'the evidence . . . is all of it ultimately derived from Spanish sources' is beneath comment.)

There is the bias created by the presence of a dominant his-torical personality on a given side or in a given age. For the long period during which Charles V and Francis I were faced off against each other we have the *Correspondenz des Kaisers Karl V. Aus dem Königlichen Archiv und der Bibliothèque de Bourgogne zu Brüssel*

[1] Samuel Rawson Gardiner, *History of England from the accession of James I to the outbreak of the Civil War, 1603–1642* (10 vols, London, 1883–4). At I, pp. 214–15, regarding the establishment of the Spanish pensions in 1604, he cites the Spanish pension-list memo (dated 18 July 1605) that Algernon Cecil refers to (and which does list Salisbury along with the rest), and adds 'Compare [but does not cite in support here] Digby to the King, Sept. 9, 1613 [when Digby was about to discover the details of these pensions], Dec. 16, 1615 [the item Cecil lacked a key to], April 3, 1616, *S. P. Spain.*' At II, 216–17, regarding Digby's discovery of the pensions, he cites Digby to James, 8 August and 24 December 1613. At II, p. 346, in a chapter entirely devoted to Somerset's fall, he makes his only direct use of the challenged document, and exclusively regarding James's query about Somerset, with no mention of Salisbury. Actually, the Digby letter that clinches the matter (Spanish documents being inherently unbelievable) is that of 24 December 1613.

(3 vols, Leipzig, 1844–6) and the *Aktenstucke und Briefe zur Geschichte Kaiser Karls V. Aus dem K. K. Haus- Hof- und Staats-Archiv zu Wien* (Vienna, 1853) edited by Karl Lanz, the *Correspondence of the Emperor Charles V and his ambassadors at the courts of England and France, from the original letters in the imperial family archives at Vienna* (ed. William Bradford, London, 1850), the *Correspondence de Charles-Quint et d'Adrien VI* (ed. L. P. Gachard, Brussels, 1859), which in addition to eighty letters between those two contains another fifty-one from Charles to the Duke of Sessa in Rome, publications from scattered repositories such as the *Recueil de lettres de Charles-Quint conservés dans les Archives du Palais de Monaco* (ed. L. H. Labande, Paris, 1910), and literally carloads of other such published documents by, about, or associated with the emperor who gave his name to the age, but we have precious little on his principal rival. The *Catalogue des Actes de François Ier* (10 vols, Paris, 1887–1908) includes an appended section on 'Ambassades et missions' and its 1,172-page index can be a gold mine, and there is some separate publication of diplomatic documents, including a few early publications, but the quantitative contrast is enormous. The international involvements of Charles V naturally produced a great deal more documentation to begin with than those (and the less developed government machinery) of Francis I did, but the ratio is not that of carloads to handfuls. And even what has been published on the French side often yields to the same bias, as in Guillaume Rebier's century-later publication of *Letters et Mémoires d'Estat des Roys . . . Ambassadeurs et autres Ministres, sous . . . François premier, Henry II & François II* (2 vols, Paris, 1660). Only Volume I pertains to Francis I, and then only to the last decade of his reign; the collection in fact not only does not focus on any French monarch or reign, but does not even pertain to any *French* period in French history, the purpose being, as stated in the subtitle, to publish materials *contenans les intelligences . . . contre les menées de Charles-Quint.*

The same bias works against publication of documents of Francis I's reign compared with more imposing holders of the same throne. We have a nine-volume *Recueil des lettres missives de Henry IV* (ed. J. Berger de Xivrey and Joseph Gaudet, 9 vols, Paris, 1843–76), separate publications such as the *Lettres autographes inédites de Henri IV* (Paris, n.d.), and even a small library of biographical works on the Green Gallant, but no multi-volume 'Recueil des lettres missives de François I', while separate publications, such as the *Nouvelles lettres de la Reine de Navarre [à] François Ier* (ed. F. Genin, Amsterdam, 1842) are as apt to pertain to another as to him—and biographically he is equally apt to appear mainly as the father-in-law of Catherine de Medici.

There is the bias of spectacular events and serious crises such as the Armada campaign or the Battle of the White Mountain. One does not argue, of course, that the Armada sent in 1588 was not more deserving of attention in diplomatic documents than subsequent ones, nor that the overthrow in Bohemia and its ramifications should not, as they did, have dominated ambassadors despatches, nor that historians should not be glad of it: more important events, crises, etc., deserve and require more extensive documentation. Yet one must note two negative effects from the historian's point of view.

Firstly, the miscellaneous information that provides the historian with such marvellous plunder, drops almost entirely from the ambassador's despatches and the councillors' discussions, unless it is directly related to the crisis. The economic, social, cultural and other data that may have been flowing in substantial quantities from foreign embassies in previous years disappear with the advance of the Armada or the pro-Imperial armies, and do not return to their customary quantity until the crisis is past—an irreparable loss of priceless evidence that would otherwise have continued to be routinely produced.

Secondly, such crises not only dominate diplomatic reports, council records, etc., but vastly inflate the quantity of them, often on such a scale as to be simply unmanageable. The historian who could examine, during the time available to him, essentially all the relevant documents dealing with relations among a given group of states over a given period in quieter times simply cannot do so in a time of serious crisis. The choices available to him are simple but inexorable: base the same scope work on fewer documents (and risk going wrong at every turn), reduce the span covered (and the substantive value of the work), cover fewer states (and thus make the result narrower and perhaps nearly worthless), or alternatively, resign himself to spending a lifetime on the subject, or abandon the task entirely. The problem is not eased by the fact that the latter choice will be the least acceptable of all to the serious historian.

Technical factors also affect the quantity produced. French ambassadors may negotiate treaties of comparable importance and generally comparable complexity in, say, Brussels and Madrid. One negotiation may involve matters that require more detailed explanation to Paris (not necessarily more complex: Paris may simply be less familiar with them), and perhaps more detailed replies to the ambassador. One case may involve matters the government insists on approving at every step—thus more correspondence—while in the other the ambassador is left largely on his own. The whole business may be dragged out, the relevant documentation extended, by stalling tactics on one side or the other, dictated by circumstances surrounding one negotiation but not the other. Thus the documentation produced directly relevant to the one treaty may be far greater than the other. Further: at Brussels, 'the crossroads of Europe', the ambassador would encounter a good deal of miscellaneous information, unrelated to the treaty, that should be communicated to the home government—usually far more than at Madrid, stuck out at the end of Europe. Brussels being very near Paris, with quick and frequent mail service, the ambassador might be inclined (or expected) to write far more often than he would from Madrid, and thus apt to include miscellaneous information of a far more trivial nature than he would need to fill less frequent despatches from a more distant place. Either factor inflates the total amount of documentation to be gone through to get at the direct evidence regarding the researcher's subject, the treaty itself. If all of these augmenting factors were to fall on one side and not the other, research of

equal thoroughness might involve ten or twenty times the documentation for one than for the other, though the subjects are so
similar that the evidentiary requirements should be about the
same. One is faced not only with the question of manageability,
but of whether the game is worth the candle.

The Bias of Survival

There is obviously no greater 'bias' in the 'history' that remains
available to us in the form of surviving evidence than the fact that
some survives and some does not. But there is—rather surprisingly
—no across-the-board generalisation that can be made about the
matter that is not either false or without any practical meaning.
The most obvious generalisation is that since documents deteriorate with time, and are subject to the accidents of time, the rate of
survival declines with the age of the document. But under satisfactory archival conditions enough time has not yet passed for the
deterioration of paper of the quality then used (in contrast to
what we use now) whether it is one of 1700 or 1500: the only
'origin' variable involved is the less professional handling at an
earlier date, not the ageing of the materials. The principal time
factor thus touches the date when the document in question
began to be properly stored. One that has reposed under professional care in Simancas since 1550 is younger than one of 1650
or 1750 that spent a century or two mouldering in some dank
London loft or in some Spanish grandee's attic. As to the accidents
of time, as soon as the second (later) document has been produced
it is equally subject to them. Certainly the occasional catastrophe
destroyed no documents subsequently made, but the Napoleonic
plunderers, for example, destroyed or carted off other nations'
records of all periods. As it involves the comparative likelihood
of survival of documents from early or late in this particular
period, the passage of time makes the difference between them
ever smaller: a document of 1570 has been exposed to the ravages
of time for a century longer than one of 1670, but by now both
have shared those of an additional three hundred years—one is
dealing with a decreasing fraction of a document's life.

Other things being equal, documents written on superior quality material should last longer than those on inferior material, which deteriorates faster. But within a given government archive other things are not equal. The fair copy of a letter would be on vellum or high quality paper (or, to a king, perhaps even parchment) with extremely good lasting quality; the draft of it would have been made on lower grade and less durable paper; any memos of instruction regarding it would usually, unless there were scraps of better stuff around, have been written on mere junk paper which quickly becomes brittle to the touch and falls apart under all but the gentlest handling. But a fair copy would have gone through the mails (*to* this government, since the archive is the constant), and probably have been read by several people, handled by secretaries and clerks making minutes, copies, extracts, etc., and might be moved from one temporary file to another several times before being put in the permanent files, and even then might be pulled out again for later consultation, adding up to a considerable amount of handling; the draft, by contrast, instead of having been sent through the mails and handed about on arrival would have been put directly into the files, and even later removal for consultation might be less than for originals; while inter-office memos, if they were kept at all, would rarely ever be looked at again and repose, fragile but undisturbed, down to the present—in no great amount, but probably as high as the other two types in proportion to the numbers anyone *intended* to preserve.

In correspondence directly between governments, from one ruler to another, the type of repository used for both originals and drafts being a 'constant' (government archive as distinct from private collection), the principal variable in the question of which form of the correspondence is most apt to survive is contemporary use. Since filing of the draft in the sender's archive would normally be done directly after the fair copy was struck, while filing of the latter in the recipient's archive would typically be after having been handed around a good deal among ministers, hangers-on at court, etc., the original should be far more subject to loss than the draft (and its filing perhaps less routinely auto-matic). But any generalisation to that effect is rendered meaning-less by variables at both ends, and the difference in materials used.

On the other hand, for every letter sent there was by definition an original, but not necessarily a draft; one may merely use the draft of letter A sent earlier to the same or another monarch as the draft for letter B (such letters were largely formula, and limited to only a few purposes at that level, more *nuancés* matters being conveyed through ambassadors), leaving no draft for the latter; or the draft of letter A might be altered as needed, giving B a draft in the files but depriving A of its draft. And even if both A and B had drafts, the likelihood of their being subsequently removed from the files for consultation in writing later corre-spondence is far greater than that of later consultation of originals (the chances might be equal regarding policy decisions, but far greater for drafts as clerical references), which entails an un-questionably sound generalisation: a document removed from its archival resting-place is more apt to be lost than one left alone. On the other hand, copies are far more likely to have been made of originals than of drafts (in the case of important documents perhaps several), increasing not the chances of survival of the original itself, but of some form of the document in the recip-ient's archives. And the cheap paper used for a draft will have deteriorated far faster than the vellum or even parchment used for the fair copy sent.

Comments upon the survival of diplomatic documents (or state papers in general) almost invariably note that officials commonly treated as their own property those addressed to them and the file copies of those they wrote, and so took them with them. This is indeed true, and a source of justifiable annoyance and much inconvenience to researchers, and much un-doubted loss. But it is not a wholly one-sided affair. But remain-ing in the original government repository and survival are not necessarily the same thing, as witness, for England, the collectively massive documentation still surviving in private hands covered by the many reports of the Historical Manuscripts Commission and the numerous large collections that have eventually made their way to the British Museum.

One clearly must distinguish between 'improper' and destructive actions: it is impossible to know how much has been lost that otherwise would have been saved, or conversely how much may have been saved that would have been lost in government hands, but it is hard to believe that the Salisbury papers, for example, would have fared better in the Tower of London than in Hatfield House. In addition, many private collections run heavily to copies specially made for one's own collection that would not have been made for the government files anyway.

Private residences are presumably more subject than government archives to the ordinary hazards of life (an apt analogy would be the far higher rate of survival of art work in churches than in private hands); the best-known English example is perhaps the loss by fire of part of the famous collection of Robert Cotton. But this did not happen until 1731, exactly one hundred years after his death; the collection in the meantime had been used extensively by scholars during a time when there were no regular facilities for researchers' access to records—the Cotton library had in fact been opened to the public in 1700; and the loss was much exaggerated by contemporary rumour and subsequent tradition, in contrast to which the report of the Commons committee appointed the next year to examine the remains 'states that out of a total of 958 volumes of manuscripts, 746 were unharmed, 114 totally destroyed or injured, and 98 partially injured'. The library was turned over to the British Museum on its founding in 1753, and after some failures: 'In 1824 a new attempt was made to restore the burnt fragments, but it was not till 1842 that a successful method of repairing them was applied. Under Sir Frederick Madden's care 100 volumes on vellum and 97 on paper were renovated, and among them the valuable fourth-century manuscript of Genesis, and the chronicle of Roger of Wendover, both of which were assumed to have been destroyed.' In contrast, in Cotton's own lifetime a fire in Whitehall (1619) destroyed years of Privy Council papers, with no hope of restoration. Contemporary borrowers apparently failed to return a good many of Cotton's manuscripts, but government archives were also subject to borrowing (and borrowers' forgetfulness), and far more tempting targets for outright pilferage; much of the Cotton collection itself was in fact accumulated by one or the other of these processes.

During times of troubles private papers are often lost in the sacking of residences. This is itself rather a matter of random decision of loss and survival by the fortunes of war, but attempts to avoid such loss also have random results. Many papers were hidden, some never to be found, some to deteriorate in whatever hole was available to cache them in; yet some have been recovered in the most improbable fashion: one retired ambassador spent his last years in quarters in Lincoln's Inn. Some years later, in the course of making repairs, workmen found his diplomatic correspondence hidden in the ceiling, apparently put there to avoid seizure during the Civil War disorders.

Chance has affected documents in government care as randomly as those in private hands. As the French Revolution rolled north, the government of the Austrian Netherlands—with revolt at home and French invasion threatening—sent as much as it could of its archives to safety abroad, mainly in the Northern Netherlands, but some scattered about in other places such as Wezel as well; at the end of 1790 even some of the local revolutionaries gathered up part of the archives for transport to The Hague. As soon as the situation was seemingly restored they were brought back to Brussels, but with prospects worsening again, as much as possible of these enormous archives was loaded into wagons in a desperate effort to get them to safety in Vienna. Some of these caravans, fleeing this way and that from the shifting tides of war, actually bounced about over a good part of central Europe for a decade. In contrast, in the early seventeenth century the Spanish government of Sicily chose to transfer some documents by ship from Palermo to Messina. The Austrian shipment was a makeshift emergency flight under impossible conditions, yet all the wagons eventually arrived safely, the documents in remarkably good shape. The Sicilian one was a simple routine operation, but all the documents were lost at sea. Clearly the only generalisations one could make about such cases would be with regard to the whims of the gods.

One might describe as a bias the constant fluctuation in international relations, as it entails a constant warping of the diplomatic system and thus of the documentation produced by it: not only the contents of documents but their very existence is biased (as of any one time) by who happens to have embassies where. Nothing, of course, affects this more than a state of hostilities, during which 'normal, peaceful' relations were officially broken off. This is of course quite natural, but its importance to the pattern of diplomatic documentation is as great as the size of the anomaly involved. The anomaly hinges upon the distinction between international relations and international relationships, for a state, oddly enough, may have relations with any other state except the one with which its relationship is most critical of all—the one with which it is at war. For evidence of 'the last stage of diplomacy' one must go to the sources of military history. (The oblique results of this lack are also important to the researcher: when two states are at war with each other there are no reports from exchanged ambassadors giving news about third parties and other matters.)

And there is the warp that domestic circumstances may cause in a state's foreign relations, the documentation thereby produced, and the handling of it. For reasons that mainly amount to the accidents of birth and death, after 1516 the Duke of Burgundy had no foreign relations with the King of Spain, and in 1519–56 the Emperor had none with either; other rulers of course sent one ambassador to all three. The handling of French foreign affairs and of their records was inevitably far less orderly during the religious civil wars than it was after 1598—a fact which makes French diplomacy under Henry III and under Louis XIV very different as subjects *and* in the practical problems research in them entails. Dutch success in rebellion added a new and important member to the international community and the diplomatic system, but subsequent commercial success led to breaks in diplomatic relations with a traditional ally, England, and corresponding gaps in the documentation: quite apart from Anglo-Dutch relations, the English ambassador's usual reports from his listening-post in The Hague about events in France, Germany and elsewhere, extremely valuable sources (as other comparable ones are), become suddenly unavailable to the historian for times when there was no English ambassador there.

MISCELLANEOUS PROBLEMS

Reading the Documents

It is unfortunate that palaeography was long ago elevated to the level of abstruse science, when in fact it is merely a matter of becoming accustomed to handwriting different from what one is used to.[1] A short cut can be had in familiarising oneself with the particular kinds of hands one is apt to encounter in research by resort in advance to some of the numerous manuals on the subject,[2] but the main result of this is not to 'learn' the hands but

---

[1] This is true for the period in question here, especially after one is a few years into the sixteenth century (the problem of simply learning to *read* manuscript hands is far more difficult in the fifteenth and rather unevenly becomes easier in the earlier part of the sixteenth). But medieval palaeography is indeed another matter, not only because of similar difficulties but because of its importance in dating, identifying and analysing documents, which is true of the later period also but less frequently and in a more routine manner. Similarly, the comments made further on regarding over-analysis of documents do not apply to those of the medieval period, where it is often the only route to understanding them and where quantity does not raise the practical problem referred to. At the same time, given the undoubted importance of palaeography to medieval historiography, its inflated status in later periods may fairly safely be credited largely to the old tradition of giving a medieval training to historians destined to work in any period.

[2] Paul J. Lehmann, *Zur paläographie und Handschriftenkunde* (Munich, 1909) deals with Latin palaeography and handwriting, with a history of the former. Maurice Prou, *Manuel de paléographie latine et française du sixième au dix-septième siècle* (Paris, 1889; 3rd ed. Paris, 1910) also has a useful bibliography. Hubert Hall, *Studies in English official historical documents* (Cambridge, 1908) is an admirable pioneer work in its field, which he followed with *A formula book*

to speed up one's entry into them; like most other 'skills', real working facility comes only with use in practice. And, like most skills, once it is acquired one wonders what all the fuss was about. In spite of a certain awe one continues to hear expressed of 'palaeographic experts', that expertise is rather like that required for riding a bicycle. Both are acquired by doggedly persisting and continually falling off until all at once one does not fall off any

of *English official historical documents* (2 vols, Cambridge, 1908–9; I, diplomatic documents; II, ministerial and judicial records).

Charles T. Martin, *The record interpreter* (London, 1910) lists abbreviations, Latin words, names, etc., used in historical documents in England. Among more extensive efforts for individual countries the palm surely goes to Joã P. Ribeiro (ed.), *Dissertações chronógicas e críticas sôbre a história e jurisprudência ecclesiastica e civil de Portugal* (5 vols, Lisbon, 1810–36). See also Filemón Arribas Arranz, *Paleografía Documental Hispanica* (2 vols, Valladolid, 1965). For other aspects of 'diplomatics' see, e.g., Joseph Vendryes, *La langue: introduction linguistique à l'histoire* (Paris, 1921), in English as *Language: a linguistic introduction to history* (translated by Paul Radin, London, 1925); André Lange and E.-A. Soudart, *Traité de Cryptographie* (Paris, 1925; new ed. Paris, 1935); and Wilson R. Harrison *Suspect documents: their scientific examination* (New York, 1958). One of the more ignored aids for dating events is A. M. H. J. Stokvis, *Manuel d'histoire de généalogie et de chronologie de tous les états du globe depuis les temps les plus reculés jusqu'à nos jours* (3 vols in 4, Leyden, 1888–93), which in its some 2,300 pages also identifies a great many persons and (conversely) holders of prominent positions. For translating vaguely expressed dates (e.g., as some obscure feast day) one needs a different sort of aid, such as A. Cappelli, *Cronologia, cronografia e calendario perpetuo* (Milan, 1930). What is argued here is of course not that palaeography is unimportant but that it is only the technical beginning in reading documents aright, that that facility cannot be acquired adequately solely through manuals, and that it is only the beginning of the background that the historian actually needs. Ultimately he needs also to resort to works and aids such as A. Himply, *Histoire de la formation territorial des États de l'Europe centrale* (2nd ed., 2 vols, Paris, 1894); Gerald Strauss, *Sixteenth Century Germany: its topography and topographers* (Madison, Wisc., 1959); L. Mirot, *Manuel de géographie historique de la France* (Paris, 1929); E. Bullon, *Los geógrafos en el siglo XVII* (Madrid, 1925). For more specialised matters reference tools are often harder to come by, as for example F. Vindry's *Dictionnaire de l'état-major français au XVIe siècle*, which never got beyond the *Première partie: Gendarmerie*, published in two volumes in 1901, and that was published rather crazily, an octavo Volume I in Paris and, for some reason, a quarto Volume II in Bergerac; the latter, which contains important tables, is extremely difficult to find.

more, after which point the skill will improve with continued use but the question of ability per se to read old documents or ride a bicycle is a watershed passed. One in fact does not have to read them for very long before one inevitably surpasses the quantity one happens to have read in more modern hands and especially current ones, in which the educational fashion shifts quite frequently; the mundane nature of 'palaeography' becomes obvious when the historian discovers that he has less trouble reading sixteenth-century documents than he has reading his students' exam papers, written in some short-lived modish hand that came into style only ten or fifteen years before and is only now reaching the university level.

Perhaps the principal technical reason that adequate familiarity can be acquired only in the documents themselves is that the distinction necessarily made in palaeographical manuals, and formally taught then, between various types of hands used for different purposes in the same time and place, was not very strictly maintained in practice. Martin Billingsley, for example, in *The Pens Excellencie, or the Secretary's Delight* (1618), specifies six principal types—the Secretary ('the usuall hand in England'); the Bastard Secretary, or Text; the Roman ('usually taught to women, because they are phantasticall and humorsome'); the Italian ('meere botching and detestable'); the Court (so called because it was used in the courts of King's Bench and Common Pleas); and the Chancery—but what is perhaps more significant is that some of these classifications have additional subdivisions, for in practice they were not all that distinct. A given office might normally use a particular hand for its documents, but the stronger training of one scribe in Secretary hand and another in text, simple personal preferences for certain usages in one or the other, and even the difference between the training in the same hand between a scribe of sixty and another of twenty would all show up in their writing, producing considerable variation on the supposedly uniform calligraphy of a given office at a given time; to say nothing of the fact that higher ranking ministers might have been trained in some completely different hand and use that, or some attempted compromise between them. Thus from a pragmatic point of view the 'secretarial' hand used by a given secretariat at a given time should be understood as the quite variable one they did use rather than the rigidly-defined one they were nominally supposed to use. All the variations and combinations could not possibly be set down in a palaeographicl manual, and even if they were one would not know which applied until one got into a particular set of documents.

Formal palaeographical training, however, can help considerably with the standard usages, especially common abbreviations such as the lingering medieval 'X' or 'Xp' for 'Christ', as in '*Xpiandad*', the distinction in Spanish between VM (*Vuestra Majestad*) and *Vm* (*Vuestra merced*, the third person plural since contracted to *usted*, applicable in this period to commoners), and more obscure ones are learned fairly quickly in reading the documents themselves.

Some, however, are less systematic, or even aberrations in writing, and coping with these can require more thorough familiarity. For example, Roman numerals were often written in connected minuscule, so that four appears as a longhand iiii. This would pose no problem, but often a fancy flourish is added, a downstroke that gives the final i the appearance of a longhand j, 'four' coming out iiij; this would pose no problem either except that the scribe often preceded this final downstroke with a little upstroke that is identical to that of an i (and with the downstroke identical to a j) except for its not being dotted; thus to discover whether what appears to be iiij is the Roman equivalent of 4 or 3, one must count not only the i-like upstrokes but the dots over them—and hope one can distinguish between intentional dots, splattered ink, age spots and fly specks. If it is a matter of iiij hundred thousand pounds sterling the distinction can be an important one.

Perhaps the trickiest problem in reading diplomatic documents, however, is not that of knowing what they say but what they mean. Although the forms in which this problem occurs are numerous, one might mention five common ones here.

(1) *Contemporary usage of ordinary words* Many words of course have since altered their meaning or shifted to a broader or narrower application. Though both are perhaps at the simplest level of understanding contemporary usage of a language, the latter can be troublesome as the shift is not always so obvious. Modern usage of 'treaty', for example, is usually restricted in such a way that it does not apply to truces, but early modern usage was not so restricted, failure to recognise which has made it possible to understand the 'treaty of Vaucelles' of 1556 to be a peace settlement when in fact it was only a truce.

(2) *Archaic usages* There was a good deal of archaic usage—largely stylistic conceits—especially with regard to place names, the result of which, if one is not familiar with them, is not misunderstanding but mystification. If one reads, for example, that someone went from Aquisgran to Argentina, it may be well to know that he went from Aachen to Strassburg.

(3) *Colloquial usage* Everyone knows that 'Flanders' was commonly used generically for the entire Netherlands, and for the southern part after the split, and that 'Holland' was thereafter used generically for the northern provinces; the distinction between the *pays de pardeça* (the Netherlands) and the *pays de pardelà* (the Free County of Burgundy) is fairly well known; but at a time when Spain had Indies in two hemispheres and the Dutch were tampering with both, it is not very obvious in a Spanish document about the Dutch that '*las Islas*' refers to the United Provinces (a broad application of what really means 'the islands of Holland and Zeeland').

(4) *Imprecise usage* Some imprecise usage is sufficiently obvious to be easily detected. The Spanish were inclined to refer to all Protestants as *Luteranos*, rather as the American extreme right calls everyone to the left of them Communists and the extreme left everyone to the right of them Fascists: one quickly learns that the term *Luterano* does not exclude Calvinists and others of that heretic ilk. But many cases are not so obvious. The English had a habit of calling whatever place had been most recently discovered (by them) Newfoundland, so that what 'Newfoundland' means

in an English document depends on when it is being used, and even then it might be used for more than one place at one time, an older one still being so referred to. By the early seventeenth century, for example, Newfoundland usually means Spitzbergen —which at least is somewhat clearer than the Spanish documents, which usually call it Greenland.

(5) *Foreign approximations* The preposterous habit of trans-mogrifying into one's own language the names of places (*Cordoue*) and even persons (*le duc d'Albe*) has a more understandable corollary in this earlier period. In the case of places or persons that would be unfamiliar to the reader, the inclination in the diplomatic reports was to reproduce them accurately, but—perhaps because spelling in general was quite variable (a person might even spell his own name several different ways) and so seemed a less fixed and integral identifying characteristic than pronunciation—this was usually done by spelling phonetically in one's own language to reproduce in that language as nearly as possible the sound (not the spelling) of the foreign name: that is, not transforming the word to fit one's own linguistic pattern, as in the English 'Seville', but spelling it in a way that would most nearly preserve the correct pronunciation according to the spelling/pronunciation rules of one's own language (Seveeya). Sometimes this phonetic approximation is fairly obvious, as when the place after which the prime meridian was later named comes out Granuche in Spanish; sometimes apparently no more than a doubtful joke, as in calling the port at the north-west corner of Spain The Groin in English; and sometimes it has even become permanent in foreign usage: everyone—except, probably, an Italian—knows where Leghorn is. But in the case of more obscure places and of the sounds hardest to reproduce in the other language, identification can require reliable confirmation from the context (if one fortunately knows where the event in question happened) or from another source. A still greater uncertainty is introduced when two different sounds are necessarily reproduced in the same way. As Spanish has neither the letter K nor the sound '-ing', the English name King was normally spelled *Quin* (pronounced Keen); as this was as

close as one could come it was reasonable spelling, but Spanish ambassadors to England also had frequent occasion to make mention of Irishmen in their despatches, so that (other evidence lacking) Quin might very well mean what it says.

The above are all technical linguistic matters of letter formation, abbreviations, word usage, spelling customs, etc. In the broad area of familiarity it goes without saying that in order to get the full and correct meaning from the documents the researcher needs to be familiar with the issues at stake, the forces at work, and other such major substantive things (as defined in the documents, not *a priori*) at the opposite end of the spectrum of importance. What is perhaps less obvious as regards the factual content of documents is the overwhelming importance of trivia. That importance in practice may be illustrated by single practical examples of four important types, involving the need for familiarity with: (a) norms of conduct, etc., in a given setting so that the significance or implications of actions in that context may be accurately understood; (b) the attitudes, etc., of the writer, especially towards the recipient, and sometimes vice versa (the association of either with the subject matter being written about is obviously crucial); (c) miscellaneous personal trivia about the individuals involved in the correspondence; and (d) the broad spectrum of business, no matter how remote from the main issues of foreign policy, that such correspondence (or whatever type of document) might cover at that particular time. (For obvious reasons, the examples chosen are some that happen to have come up in the course of my own research.)

(a) There is perhaps no more glaring example of historians misunderstanding the implications of an individual's actions than that of James I of England, as in the case of his taking his hat off to receive foreign ambassadors. That historians have been overly eager to read an obsequious attitude into this to fit their preconceptions is rather baldly apparent in the fact that they mention it only in connection with the Spanish ambassador, and only one of those, that object of hatred and Machiavellian caricature Gondomar, when in fact James did it, of course, with all foreign ambassadors. 'Of course' because it was routine protocol for an adult male monarch to do so: to fail to do so was a very specific and very strong declaration of anger with the ambassador or with his government, not too far short of a threat of breaking off relations, but historians of that reign have managed somehow not to know that. The latter fact makes this a particularly useful example not only of the trivia aspect (here involving mere ritual, not a matter of substance) of the proper extraction of the correct meaning from documents, but of four others as well: the unwisdom of carrying preconceived notions to the sources, of taking for one's own the prejudices of the time, of taking an insularly national approach, and of too confidently assuming that one's sources, prejudices aside, knew what they were talking about. The application of this first example is obvious. That the historians shared with contemporaries both anti-Catholic and anti-Spanish prejudices (as well as anti-James ones) is equally so. Had they been less insular and looked beyond England at the time they would have discovered the obvious, that the king's 'obsequious' behaviour was common European protocol, and would instead have recognised as exceptional and therefore significant any departure from it, not normal conformity to it. And had they done this they would, of course, have realised that their sources, in addition to being hostile commentators and therefore doubtful ones, did not themselves know what was usual conduct at an adult male court, there having been none in England since 1547, sixty-six years before the 1613 incident in question and thus before most of the critics were even born (and they in the nature of things had of course seen little of court customs in the previous years of James's reign).[1] The historian, who is properly the judge of his sources, not the regurgitator thereof, clearly needs not only to be sufficiently familiar with custom (and much else) to understand the actual meaning of a document's contents but to be able to judge the same familiarity of the writers of those documents.

[1] Protocol was not precisely the same in all times and places, nor was what was locally 'recognised' always adhered to, variations in practice which provide a rough but useful index of the degree to which given states partici-

(b) Regarding attitudes: A letter from the Archduke Albert, nominal co-sovereign of the southern Netherlands (1598–1621), thanking Philip III of Spain for having granted a favour Albert had requested for a third party, closes '*Beso los pies de Vuestra Majestad.*' Verbal foot-kissing of the Spanish king was mere court formula at the time, a completely conventional closing to what seems a routine bread-and-butter acknowledgment of a routine favour granted, indistinguishable from countless others like it. (The format of the letter as a whole is in fact a standard one for such business.) But if one is familiar enough with their relationship to know that Albert detested his royal brother-in-law, in his opinion an upstart of no discernible merit who had inherited a throne that would otherwise have gone to Albert's wife Isabel, and *never*, ordinarily, used this obsequious convention, its use (mandatory for practically anyone else) immediately alerts one to the fact that he is much more than ordinarily grateful, that the request in question was apparently quite out of the ordinary and should be looked into further by the researcher.

(c) Regarding personal trivia: A letter from an ambassador is clearly to one of two secretaries of state but does not indicate which one; as they belong to competing court factions, the implications of the letter (the meaning itself) would be radically

pated in the mainstream of diplomatic activity. For example: after the initial formalities of the ambassador's presentation were over the monarch normally put his hat back on, and according to hat protocol in the West the ambassador, being symbolically the alter ego of his own monarch, could do likewise; but on one occasion in the late sixteenth century the Russian emperor, claiming superiority of rank over the mere king of France, refused the French ambassador permission to cover, and when the latter did so anyway the Tsar was reported to have met the affront by having the ambassador's hat nailed to his head. The aggressive gambits employed by the English ambassador, Sir Jerome Bowes (d. 1616), on hearing of this, and indeed throughout his residence (he was not allowed to carry a sword at his initial audience, so 'since he might not go as a soldier', he went in his nightgown, nightcap and slippers) were by contrast not only tolerated but highly successful, gaining him high regard not only at home but from the Tsar himself; some of the more outrageous incidents on both sides are conveniently summarised in the *Dictionary of National Biography* (*sub* Bowes), with references to fuller accounts.

different depending upon the addressee. Fortunately, in a formula that almost always refers to the addressee's wife the writer closes by sending his respects to '*mi señora doña Constanza*' : fortunately, that is, if the researcher knows that one possibility is married to a Constanza, the other to a Beatriz. There are few facts less important to history per se than the Christian name of a secretary's wife, but in a case such as this it can be of critical importance in the process of *writing* history.

(d) Regarding miscellaneous business: A Spanish ambassador makes some bland-seeming comments about someone he calls '*el vecino de Bilbao*' (literally, 'the resident of Bilbao'), an oblique reference that would not normally excite any particular notice on the part of the researcher. As ambassadors (including this one) often gave considerable attention to the literary quality of their correspondence, and as stylistic conventions of the time favoured an occasional cryptic reference (often a joking allusion to a mutual acquaintance) there is nothing at all sinister to suggest that the writer is being designedly secretive here, nothing to alert the researcher to any special importance of the subject nor to any important meaning in the seemingly routine remarks about some unnamed person. '*Vecino*', of course, also means 'neighbour', but that would refer to a neighbouring *city*, and as it is obviously a person being spoken of that would make no sense at all. Unless —there is always an 'unless' in cases like this—one is aware of a carefully-suppressed scandal involving a government clerk in Madrid recently caught stealing documents for the English ambassador—and that his name was Josef de Santander. Then a seemingly banal passage comes to life, and turns out to be loaded with import for the whole of Spanish policy at the time.

Authenticity and Authoritativeness

Among the manuscript sources in question here, the problem of 'authenticity' is mainly limited to that of whether a given unidentified document is really a copy of some unseen 'original' or only an excerpt or summary or even an early draft. Forgery— the type of problem that comes most readily to mind in connection with 'authenticity'—is extremely rare, and then seldom a danger to the researcher. Modern forgeries are rare simply because the sheer quantity of authentic documents would make their scarcity value nil, and most of the people writing them are too obscure to have any 'star' value. A document purportedly signed by someone of the rank of Queen Elizabeth or Philip II might find a buyer, but any archive interested in purchasing documents, even if the forgery went undetected, would not be interested in only one or a few unless the contents were rather unusual, in which case the forgery almost certainly *would* be detected. None of this would prevent their being palmed off on an oil millionnaire who wanted them for his private library; but few historians (alas) travel in those circles anyway.

As indicated elsewhere, some diplomatic correspondence was intercepted and altered, and whole documents were occasionally forged, and these can present a problem for the historian, but as also stated elsewhere those shenanigans could not, in the nature of things, be practised successfully for very long, and often there were overriding reasons not to practise them at all. Thus contemporary forgeries are also very rare. They are also usually fairly readily known to the historian: they can themselves sometimes be quite important historical facts, but they are not particularly important in the long run as pitfalls in research.

The problem of authenticity of *contents*, however, is quite another matter. In a variety of ways and for a variety of reasons diplomatic documents, including correspondence both from and to ambassadors, were often intended to deceive. Some examples of intentional deception written into an ambassador's formal Instructions have been discussed in Chapter 2. Later letters to the ambassador could be equally deceptive, intended to mislead a monarch or minister it might be formally shown to, or any of their agents who might get a look at it. One might write an entirely false letter (which the ambassador would know to be so, and thus not himself be misled by), but one needs the ring of truth—of documentary authenticity—to make such a gambit convincing. The better way, therefore, was to incorporate the falsehoods into the regular, authentic letter to the ambassador, along with all the usual routine things found in such a letter and with as much verifiable truth as could be safely revealed, and to write a second letter to accompany the first one, advising the ambassador of (for example) what the government's policy decision had *really* been. The former would then be formally shown, or just left lying about in the embassy for prying eyes to see. Whether the ploy was successful or not in any given case, the second letter will clear the matter up for the researcher—provided, of course, the ambassador did not do the security-conscious thing and destroy it. One encounters fairly frequent examples of the overriding letter, but there is simply no way of knowing how many others have not survived and thus how many authentic *documents* with falsified *contents* continue to deceive unknowing readers as they were intended to deceive certain contemporary ones.

An ambassador's own reports home or his letters to others can be equally disingenuous. At one point during Gondomar's tenure in England the Duke of Savoy published a small volume of letters from the King of Spain to his governor in Milan, outlining warlike Spanish plans in Northern Italy that belied their publicly proclaimed peaceful ones. One can learn from Gondomar's letters to Madrid and to the Governor of Milan and to other ambassadors and officials abroad exactly how the letters were obtained. The Madrid-Milan courier normally went by land as far as Villefranche and then skirted the mountains and the Savoy neighbourhood by taking a ship to Genoa, then proceeded by land. On this occasion the courier arrived a bit late at Villefranche and missed the ship he had intended to go on, and during the delay while he was waiting for the next ship to depart for Genoa some of the Duke of Savoy's agents waylaid him and seized the letters. Gondomar wrote to all sorts of people complaining that this was a dismal thing to do, and in the process spelling out all this detail. The fact that the dates of the published letters ranged over a far longer period of time than any single despatch would normally ever contain can be explained by saying that some of them were duplicates of letters sent earlier. All of which is very interesting and certainly explains the matter, except that the documents were stolen in Madrid from government files by the same Josef de Santander mentioned earlier. It was in fact the one-too-many coup, betrayed by publication, that led to Santander's discovery and downfall (an habitual gambler with heavy losses, he had taken this extra job with a second employer and, caught, was thus lost to John Digby's services). Gondomar's concern, since no one would believe a public denial of the authenticity of the letters themselves, was to save as much face for Spain as possible by at least concealing the fact, which he found horribly shaming, that there had been a spy—one of the king's own subjects—right in the centre of Spanish government. His proposed solution, instead of letting the matter leak out in the course of a formal trial or even summary punishment, was to suppress the whole matter by hiding Santander away in some dark dungeon in one of Spain's African possessions (which was apparently actually done) and, to eliminate that problem of secrecy, lock his wife away in the remotest mountain nunnery that could be found (I am in fact uncertain what actually became of her). And to divert attention from the true locale of the deed he wrote the alternate facts of the case to all sorts of people. To those he trusted he admitted the fabrication (usually separately) and urged them to spread it around in the same plausibly outraged fashion. But if the researcher has not seen these references to other (unspecified) actual facts and is not acquainted with the Santander incident he is apt to read these very convincing accounts of what happened as they were meant to be read, as the actual facts of the matter. The documents are authentic and the event is authentic; all that is false are the facts.

During the same period James I found a serious (pro-Spanish) security problem in his own Privy Council, so he withheld from their usual perusal all the despatches from his ambassador in Madrid, John Digby. As they began to be troublesome about it, it became necessary for Digby to send reports for them to read. Thus there is a long stretch in Digby's reports when it is often unclear how much is for real and how much just to keep the Privy Councillors busy and happy.

Even when the contents are not intended to be deceptive they still pose a question of reliability, especially that of authoritativeness, particularly in ambassadors' despatches. As these comprise the greater part of diplomatic documentation, were governments' principal source of factual information for the conduct of their affairs, and are often the historian's principal source not only for diplomatic history but for at least some aspects of the wide spectrum of subjects reported upon—political, economic, and so forth—the quality of the information they report is obviously important to the researcher. And the inevitable fact is that the authoritativeness varies a great deal from one ambassador to another, from one subject to another with regard to given individuals, and in a broader way according to what country the ambassador represents regardless of the individual, and what country he is reporting from.

Although some of them overlap a bit at the edges, one may distinguish five basic types or sources of information to be put into these reports: (1) Matters of common knowledge—publicly circulated news and rumour, especially that derived from the almost institutionalised exchange of 'gossip' (not then so pejorative a term) among individuals, often the most important local medium of news circulation in the period. (2) Publicly available knowledge that the ambassador specially collected, the sort of information governments now get (in addition to consular reports) through the shipping columns, financial pages, obituary notices, and other pertinent sections of the local newspapers, from published government statistical reports, and so on. (3) Lower-level contacts in and around the court—in a position to hear things and sometimes to witness them, but not themselves of the decision-making inner group—who, if sympathetic or suborned, might pass on the information available to them. (4) Top people, who were in a position to know first hand of the more secret events, plans, etc., because they had a direct hand in them. (5) Espionage, especially as an alternate route to information otherwise available only to the inner group. There was great variety in use of and access to these various sources.

The best known and most widely used ambassadorial sources are those of the Venetians, large numbers of their reports having been calendared by the nations reported from, some *diarii* published, and, best known of all, the *Relazioni* they delivered to the Doge and Senate on their return from individual embassies, which were quite numerous as these rotated quite frequently. This is appropriate in one sense, as the Venetian ambassadors were assiduous reporters, collecting and relaying information on a wide variety of subjects great and small, often in considerable detail. They were particularly thorough in collecting large quantities of information that was locally common knowledge or otherwise publicly available (the first two types mentioned above). But for inside information about, for example, coming changes in government policy, Venetian envoys usually had to rely on the same public sources or, at best, low-level contacts in government service. They seldom had *entrée* to the inner circles of government, nor did they have much of an espionage apparatus compared to some others. Thus the historian simply cannot give the same credence to a Venetian report on the secret actions or intentions of the host government that he more safely can to one on, say, shipping movements.

For others, access to restricted knowledge was imbalanced in other ways. Around the beginning of the Thirty Years' War the Brussels envoy to London had a highly developed spy apparatus but had little direct access to highly placed persons, while the Spanish resident had high level *entrée*, including frequent access to the king himself, but made little use of spies.[1] As they represented two branches of the same firm this was a nicely complementary matching of strengths and weaknesses, but not of course for the historian using only one of the two sets of reports. Further, with the English court factions split along foreign policy lines, the Spanish ambassador's access was mainly to those favouring a

---

[1] A situation I have described in *The Secret Diplomacy of the Habsburgs, 1598–1625* (New York, 1964), especially Chapters 10 and 11.

Spanish alliance; the French ambassador also had access to Privy
Councillors and such, but mainly the pro-French ones, especially
the Scots at court; the access of the Dutch resident was also of
course among the anti-Spanish group, but with emphasis not
among the Scots but among the English Calvinists and near-
Calvinists. This is of course true of other places as well as England:
in the 1580s and 90s the Spanish ambassador to France was often
more an envoy to the Catholic League than to the king. These
various groups not only gave different slants to the information
they gave, but their own access to information of any reliability
was often on entirely different matters. In Spain, in fact, foreign
ambassadors seem to have had little access, social or otherwise, to
top ministers and other knowledgeable officials, or even to
routine information directly, in considerable contrast, for example to London. The Spanish ambassador in London got his
information on trade, customs laws, and such directly from the
English (no doubt partly because it was more readily available
there, partly because there were almost no Spanish nationals
resident to help him), while the English ambassador to Madrid
got most of his comparable information from English merchants
in Spain. And the variation could also be personal. The first
Spanish resident in London after the peace in 1604, Pedro de
Zúñiga (whose Instructions are examined in Chapter 2), neglected
the making and maintaining of high-level contacts at court in
favour of a policy of courting support for Spain among the
English Catholic laity; his successor, Alonso de Velasco, reversed
this policy but did not really have the social and political talents
needed to be successful; his successor, the later Count of Gondomar, did have, and put them to extremely good use; while his
successor, the Marquis of Hinojosa, was so maladroit that he
managed to alienate practically the entire English court.

Information from these various sources was naturally varied
in content and authoritativeness, being subject to a built-in
variation in access. It was also subject to a wide variety of distortions according to the motives, prejudices and such of the
information giver. Thus the validity of a report is not guaranteed

either by the accuracy of the reporting or the knowledgeability of the source. Since James I kept foreign policy largely in his own hands, Gondomar had the most authoritative possible source available to him in his frequent and quite intimate access to the king himself, and he reported many of their conversations almost verbatim. Yet he did so with reason (instead of reporting their contents as facts), for James managed to obscure his intentions very effectively by mixing an ample amount of undoubted truth with an uncertain amount of outright lies. James opened his heart to the ambassador on many occasions, but when he had done so the ambassador could seldom be sure what to believe and what not; his detailed accounts of these occasions leave the historian in precisely the same position, at least until he checks further documentation. One naturally needs to know both the ambassador and his source in order to judge the reliability of such reports, but even that can be a problem if the document is misleading about who they really are. The Venetian reports, for example, in this same period contain an estimate of the population of England, broken down according to religious inclination, apparently made by the Venetian ambassador, but one finds an identical estimate in the Spanish ambassador's reports five years earlier: whatever critical criteria one applied to it based on what one knows of the individual Venetian ambassador would, of course, be completely invalid.

All of this has to do simply with the quality of the information the ambassador got. There remains the problem of what he did with it. Quite apart from the partial and often partisan nature of the information available to him, the distortions he himself introduced in its transmission were many and varied. The same Count of Gondomar provides convenient examples of five of the more conspicuous types—especially appropriate since he is generally counted one of the ablest ambassadors in history.

(1) *Naïveté* Especially at the beginning of his mission (his first experience with diplomacy) he tended to believe too much of what he was told and to assign unmerited substance to what appeared to him victories in debating given diplomatic points.

(2) *Religious bias* He fairly quickly discarded his more ex-aggerated notions—the typical Spanish view at the time—about the condition of Catholics in England, but he could never take the Anglican church seriously as a religion and thus underestimated the reality and strength of Protestant belief. Their practices and pronouncements were so diverse that they obviously did not know *what* they believed, and the truth of Catholic doctrine was so manifest that anyone who did not practise it was obviously prevented from doing so or—the only alternative left—an atheist. The result for his diplomacy was a crippling fantasy of instant conversion of the entire nation if only toleration were granted. The result for his reporting was to limit his treatment of the subject mainly to anecdotes about the grotesqueries of this heretical sect, both their scandalous conduct in church and such absurd practices as using ordinary bread for communion. Some are quite amusing, such as that of a woman returning from market with a live goose under her arm who met a woman friend on the way to communion who insisted she come along in spite of having the goose with her; they happened to sit in the front row, and just as the priest was about to elevate the Host the goose snaked out his neck, grabbed it, and ate it; Gondomar was reliably informed [sic] that several people, shocked, were con-verted to Catholicism on the spot. Or the time in Scotland when Archie Armstrong, the king's jester, sneaked into the sacristy while the sermon was still going on and ate up all the bread and drank all the sacramental wine, so that there was none when it came time for communion; whereupon Archie sauntered out through the body of the church and told the assembled company that they could have lunch whenever they wanted but he had already had his; again Gondomar was reliably informed that several disgusted spectators were instantly converted to Mother Church. Such stories (to this reader at least) can be entertaining, and they are certainly important evidence of an ambassador's blinding prejudice, but they are no substitute for a serious analysis of the strength of Protestant feeling, either for his own government or for researchers.

(3) *Ignorance* The ambassador may be insufficiently familiar with his subject, especially on matters of detail which he may be inclined to translate into terms familiar to his reader. Gondomar, for example, explained the English office of Lord Treasurer as being equivalent to the Spanish one of *Contador Mayor*, which is not at all comparable in rank or political power (he himself had once held that post, which may have led him to overrate its importance). And sometimes an ambassador just did not know what was going on. On one occasion John Digby in Madrid had nothing much to do, so to stir up a bit of action and see what would happen he sought an audience with Lerma and complained about current Spanish support for Irish rebels. Lerma, caught off guard, did not know of any such thing, or even of any current Irish rebellion, but he also could not be sure that it was not true since it would not have been the first time—maybe the Spanish ambassador in England was doing it, or some such. Flustered by the unexpected protest and alarmed that the matter—whatever it was —might unexpectedly have complicated Spanish affairs, he sought to bury them both under a strong formal declaration of Spanish friendship towards England for Digby to relay to his master, and himself repeated this in a letter to England meant to be a formal statement of policy. James accepted this as such and replied in kind to the Spanish ambassador, which the latter promptly reported to Madrid, complete with a gratifying description of the king's personal reaction to Lerma's letter. Thus at a critical time, when relations between the two countries were dangerously strained, for a variety of reasons, some badly needed additional formal structure was built into a very tenuous peace. This makes the transaction rather important, but—unlike James, who had been clued in, and of course Digby, who was understandably rather pleased with himself—the Spanish ambassador acted in it and reported on it completely unaware (as was the government in Madrid) that the whole thing originated in a put-on by a whimsical envoy trying to earn his pay.

(4) *Policy bias* Theoretically policy is decided at home and executed abroad, the ambassador's role being analogous to that

of a soldier who attacks on the front he is told to, not the one of his personal choice. But in practice ambassadors have policy preferences, which may or may not coincide with government policy, and which they may or may not succeed in suppressing even if they try. When a Jacobean ambassador to The Hague, for example, is a committed Calvinist (there seems to be no other kind in the period) the thrust of his despatches will be that the United Provinces should be supported at all costs against the Spanish, and the subjects he chooses to report on and the information he reports about them will reflect this, to say nothing of the twist he may put on things, such as understating military strength to make the need for help seem greater, while what would be found in the reports of an unsympathetic ambassador would be far different and probably equally inappropriate for literal belief. Gondomar, for his part, was convinced that a resumption of major war would be disastrous for Spain, that the best chance for peace in Europe was an Anglo-Spanish marriage alliance (the most binding form of treaty tie), and that such a treaty could actually be worked out in terms agreeable to both sides. As long years of intermittent negotiations hit snag after snag, the Spanish government became increasingly doubtful that such a treaty was possible, while increasing danger of major war (which eventually did occur) made Gondomar increasingly concerned to convince his government otherwise; his despatches show it, not only arguing in favour of the treaty but giving an unrealistically rosy picture of its prospects of success, and this not only by inaccurate assertion but by emphasising subject matter whose undistorted facts tended to support that conclusion and neglecting those that did not. In this latter respect he was not necessarily being consciously dishonest, but neither was he working with equal zeal to prove and disprove his own case. Most to the point, there was nothing unusual in it: in reading at most any diplomatic report the researcher must adjust (and learn how much to adjust) for the prejudices, opinions, etc., of the writer.

(5) *Advertisements for oneself* Venetian ambassadors were largely career diplomats, and they naturally wanted to appear to

do their job well. For the English an ambassadorship was a standard step up the ladder to secretary of state or other comparable promotion in the service of the crown. Spanish ambassadors were already near the top of the ladder—the position ranked far higher in the Spanish scheme of things, and was held by men of far higher origin—and so there was usually no higher appointment left to receive that they were eligible for except membership of the Council of State, but they desired that, and of course honours and rewards, including (if still lacking) a title of nobility to pass on to a man's posterity as a mark of distinction and a public reminder that his house had served the crown well. French ambassadors, being somewhat lower in social origin than the Spanish (but higher than the English) and less far advanced up the hierarchy of government positions, had both social and professional advancement to think of (as well, of course, as financial). Whatever the details, it was in the interest of almost any ambassador to look good in the eyes of his own government, and against his interest to appear the reverse. Thus in their regular reports of their activities they tend to perform masterfully at all times, to win all debates, say only witty things (or daring or shrewd or point-clinching ones), and find success in all their manœuvres; they fail, when results could neither be revised into success nor quietly left unmentioned, only because of chicanery, bad faith, or unreasonable refusal to see reason on the part of others. Gondomar provides a particular example here too (half the despatches of most ambassadors would be valid examples): he is widely known in history for having taken a strong line with James on various occasions almost to (or beyond) the point of bullying, and got away with it, this necessarily on the basis of his own reports since these exchanges usually took place in private and James naturally did not broadcast details of his own humiliation; but the ambassador in fact often speaks to the king far more daringly in his official reports than he does in his other records of the same conversations.

The most obvious way for the researcher to have some idea of how much to discount (or add) for all of these various factors is to have the greatest possible familiarity with the writer and the other persons or elements involved and his relationship to them. Fortunately this provides one fairly reliable criterion: when the ambassador is clearly speaking against his own interest one may fairly safely assume that things went at *least* that badly. For the rest, one is dealing at best with *degrees* of sureness. But there is one excellent means of 'controlling' almost any ambassador's reports on most things (and is really indispensable in handling diplomatic reports as sources in any case): comparing them with reports on the same matters by other ambassadors to the same court. As these will normally be written by men with various different interests, biases and sources, no one of them will necessarily be *the* authoritative version to which all others should conform, but they will often serve to confirm the version one wishes to check; that version will often be corrected by one that is clearly more authoritative; and, when specialised knowledge (such as what went on in a private conversation) is not involved, one can often usefully find where the consensus lies. In one way or another the researcher can usually sort out the truth by such comparison of parallel reports. Except, of course, that of who was the real hero of an event in which several ambassadors were involved: it will normally turn out that each of them was.

In general, reading such documents is no more 'risky' from the point of view of accuracy than is reading a present day newspaper of a particular political persuasion: in both cases the crucial thing is to know what that persuasion is, and make the necessary allowances.

Dating and Identification

Knowing the date of diplomatic and related documents in this period is fortunately much less of a problem than in earlier periods and for domestic and private papers in this period; most were dated at the time. What this date actually means, however, can be less clear. In a letter it is normally a part of the signature and thus presumably of the date of signing, but this does not necessarily mean that the text might not have been drafted weeks, months, or even (in a specific case that comes to mind) a couple of years earlier. Nor does signing mean sending, which may have been deferred for some time for some reason of policy or delayed by the lack of a courier. And sending, of course, does not mean receiving: as noted elsewhere, a dispatch known to have been sent on the first of the month that would normally reach its destination in ten days cannot without evidence be assumed to have arrived by the tenth as it may have been delayed days or even weeks in transit—obviously an important matter when dealing with the basis upon which the addressee subsequently acted.

In English documents after October 1582, if Old Style or New Style is not specified, internal evidence may indicate which it is. If not, familiarity with the customary procedure of the writer may provide the answer: in the early seventeenth century, for example, letters written in England, whether destined for someone at home or abroad, usually were dated old style, those between ambassadors abroad usually new style (it seems to have been rather a fetish, to demonstrate their worldliness to each other), while those written home by ambassadors abroad could be either (though individuals were often consistent in which they used). If a partial date reads, for example, Tuesday 9 April, without giving the year, the year that it would have to be (the only year within the possible span in which that date fell on that day) can be readily had from a perpetual calendar. These are also often indispensable for translating internal evidence (either of the date of a letter or of an event) such as a statement that 'I could not see the king until yesterday because he was celebrating Palm Sunday the day before'. Often the specific date of a given letter can be found when the receipt of it is acknowledged in the reply to it.

The parallel problems of identifying the writer (often not noted on a copy) or the addressee (often missing even in the original, where it may only have appeared on an outside address since lost) or even persons referred to in the text may be solved by internal evidence or replies. Any of these may also be clarified in other letters by the same writer, either to the same addressee or to others—parallel but slightly variant correspondence can be extremely valuable in this regard as well as others—either by more revealing internal evidence or because they are named there. These avenues are equally useful for clarifying vague allusions of other types, to places, events, and so forth.

The Time Factor

The foregoing considerations, however, deal only with the problem of discovering the precise dates of documents, not with the further question of what those dates mean—a matter of considerable importance if one is to judge aright the relevance, the meaning in a purely historical sense, of the documents and their contents. This time factor is of two types: the one in relation to the document's writing and sending, the other in relation to its receipt and potential effect.

The date on a manuscript letter or other document—assuming it to be authentic (e.g., dated by the actual writer) and correct— is surely the most precise and specific piece of historical data one may ever encounter. It constitutes a precise, unambiguous, unequivocal datum in terms that are universally understood and universally agreed to (or in others that can be translated into such terms): 10 April 1609 ns. has one universally agreed-upon meaning and no other, and no other date expressed in the same set of terms (those of the Gregorian calendar) has that meaning— each day is unique, with a unique calendar label. But this almost excessive certitude is misleading, for the relationship between the specific date and the specific document to which it is attached (again, assuming it to be correctly so, in the conventional sense) is not nearly so certain as one might suppose.

The most obvious reason for this is that a good many such documents (practically all that are of government origin) take more than one day to write. The least troublesome case of this is when the document went through only a few days of consultation and drafting, after which a fair copy was made, dated, signed and sent off. In this sort of case, where dating and sending coincide or vary only a day or so, problems for the historian begin to accrue only when the process of drafting has been so drawn out and the evidence of it is so unspecific that one cannot be certain when the letter was actually written—a matter of considerable importance for understanding the shaping of policy when different and often conflicting motives for taking the decision that gave the document its final shape (e.g., the occurrence of further events or the arrival of further news from abroad) came into force at various times during the possible period of drafting. This problem becomes even more severe when the document was not dated immediately upon being drafted. A foresighted government may, for example, make drafts of possible treaty proposals (which confusingly, may end up being the actual later ones) when it has not yet even become clear whether negotiations will be possible; it may be months or even years before the situation develops to the point of making the draft usable, whereupon it may be dated, submitted for discussion, and processed out as declared policy. The document, now approved, is presumably relevant to the current situation and so to events since its drafting, but in no way owes its origin to them—a fact that has considerable importance for the conclusions the historian may be inclined to draw from the *apparent* timing.

Or a government may contemplate sending a resident somewhere, draw up his Instructions, then for one reason or another defer his departure or defer making the actual appointment. As with other drafted documents, the ambassador's Instructions may lie around for as much as two or three years, then be dated and used unchanged. Knowledge of this can tell the historian several possible things (and lack of knowledge of it can hide them from him): that nothing has happened in the intervening period to change policy; that something may have happened but policy has not caught up with events; or that it has, but the Instructions simply do not reflect it—perhaps the ambassador is inadequately or even deceptively instructed. These things the historian must puzzle out as best he can; the one thing that is absolutely certain (once he knows the facts of timing) is that the Instructions, whether they reflect actual policy or not, in no way owe their origin to events in the intervening period. This practice, though troublesome to the historian, usually reflects clerical efficiency, not carelessness or laziness, with documents drawn up in advance for use when actually needed, requiring only a date and signature, or at the most the striking-off of a new fair copy. But one does wish they had corrected the date on the old one, so that we might know both.

Scattered Documentation

The matter of Spanish pensioners at the court of James I, which appears in the set of Secret Instructions examined in Chapter 2, provides a useful example of the problem presented to historians by incomplete evidence and scattered documentation. One must start first with the documentary background.

During the 1603–4 negotiations for the Treaty of London, the Spanish peace delegation, headed by Juan de Velasco, duke of Frías, Constable of Castile, and Juan-Baptista de Taxis, count of Villamediana, also negotiated the establishment of a body of Spanish pensioners in the English government (and Scottish and Irish as well), royal households, navy, etc.: Secretary Cecil, Lord Treasurer Dorset, Lord Admiral Nottingham, Devonshire, Northampton—a beginning total of fourteen, which death, resignation, etc., reduced in a few years to about half that number. The need for newly-appointed ambassadors (and occasionally the Madrid government) to be fully informed on this set-up generated, between its establishment and its exposure in 1613–14, a series of documents—new memos and copies of old ones— beginning with those left (1) by the Constable (Dover, 9 September 1604) for Villamediana, who remained as interim ambassador, giving names and amounts initially agreed upon, and (2) by Villamediana (London, 18 July 1605) for his permanent replacement, Pedro de Zúñiga, bodily incorporating (1), then detailing subsequent developments and listing the new (higher) amounts. In 1607 Zúñiga simply left his replacement, Alonso de Velasco, a copy of (2), but, having a continuing hand in affairs after his return to Spain, submitted on request (3) a subsequent memo (apparently to Secretary of State Juan de Ciriza [? place], 6 June 1610) dealing with payments and other developments through July 1609. Zúñiga (who had meanwhile been in England on an extraordinary embassy in 1612) was later asked to supply briefing for Sarmiento, Velasco's replacement, which he did by sending Secretary Ciriza further copies of (2) and (3), updated by (4) a one-page covering memo ('from home', 27 March 1613).[1]

It was this latter batch of documents that John Digby, the English ambassador in Madrid, got his hands on in December 1613, copying them as completely as time would allow before his agent had to return them to the files. He notified James of his discovery in a long, tortuous, embarrassed letter: knowing that the information was political dynamite that could backfire on him badly if it went through the wrong hands, he begged leave to come home and show the lists personally to the king,[2] leave which James subsequently granted. The most immediate result for the historian is to put him in the same position as the compromised ministers—denied a look at what Digby had actually come up with. If the historian pushed on he would find Digby's lengthy summary[3] of it two years and one volume later in the same Public Record Office State Papers Spain, but that is not a

[1] Regarding (3): Zúñiga somewhat ambiguously says he is enclosing a copy of the paper Villamediana left him (2) and of 'the other I left . . . Velasco' without mentioning dates, but I have encountered no other Zúñiga–Velasco memo on the subject, and the enclosures still to be found in *Est.* 2514 with the signed original of (4) are definitely copies of (2) and (3), the latter in the same hand as (4).

That Ciriza should have to keep coming back to the same former ambassador with requests for copies of a crucial government document is a revealing measure of the limits of bureaucratic efficiency, even when it involved perhaps the best secretary at the time in Europe's most fully developed administrative apparatus.

The ambassadors' despatches themselves contain fairly frequent mention of these pensioners, some of which had come to Digby's hand and alerted him to the situation, but without details; having given James notice of this he was ordered to press on to what both referred to as the Main Discovery.

[2] Digby to James, Madrid, 24 Dec. 1613 os, SP94/20/189–95.

[3] Digby to James, 16 Dec. 1615 os, SP94/21/198–205.

really satisfactory substitute for the real thing. The obvious place
to look, of course, is in the state papers in Simancas and, if
unsuccessful, in the Biblioteca Nacional and other miscellaneous
collections, including the Spanish papers in the British Museum
that Gayangos catalogued.[1] In fact several copies of the Villamediana memo are to be found scattered about, including some of
those whose origin is outlined above. As to the copy Digby
actually saw, once it and the two Zúñiga memos were safely
returned to the secretariat (the agent seems to have brought Digby
the whole batch of related items together) and the Spanish were
done with consulting them (including having a copy struck off
for Sarmiento's use) and had presumably filed them somewhere,
they eventually made their way into a small *legajo* formed
several years later bearing the contemporary label 'Original
consultas assembled [*resueltas*] for His Majesty on English matters
of the years 1615–1616–1617' (and the notation 'Those that deal
with the marriage negotiations are in a separate *legajo*'). These and
several other items later became part of the larger archival
legajo Est. 2514.

In dealing with this matter at some length, S. R. Gardiner,
the standard and still indispensable historian of England in the
period, of course examined the whole series of Digby correspondence,[2] and of course he pushed on beyond the English
documents. Given the comprehensive scale of Gardiner's research
and the number of copies of the Villamediana memo scattered
about, it is not surprising that he found one. It is quite remarkable,
however, that, working in the mid-nineteenth century with no
effective catalogue to guide him, the one he came up with was the
specific copy Zúñiga supplied Ciriza in 1613, precisely the one
Digby saw and copied, the very crux of what both Digby and
James referred to as 'the main discovery', with which Gardiner

[1] Pasqual de Gayangos, *Catalogue of the manuscripts in the Spanish language
in the British Museum* (ed. E. A. Bond, 4 vols, London, 1875–93).
[2] And cited the most pertinent items: *England*, II, 216–17 (re Digby's discovery of the pensioners), 346 (re Somerset's fall); on establishment of the
pension set up see the following note.

was so seriously concerned; it is equally remarkable that he completely failed to recognise it as such, citing it merely as 'Memoir left by Villa Mediana', ignoring the two adjacent Zúñiga memoirs that make the connection plain and the historian's knowledge of what James actually found out about his ministers more precise.[1] The explanation is perhaps partly that, concerned primarily with English history, he was insufficiently concerned with the details of what was going on 'locally' elsewhere to be properly attuned for detecting this sort of connection; if so, it is an unconcern that the historian cannot well afford. But at least part of the explanation must be the scattered nature of the necessary documentation—in this case partly in London and partly in a castle in a tiny village in Old Castile—and the consequent distance in time between at least the initial handling of the one and the other. Unfortunately, it is a factor that operates powerfully on the process of historical synthesis: the foregoing example was chosen largely for its comparative simplicity and the greater familiarity to most readers of the subject matter; space and the reader's patience permitting, almost endless examples of far greater consequence could be cited as well. Wide research in the archives of various countries is indispensable to proper diplomatic history, scattered documentation a built-in problem that is not always easy to overcome.

It is one to be coped with, however, and not avoided, for two very basic reasons. Given the fact that unilateral diplomacy is both conceptually and pragmatically ludicrous, it follows that proper research in diplomatic documents must be at least bilateral. And given the uneven nature of diplomatic reports discussed above, it is imperative that they be 'controlled' by monitoring the parallel correspondence of at least one other ambassador (preferably more than one) reporting from the same place (indeed, the latter often becomes a principal source for diplomatic events of which he is only an observer, not a participant). Both of these usually involve not only 'foreign' documentation but foreign

---

[1] The citation in Gardiner, *England* (1883 ed.), I, 215 n1, as *legajo* 2544 (which consists of documents of 1670) is clearly a misprint: *sc. Est.* 2514.

archives, making dispersal of documentation merely a routine fact of life.

A special kind of locating problem is created for the historian, whose area of research is usually topically broad but chronologically restricted, by the organisation of documents into long-span one-topic groups. When this was done by original plan with folders clearly labelled and clearly catalogued 'Treaties with France, 1525–1659' or some such, it causes no problems, and in fact can be as much of a convenience to the researcher as it was to administrators at the time. But when it was done to serve immediate consultative needs the result is far different. Then the same batch of papers may be labelled 'Treaty negotiations, 1659', giving the historian of the Treaty of Cateau-Cambrésis no way of knowing that documents relating to it, procured from their regular place in the archives for consultation a century later, even exist, since they are catalogued under the later date, far beyond his period of interest; or an archivist may have noticed that the bulk of the documents are of 1559 and catalogued the whole *legajo* as relating to that date, thus concealing its relevance to the historian of the later treaty. In another type of case, documents of one period, procured at a substantially later date, may have been filed with the papers relating to their acquisition and remain filed and catalogued under that later date.

Simancas K1680A is a fairly typical example of the former and a rather extreme example of the latter. Ostensibly it is a batch of miscellaneous treaties, powers, renunciations, etc., regarding royal marriages, covering the four decades 1518–57. This span is already in some imbalance: of the eleven pertinent items, one is of 1518, one of 1525, and three of 1530, the remaining six a quarter century later, 1552–7. And one of the 1530 items proves to be an 'Inventory signed by Francis I of the papers he turned over to Charles V regarding the kingdoms of Naples, Milan and Genoa (1530)'; included with it are two dozen items, fourteen of them ranging from the 'Investment of the Kingdom of Naples made by Clement IV in favour of Charles I (1265)' to the 'investment of the Kingdom of Sicily conceded by Eugenius IV in favour of King Renato (1416),' including two 1396 items on the cession of Genoa to the King of France and two of 1409 on the investment of Naples and Sicily to Louis d'Anjou, the remaining ten spanning 1419–1515, dealing with the disposition of the thrones and territories of Sicily, Naples, Milan and Genoa. To these have been added the renunciations of Philip II's wife Anne and of Philip V of their rights to the French throne in 1571 and 1712 respectively, a 1510 letter of payment of 25,000 *louis d'or* by the Emperor Maximilian to Ferdinand the Catholic, and a 1515 letter from the Queen of France announcing the birth of a daughter: topically and chronologically rather miscellaneous to say the least. With the documents ranging across five centuries, from late medieval and Renaissance Italian history to the problem of European hegemony in the early eighteenth, it seems inevitable that historians for whom one group or another are important will fail to discover their presence in so miscellaneous a group.

Perhaps because they are *faits accomplis* and thus not so actively tied in a functional sense to the context of continuing affairs with one country, treaties themselves (as distinct from renunciations, draft protocols and other documents regarding their negotiation) are much more apt to be filed in broader multinational groups covering a correspondingly shorter span of time, often associated with a coherent historical period, as in the case of Simancas K1614A, which consists of three related Spanish treaties: with the Hanseatic League (Münster, 1647), with the States General (Münster,1648), and with France (Pyrenees, 1659). But organisational coherence is neither universal nor without aberration when practised: the Belgian manuscripts taken to Vienna in the 1790s, for example, include a large and rich *liasse* otherwise relating entirely to Habsburg relations with Denmark 1514–1627 but including, for no very obvious reason, a Habsburg-Scottish treaty of 1541. Nor are treaties immune from displacement for consultative purposes: only five *liasses* away from the above one is one containing four Franco-Burgundian treaties from the Treaty of Arras, 1435, to the Truce of Picardy, 1537— plus a small miscellany of 1558 documents relating to preliminary negotiations for the eventual (1559) Treaty of Cateau-Cambrésis, which almost certainly explains the presence of earlier treaties here.

The Problem of Quantity

Historians working in diplomatic documents have often fallen into the twin traps that massive quantity presents: a desperate thrashing about in an unmanageable sea of necessary documentation, and the compensatory false rationale that a handful of documents are enough. That the former is wholly ineffectual is obvious. That manageability is irrelevant to sufficiency is equally so: the notion that what one can read or happens to find ready at hand is a sensible measure of what one *needs* to read or find seems outlandish; however—defensively but persuasively couched in the plausible terms of common sense, moderation, and an appropriate avoidance of making a fetish of archival research—it has in fact been treated as axiomatic by many. It of course will not do. A document that states what policy is, though authentic, authoritative and accurate, may be completely invalidated by a subsequent one in another *liasse*, and perhaps another archive. One must read them both, and everything in between. Which returns one to floundering around in an unmanageable sea of necessary documentation.

It is basically a question of impossibility. It is impossible to read all the relevant documents about all the relevant aspects of the issues, and their ramifications, and all the collateral factors that impinge upon them, yet it is impossible to write truly satisfactory diplomatic history without doing so. This is unfortunate, but admitting it from the start has the virtue of freeing one for the pragmatic task of finding ways to cover more ground and to reduce the amount of ground to be covered.

It is quite true, as is often said, that 'you can't read it all', but one can read a good deal more if one does not fall into the amateur's trap of treating all Historical Documents with equal reverence. After having found the evidence for his subject—the literally 'research' part of his task—the historian's role is a discretionary one with regard to that evidence: its accuracy, relevance, cause-

and-effect relationships, and all the rest. It follows that he has as well a discretionary role with regard to the documents themselves, as distinct from their contents—or, the two being inseparable, as defined by their contents.

The rather common failure to exercise this duty of discretion is oddly a result of over-commitment to 'accurate' research, to the supposed need to subject every document to painstaking analysis in order to ascertain its full and precise meaning. There are two things wrong with this: it is self-defeating, and it is more often than not superfluous, and therefore perhaps also distorting.

Firstly, what one is seeking is the fullest knowledge possible about a particular matter, such as French policy towards the Papacy in a given period, or an aspect of it, and the eivdence for that is strung over a great many documents: to extract the full and precise meaning from a few documents down to the last comma, while failing to examine all the rest for lack of time, is clearly no way to acquire full knowledge of the subject, or even a knowledge of the place of those few documents and their contents within the whole—it is precisely as useful as focusing one's examination on one detail of a large painting and ignoring the rest.

Secondly, not all documents, or all statements in documents, are worth such a searching analysis, or even susceptible to it. If the ambassador says it snowed, it snowed—and that's about the size of it: perhaps interesting, perhaps important, but not subtle and not complex. Though one may sensibly take five seconds to ruminate upon its possible impact upon relevant affairs, the result is a realisation that bad weather may slow this despatch from arriving in its usual time or prevent an army from marching: perhaps important, but a matter of common-sense practical associations, not of internal analysis. And, just as snow under continued analysis eventually turns to water, which is a very different thing, so excessive analysis of a limited fact can turn it into something else, extracting from it more meaning than it actually contains: internal analysis of the concrete must either lead nowhere or to a distortion of fact.

The two taken together, of course, mean that while analysis

of the evidence is indispensable, the evidence is in the whole body of relevant documents and so it is to that body of evidence, not to a few isolated documents, that the analysis should be applied. And in order to do so as widely as possible, one might paraphrase Francis Bacon: some documents are to be studied, some to be read for their narrative or descriptive content, some to be skimmed for whatever relevant bits there may be, some to be recognised as useless and so discarded: handling historical evidence is a combination of analysis and synthesis, but one will never practise either on a wide enough scale until one has perfected the art of rejection.

One important aspect of the problem is not the quantity of directly relevant documentation that must be looked at, but of miscellaneous material that must be ploughed through to get at it. If one supposes the researcher to be concerned with the breaking of Franco–Spanish relations in 1667, a fairly typical example would be the 'minutes of despatches for [sic] the marqués de la Fuente', Spanish ambassador to France, for the nine-month period January–September 1667, comprising about half the smallish Simancas *legajo Estado* K1411 (the other half relates to 1669). Of the twenty-two miscellaneous documents included, five, largely intelligence reports, have to do only with the French context in general (in their unnumbered order in the *legajo*: 1, 3, 5, 9, 10), one with a minor matter satisfactorily settled (8), and five merely with the implementation of the shuttling of ambassadors (2, 4, 11, 17) and the governing of their residencies (16)—totalling exactly one half of the twenty-two items. Only the other half can be said to deal with matters of substance, and three of these come at or after the outbreak of war (20, 21, 22), and so post-date the researcher's principal concern. That leaves only eight, and a very mixed lot at that. The researcher goes, in this initially impressive assemblage of documents, from the appointment of a new ambassador to the outbreak of war with a mere four items involving areas that affect Franco-Spanish relations (6, 7, 13, 14), three others regarding military plans and actions leading to war (12, 18, 19) and only one (15) involving actual negotiations—and these irregular. Clearly, this neat packet is only one of many that must be consulted, analysed and synthesised—but first weeded—in order to discover and reproduce an accurate picture in the relevant terms of issues, events and diplomatic actions about them.

Within a given available amount of research time, access to archives, etc., the problem of quantity is essentially one of compromise between breadth and depth. There are a number of ways of attacking the problem, one of the most useful of which is the case-in-point method of dealing descriptively and analytically with a particular type of matter via a single representative example of it (or a few, as the topic requires). But where one must make a straightforward choice between greater breadth of coverage at the price of depth of treatment or vice versa, there is much to be said for opting consciously for a focused treatment specifically of some relatively narrow subject where one's attention and closest research can be concentrated within a relevant but manageable field. Naturally one still requires extensive attention to the broader context; due respect for the shape and scope the documents give their own subject; and careful coverage of all relevant aspects of whatever the subject at the centre may be.

What can be done (and sometimes what cannot) in extracting more useful historical knowledge from concentrated evidence of limited topics than can be had from the dispersed, thin and often superficial evidence of an unmanageably broad one can be seen from what has been done in the past. The point is urgent enough to warrant mentioning several of these special focuses (many are obvious) and some examples of treatments of them.

One State's relations with Europe When it involves a preponderant power it amounts almost to a bilateral treatment on a grand scale, as in J. B. H. R. Capefigue, *Louis XIV, son gouvernement et ses relations diplomatiques avec l'Europe* (new ed., 2 vols, Paris, 1844) and Louis André, *Louis XIV et l'Europe* (Paris, 1950). Such studies can be particularly useful, but the scope is enormous, with attendant difficulties.

One State's relations with one area E. Gossart, *La domination espagnole dans les Pays-Bas à la fin du règne de Philippe II* (Brussels, 1906); G. Zeller, 'La France de l'Ancien Régime devant la question des Pays-Bas', *L'Information Historique*, 10ᵉ année, December 1948; A. T. Anderson, *Sweden in the Baltic: a study in the politics of expansion under King Gustav Adolphus and Chancellor Axel Oxenstierna* (Berkeley, 1947). If the territorial focus is narrow enough, the treatment (within a given amount of research and evidence) can be considerably extended chronologically, as in Gustave Saige, *Le protectorat espagnol à Monaco. Ses origines et les causes de sa rupture* (Monaco, 1885), which manages to cover the period 1524–1641 in 170 pages.

One State's policy towards one other L. Anquez, *Henri IV et l'Allemagne: d'après les Mémoires et la correspondence de Jacques Bongars* (Paris, 1887); H. Brugmans, *Engeland en de Nederlanden in de eerste jaren van Elizabeth's regeering* (Groningen, 1892).

One set of bilateral relations Edward P. Cheney, 'England and Denmark in the later days of Queen Elizabeth'. *The Journal of Modern History*, I, No. 1 (March 1929), pp. 9–35; Joseph Lefèvre, *L'Angleterre et la Belgique à travers les cinq derniers siècles* (Brussels, 1946); Henri Lonchay, *La rivalité de la France et de l'Espagne aux Pays Bas, 1635–1700* (Brussels, 1896); Francesco Verneau, *Il conflitto anglo-francese da Luigi XIV alla Pace de Vienna . . . 1660–1783* (Bologna, 1939); Max Braubach, *Versailles u. Wien von Ludwig XIV. bis Kaunitz* (Bonn, 1952).

Bilateral relations between monarchs L. A. Prévost-Paradol, *Elizabeth et Henri IV 1595–1598* (2nd ed., Paris, 1863); Martin Philippson, *Heinrich IV. und Philipp III. Die Begründung des französichen Uebergewichtes in Europa 1598–1610* (3 vols, Berlin, 1870–6).

Bilateral politico-economic relations I. Lubimenko, *Les relations commerciales et politiques de l'Angleterre avec la Russie avant Pierre le Grand* (Paris, 1933); Fernande Delfosse-Benay, 'Les relations politiques et économiques entre les Pays Bas et l'Angeleterre a l'époque des Archiducs (1598–1621)' (an unpublished *mémoire de licence*, University of Brussels, 1939–40).

Two States with a third-party focus Arthur Horniker, 'Anglo-

French rivalry in the Levant from 1583–1612', *The Journal of Modern History*, XVIII (December 1946), 289–305; Dieter Albrecht, *Richelieu, Gustav Adolf und das Reich* (Munich, 1959).

Foreign intervention J. W. Thompson, *The wars of religion in France, 1559–1576: the Huguenots, Catherine de Medici, Philip II* (Chicago, 1909): P. Champion, *Charles IX, la France et le Contrôle de l'Espagne* (2 vols, Paris, 1939); I. S. Révah, *Le Cardinal de Richelieu et la restauration du Portugal* (Lisbon, 1950).

A particular issue Manuel R. Pazos, 'Del conflicto entre Paulo V y Venecia. El embajador de la Serenisima en España y el entredicho', *Archivo Ibero-Americano*, IV (1944), pp. 32–61, is a particularly good example of a bilateral dispute with a third party involved.

One State's handling of one issue M. Ritter, 'Die pfalzische Politik und die böhmische Königswahl von 1619', *Historische Zeitschrift*, LXXIX (1897), pp. 239–83, or F. Kunz, *Oesterreich und der spanisch-englische Heiratsplan vom Jahr 1623* (Wien, 1895).

A special event H. F. Delaborde, *L'Expédition de Charles VIII en Italie. Histoire diplomatique et militaire* (Paris, 1888).

Many very small topics that are capable of supporting only brief treatment, though important to broader matters, unfortunately cannot be dealt with satisfactorily in isolation, but many can—Charles Paillard, 'Détournement, au profit des huguenots français, d'un subside envoyé par Philippe II à Catherine de Médicis' (*Revue Historique*, 1876, II, pp. 490–9) being an excellent example for its brevity, its importance, and its self-sufficiency.

Frontier disputes Henri Hauser, *Le traité de Madrid et la cession de la Bourgogne à Charles-Quint: étude sur le sentiment national bourguignon en 1525–1526* (Paris, 1912); José Luis Cano de Gardoqui, *La cuestión de Saluzzo en las comunicaciones del imperio español, 1588–1601* ([Valladolid], 1962); Edouard Rott, *Henri IV, les Suisses et la Haute Italie. La lutte pour les Alpes, 1598–1610* (Paris, 1882); Gaston Zeller, 'Saluces, Pignerole et Strasbourg, la politique des frontières au temps de la prépondérance espagnole', *Revue Historique*, vol. 193 (1942–3) and *La réunion de Metz à la France, 1552–1648* (Paris, 1926); G. Bardot, *La question des Dix*

Villes impériales d'Alsace . . . 1648–1680 (Paris, 1899). The fact that France's territorial rivalry with her neighbours involved her with Spanish domains on all sides (for the whole of her northern and southern frontiers and part of the eastern) and thus coincided with her rivalry with the preponderant power naturally served to heighten both those rivalries. As even this brief list indicates, French expansionist pressures eastward, a mixture of the acquisitive and hegemonic, were inextricably combined with rivalry for domination of strategically important areas.

Peace treaties Individual treaties and congresses have been successfully dealt with on various scales: J. Thomas, *Concordat de 1516; ses origines, son histoire au XVIᵉ siècle* (3 vols, Paris, 1910); Baron Alphonse de Ruble, *Le traité de Cateau-Cambrésis, 2 et 3 avril 1559* (Nogent-le-Rotrou, 1889); Arthur Erwin Imhof, *Der Friede von Vervins* (Aarau, 1966); F. Dickmann, *Der Westfälische Frieden* (Münster, 1959); Père G. H. Bougeant, S.J., *Histoire des guerres et des négotiations qui précédèrent le traité de Westphalie* (3 vols, Paris, 1751). The value of 'limited' background studies has no better example than Joseph Cuvelier, 'Les préliminaires du traité de Londres (29 Août 1604)', *Revue belge de philologie et d'histoire*, II (1932), pp. 279–304, pp. 485–508, absolutely basic to its subject (though a recent monograph on that treaty was written in apparent unawareness of its existence). Abortive negotiations deserve a good deal more attention than they have received: E. F. Hamy, 'Conférence pour la paix entre l'Angleterre et l'Espagne tenue à Boulogne en 1600. Etude historique suivie d'un choix de lettres relatives à ce sujet', *Bulletins de la société académique de Boulogne-sur-Mer*, Vol. VI.

A single alliance Father Luciano Serrano's *La Liga de Lepanto, 1570–1573* (Madrid, 1918), is an excellent example of how useful as well as viable such a 'narrowly' topical treatment can be, as it is part of a very fruitful lifetime of work on a subject not very much broader, Spanish-Papal relations in the period. The most important alliances, however, from the point of view of diplomacy, have been largely ignored. Whether one considers war 'the last stage of diplomacy', which makes diplomacy essentially a matter of extortion, a device for acquiring the gains of war without the expense, or considers diplomacy the imperative rational alternative to the horrors of war, the assumption is that diplomacy—spies and all the other unfriendly trappings apart— is most importantly a system of *peaceful* settlement of international disputes. It therefore seems quite paradoxical that 'diplomatic historians', as well as others, have mainly recorded the system's failure and not its periods and occasions of actual success in achieving its principal purpose. In the case of alliances, most of the historical work has been on alliances for war—definitely the point of maximum intensity in international relations, but essentially a military matter, after peaceful diplomacy has broken down. Being mainly crisis oriented, historians have largely ignored alliances through which the peace was *kept*, not aban- doned, which one might describe as pure diplomacy in both senses. It is a potentially fruitful field well worth being tapped; diplomatic historians might even learn something useful about how the techniques of diplomatic peacekeeping actually work— not a bad thing to know.

Career biography As the diplomatic historian is apt to be working heavily in the papers of one particular ambassador, the notion of giving the study the form of a career biography of him almost inevitably arises, but if the man moved about very much it is not a very good one, unless one is intending a sort of Cook's tour of several embassies, courts, countries and diplomatic issues, or—fairly unlikely—the particular individual is more important than are the events, issues, etc., involved. To deal with any ambassador's activities one must have an adequate depth of know- ledge both of the person (to understand his actions, correspond- ence, etc., accurately) and of the locale of his embassy (the con- text of monarch, ministers, etc., he will deal with), the issues being dealt with, and so forth. As the former is a good deal easier to come by than the latter (and one assumes here that the time and resources available make possible research on a scale larger than that of one ambassador's tenure at one court) the choice is obvious: better for the historian to put himself in the place of the receiving monarch and deal with the same (continuing) set of issues between the same pair of states than to follow the ambassador to another embassy and thus to an unfamiliar context—setting, issues, etc.—and, not least important for the historian, sources.

When a given ambassador served only in one country, but for as long a span as the historian intends to cover, one automatically gets these benefits of local continuity while still dealing with just the one envoy (which happens to be true of my own forthcoming work on Gondomar, which I sometimes refer to inexactly as 'career biography'). When this is not the case, this double benefit can sometimes be taken advantage of by dealing with just a single mission—and to good effect, if it is a sufficiently important one. Two excellent examples of this approach are De Lamar Jensen, *Diplomacy and Dogmatism: Bernardino de Mendoza and the French Catholic League* (Cambridge, Mass., 1964) and Herbert H. Rowen, *The Ambassador prepares for war: the Dutch embassy of Arnauld de Pomponne, 1669–1671* (The Hague, 1957).

All of these, and others like them, are of course expedients, but they are honest and honourable ones. For the historian working in the sources of the history of the great powers in this period (as distinct from surveys necessarily based on modern secondary works) they are also necessary ones. As was noted at the start of this book, states produced an enormous amount of documentation in handling their affairs—its production, in a very true sense, *was* the handling of those affairs—and the other source material, such as contemporary publications of various kinds, is also vast and often crucial. Technique, practice and judgment all speed up the process and let one plough through much more than would otherwise be possible, but for adequate depth of treatment one has to carve a slice that matches feasibility. Fortunately, as indicated above, there are many possible ways of slicing, and fortunately that slice need not be so thin as to be not worth doing.

The sources are there, and a great deal has to be got through to deal adequately with the subject. But a great deal can be. Clio told me so, and women never lie.

Index

Index

Index

Doucet, R., *Les institutions de la France au XVIe siècle*, 35

Duchesne, André, *Bibliothèque des autheurs*, 198

Du Perron, Cardinal Jacques Davy, *Ambassades et Négotiations*, 158

Duro, Fernandoz, 190n.

East India Company, 244

Edmondes, Thomas, 150

Edict du roy, 228

Edict of Nantes, 164

Edward the Confessor, 265

Egerton, Francis Henry, 137n.

Egerton MSS, 137

Eighty Years War, 155

Elizabeth I, Queen of England, 163, 207, 240, 244, 303

Ellis, 270

Elton, G. R., *England*, 33n., 66n., 94n., 127n., 162n.; *The Tudor Revolution in Government*, 34

Elzevier, 216, 219; *Republics*, 216, 218

Enciclopedia universal ilustrada, 173

Encyclopaedias, 214

Emmison, F. E., *Tudor Secretary*, 34

England, 28, 34, 49, 54, 56, 57, 58, 59, 90, 103, 123, 133, 134, 150, 158, 161, 163, 178–9, 246, 269, 272, 277, 278, 280, 293, 299, 312, 318–21

English Civil Wars, 223

English merchants, 105, 115–16

Estado, Secretary of, 130

Estat General des Affaires, 223

Estoile, Pierre de l', 168

Eugenius IV, 322

Evangelical Union, 248

Evans, F. M. G. (Mrs Higham), *The Principal Secretary of the State*, 34

Expedition du duc de Guise à Naples, 165

'Extraits de la correspondance Jean Thomas de Langosco', 155

Fatio, Alfred Morel, 180, 185; *His-toriographie de Charles-Quint*, 170, 191n.; *L'Espagne*, 184

Ferdinand of Aragon, 20n., 24–25, 104, 323; and Isabel, 190, 191

Figueroa, Christobal Suárez de '*Plaza Universal*', 215

Financial Times, 227

Florence, 23, 26, 27, 247

Flysheets, 207

Folieta, Uberto, 198

Foppens, F., *Auberti Miraei*, 204

Fornes, Francisco, *La catalona verdad contra la emulación*, 211

France, 21, 27, 28, 35, 49, 53, 55, 56, 57, 59, 63, 71, 123, 126, 127, 129, 133, 134, 135, 143, 150, 162–7, 168, 169, 172, 176–8, 195, 210, 211, 213, 270, 271, 277, 278, 279, 280, 284, 291–3, 326; king of, 54

France, Renon de, *Histoire des troubles des Pays-Bas*, 183

Francis I of France, 154, 198, 220, 283, 284, 322; letters of, 285

Franklin, Alfred, 176; *Les sources de l'histoire de France*, 151

Frederick V, 244

Frías, Duke of, 318

Fuentes naratives de la historica de España, Las, 174

Fueter, 205

Fuertes y Biota, Antonio, *Anti-Manifesto*, 212

Gachard, L. P., 180, 185, *Les monuments de la diplomatie Venetienne*, 220; *Notes sur les Commentaires*, 170n.

Gallardo, Bartolome Jose, *Indice de manuscritos de la Biblioteca Nacional*, 138n.

García, Carlos, *Antipathie de François et des Espagnols*, 212

Gardiner, S. R., 67, 81, 115, 117, 282, 283, 320, 321

343

Index

Index